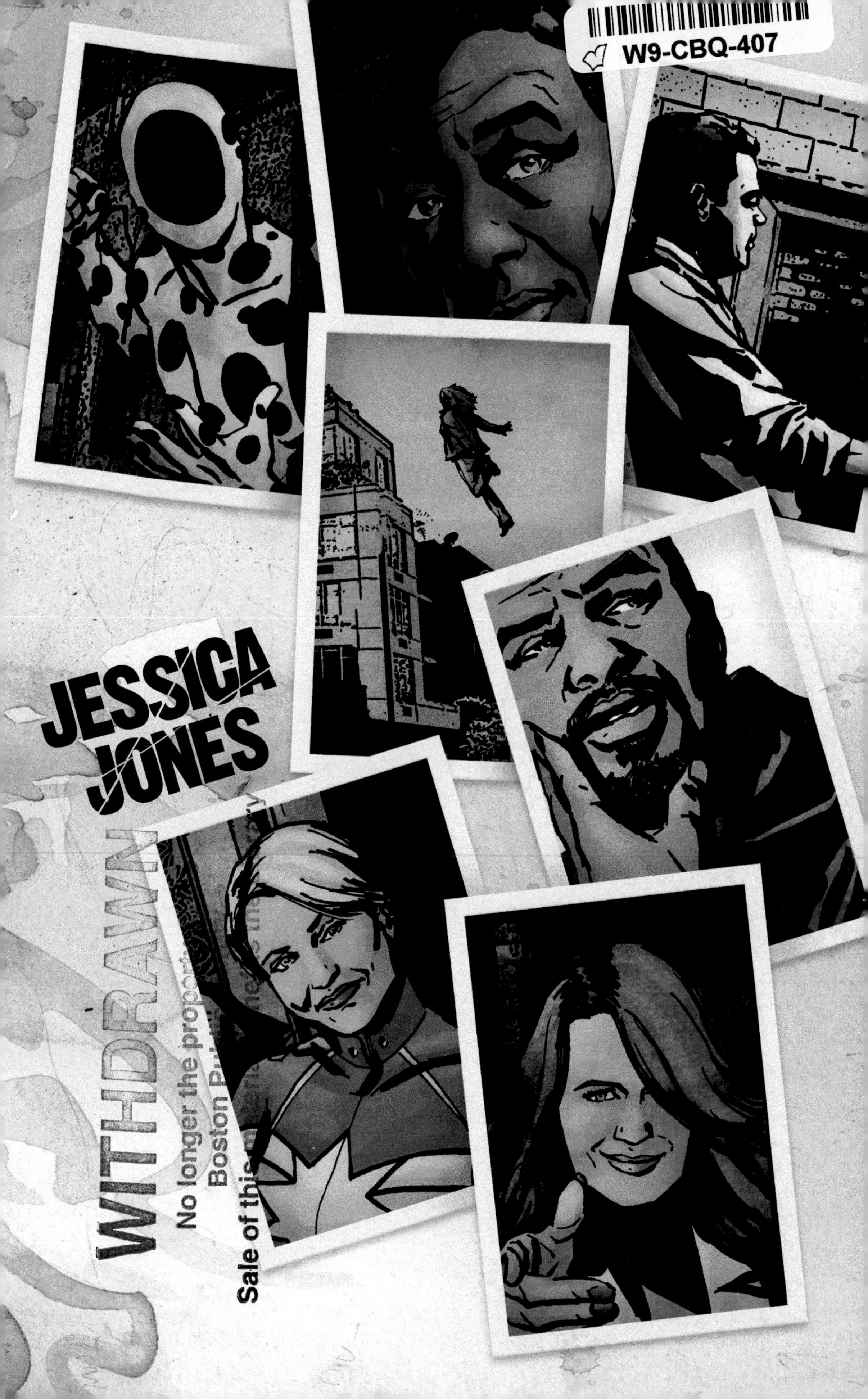
JESSICA
JONES

Jessica Jones, a former costumed super hero, is now the owner and sole employee of Alias Investigations--a small private investigative firm.

But dark secrets from her super hero past haunt her, affecting her relationships and happiness.

JESSICA JONES

UNCAGED!

Writer: **Brian Michael Bendis**
Artist: **Michael Gaydos**
Color Artist: **Matt Hollingsworth**

Letterer: **VC's Cory Petit**
Cover Art: **David Mack**

Assistant Editor: **Alanna Smith**
Editor: **Tom Brevoort**

Based on characters created by **Brian Michael Bendis** & **Michael Gaydos**

Collection Editor: **Jennifer Grünwald** • Assistant Editor: **Caitlin O'Connell**
Associate Managing Editor: **Kateri Woody** • Editor, Special Projects: **Mark D. Beazley**
VP Production & Special Projects: **Jeff Youngquist** • SVP Print, Sales & Marketing: **David Gabriel**
Book Designer: **Jay Bowen**

Editor in Chief: **Axel Alonso** • Chief Creative Officer: **Joe Quesada**
President: **Dan Buckley** • Executive Producer: **Alan Fine**

JESSICA JONES VOL. 1: UNCAGED! Contains material originally published in magazine form as JESSICA JONES #1-6. First printing 2017. ISBN# 978-1-302-90635-1. Published by MARVEL WORLDWIDE, INC., a subsidiary of MARVEL ENTERTAINMENT, LLC. OFFICE OF PUBLICATION: 135 West 50th Street, New York, NY 10020. Copyright © 2017 MARVEL No similarity between any of the names, characters, persons, and/or institutions in this magazine with those of any living or dead person or institution is intended, and any such similarity which may exist is purely coincidental. **Printed in the U.S.A.** DAN BUCKLEY, President, Marvel Entertainment; JOE QUESADA, Chief Creative Officer; TOM BREVOORT, SVP of Publishing; DAVID BOGART, SVP of Business Affairs & Operations, Publishing & Partnership; C.B. CEBULSKI, VP of Brand Management & Development, Asia; DAVID GABRIEL, SVP of Sales & Marketing, Publishing; JEFF YOUNGQUIST, VP of Production & Special Projects; DAN CARR, Executive Director of Publishing Technology; ALEX MORALES, Director of Publishing Operations; SUSAN CRESPI, Production Manager; STAN LEE, Chairman Emeritus. For information regarding advertising in Marvel Comics or on Marvel.com, please contact Vit DeBellis, Integrated Sales Manager, at vdebellis@marvel.com. For Marvel subscription inquiries, please call 888-511-5480. **Manufactured between 3/17/2017 and 4/18/2017 by QUAD/GRAPHICS WASECA, WASECA, MN, USA.**

10 9 8 7 6 5 4 3 2 1

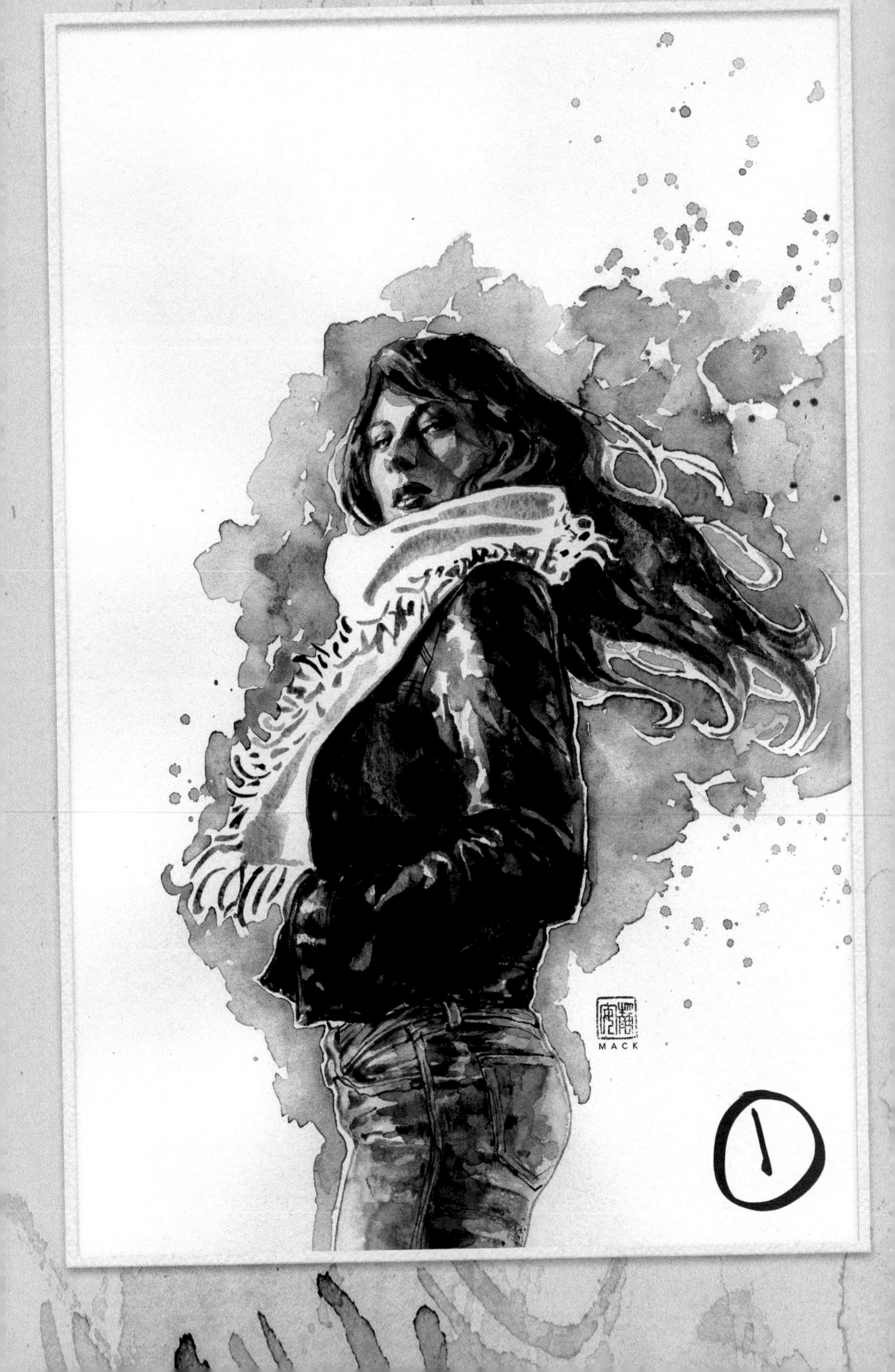
MACK
1

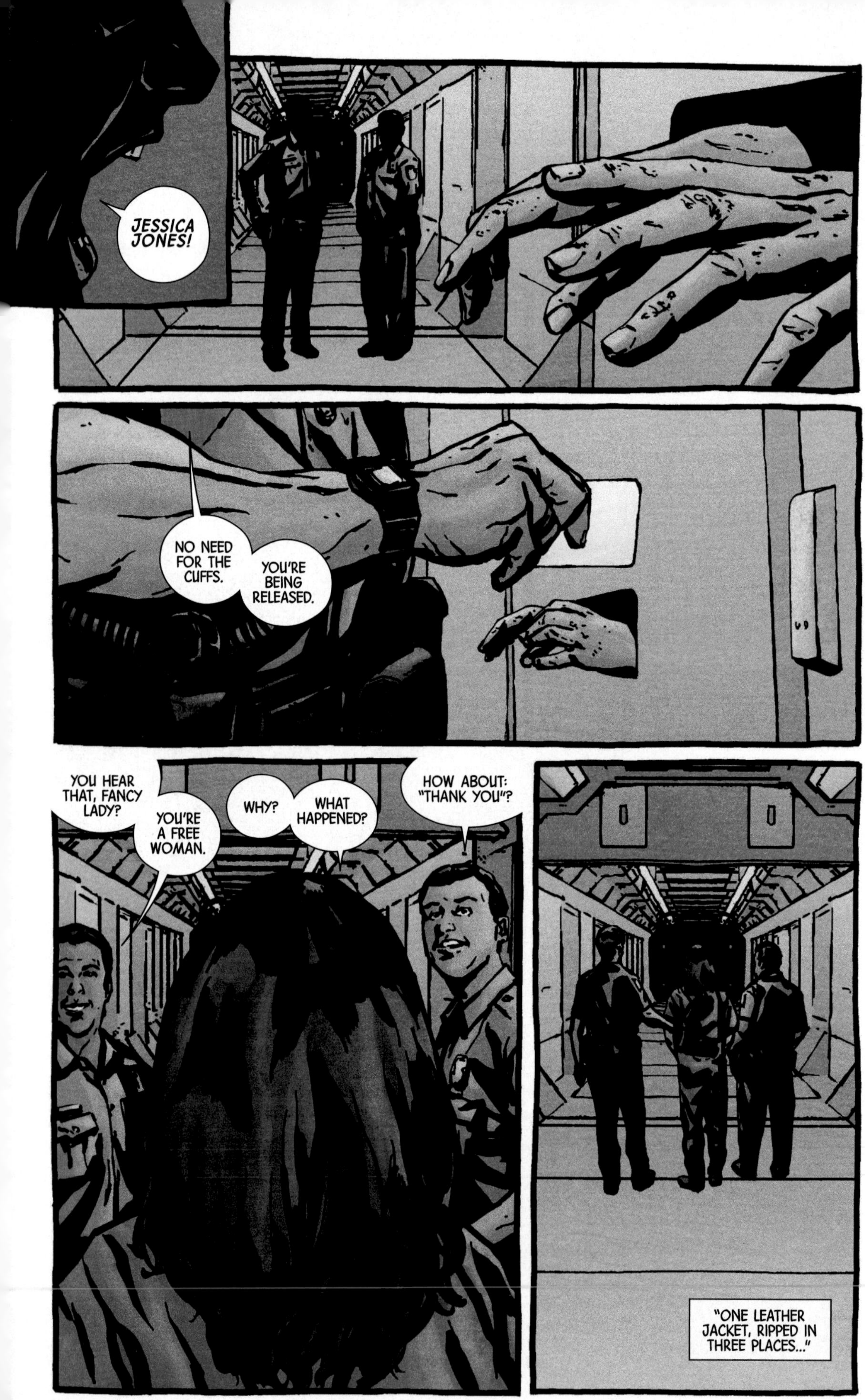
JESSICA JONES!
NO NEED FOR THE CUFFS.
YOU'RE BEING RELEASED.
YOU HEAR THAT, FANCY LADY?
YOU'RE A FREE WOMAN.
WHY?
WHAT HAPPENED?
HOW ABOUT: "THANK YOU"?
"ONE LEATHER JACKET, RIPPED IN THREE PLACES..."

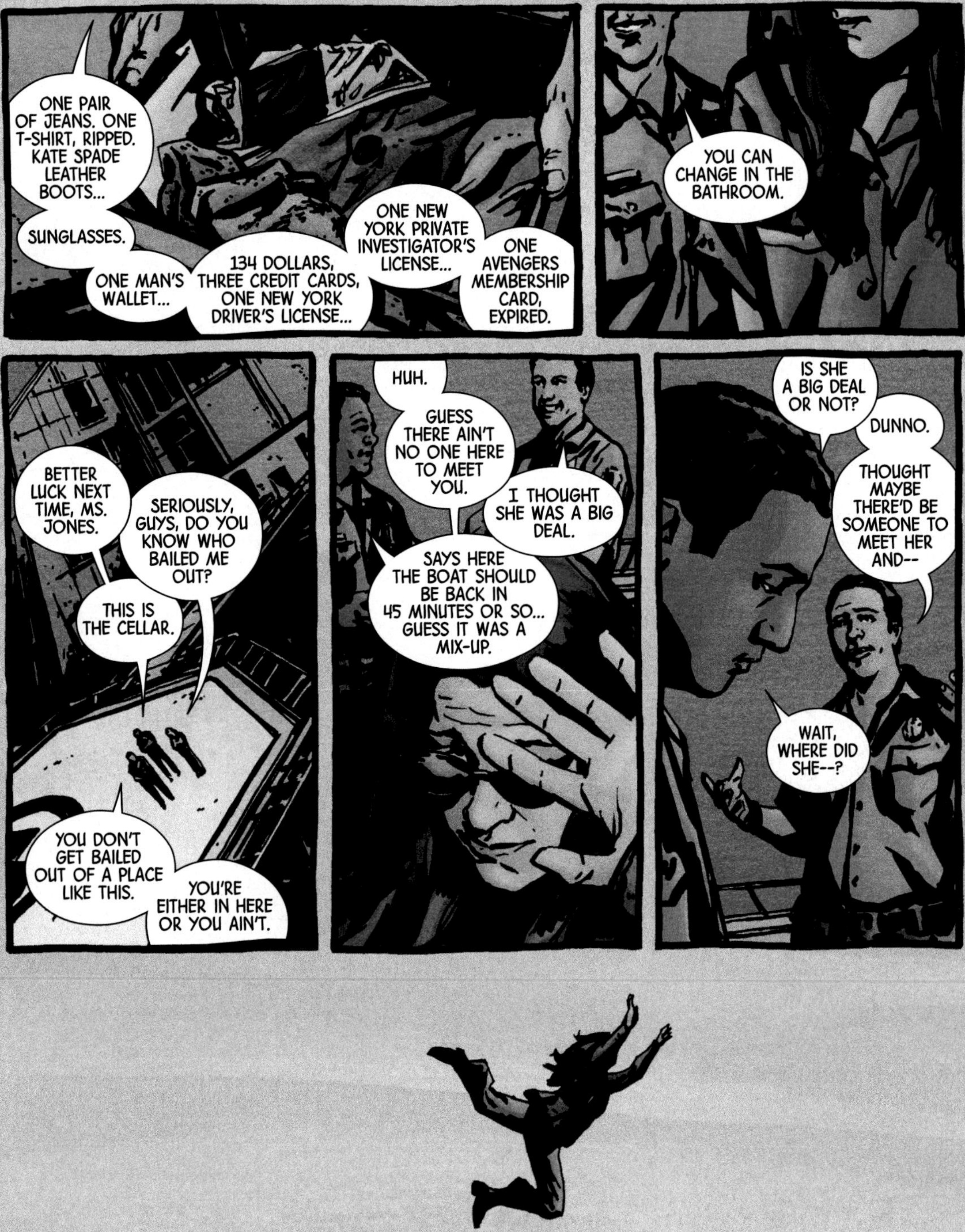
ONE PAIR OF JEANS. ONE T-SHIRT, RIPPED. KATE SPADE LEATHER BOOTS...
SUNGLASSES.
ONE MAN'S WALLET...
134 DOLLARS, THREE CREDIT CARDS, ONE NEW YORK DRIVER'S LICENSE...
ONE NEW YORK PRIVATE INVESTIGATOR'S LICENSE...
ONE AVENGERS MEMBERSHIP CARD, EXPIRED.
YOU CAN CHANGE IN THE BATHROOM.
BETTER LUCK NEXT TIME, MS. JONES.
SERIOUSLY, GUYS, DO YOU KNOW WHO BAILED ME OUT?
THIS IS THE CELLAR.
YOU DON'T GET BAILED OUT OF A PLACE LIKE THIS.
YOU'RE EITHER IN HERE OR YOU AIN'T.
HUH.
GUESS THERE AIN'T NO ONE HERE TO MEET YOU.
I THOUGHT SHE WAS A BIG DEAL.
SAYS HERE THE BOAT SHOULD BE BACK IN 45 MINUTES OR SO... GUESS IT WAS A MIX-UP.
IS SHE A BIG DEAL OR NOT?
DUNNO.
THOUGHT MAYBE THERE'D BE SOMEONE TO MEET HER AND--
WAIT, WHERE DID SHE--?

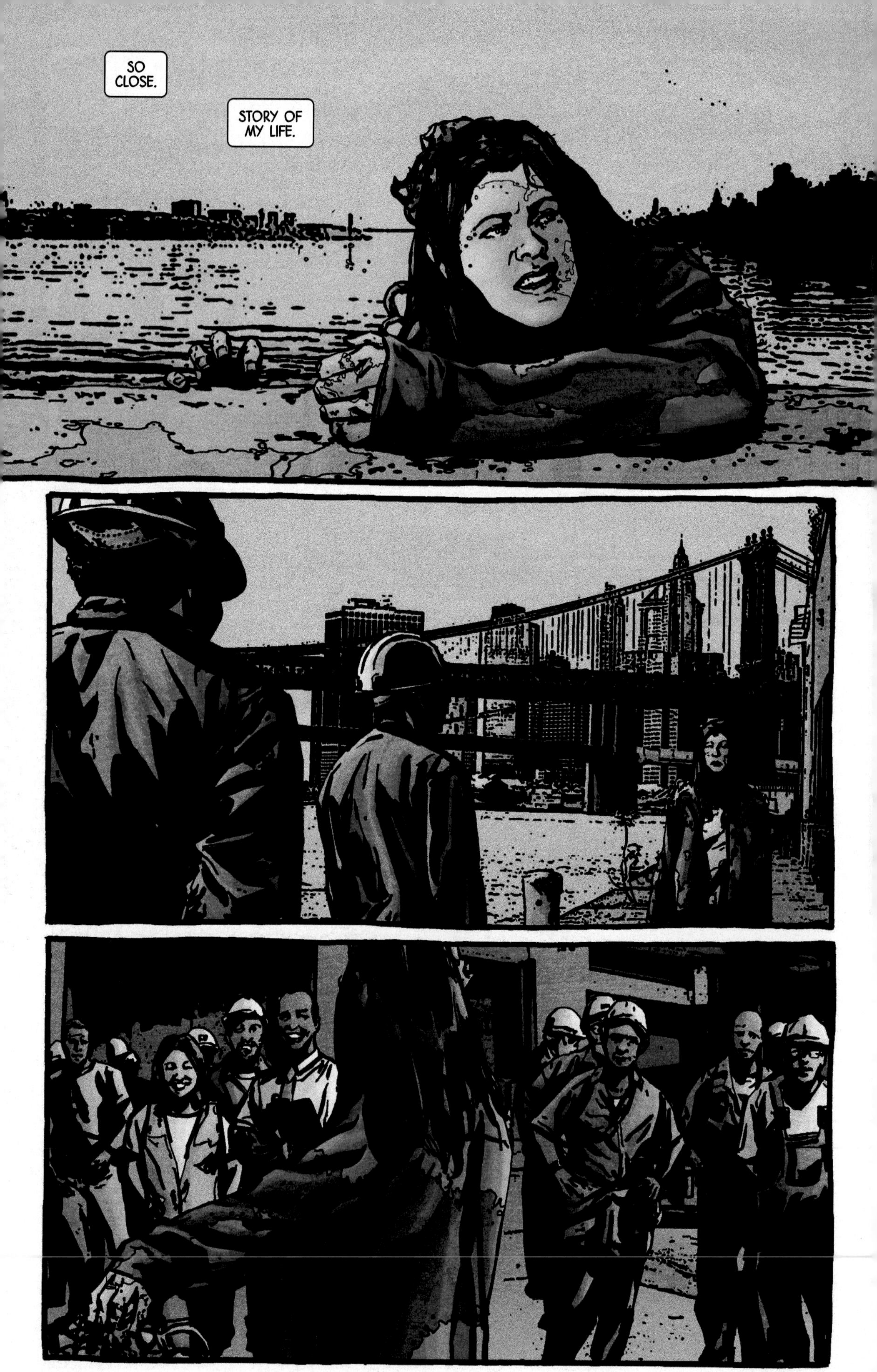
SO CLOSE.
STORY OF MY LIFE.

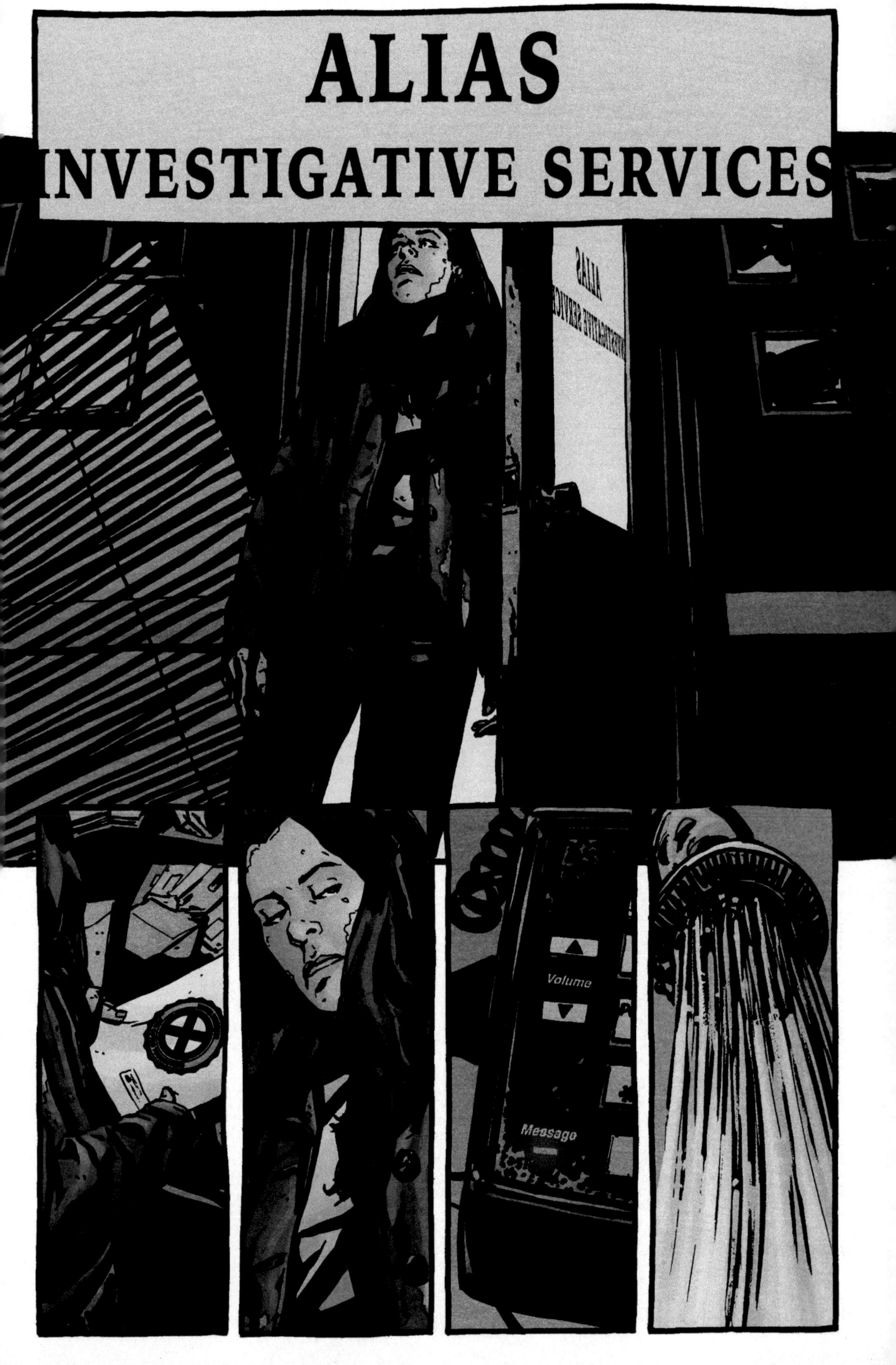
ALIAS
INVESTIGATIVE SERVICES
Volume
Message

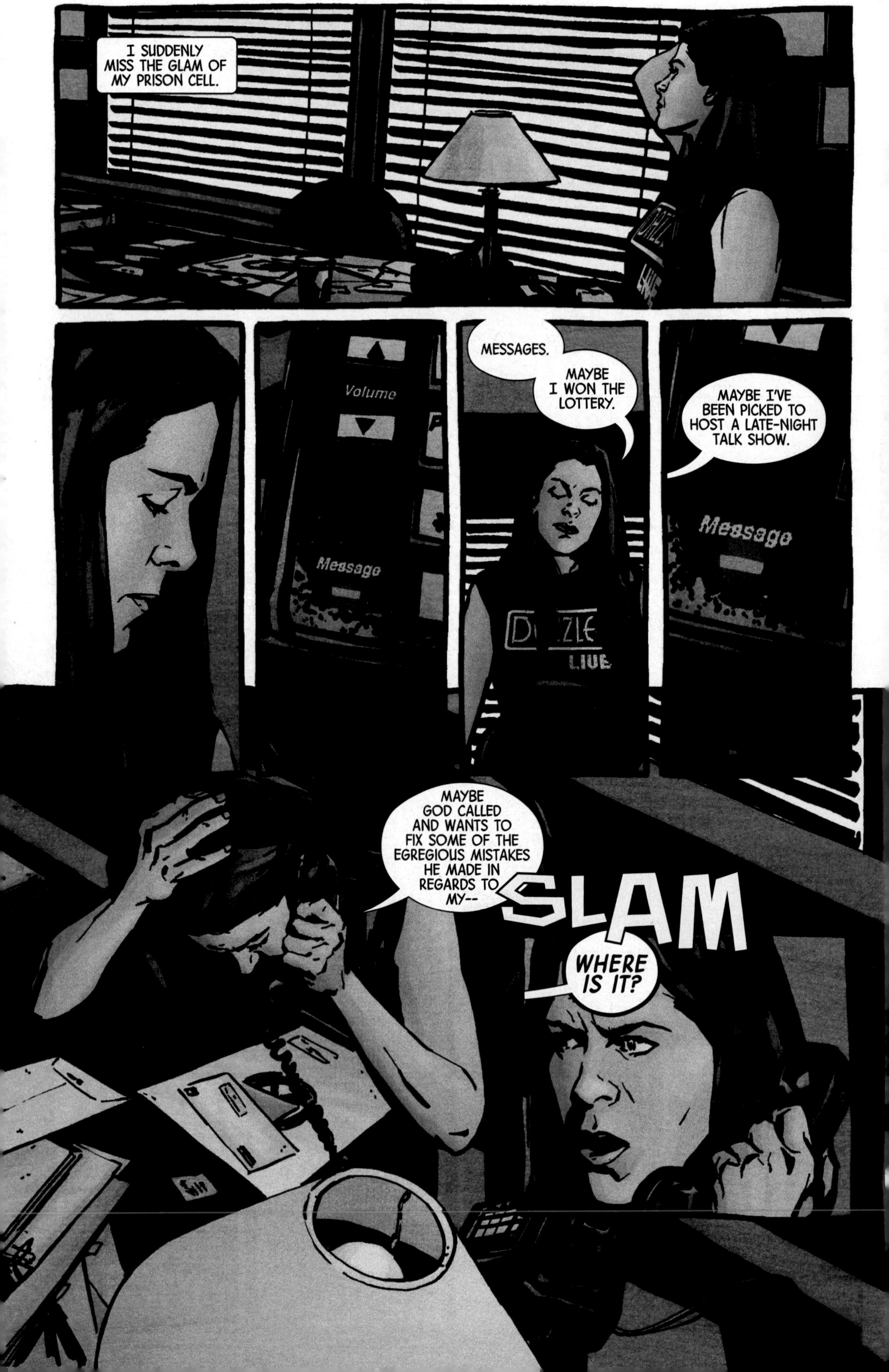
I SUDDENLY MISS THE GLAM OF MY PRISON CELL.
Volume
Message
MESSAGES.
MAYBE I WON THE LOTTERY.
DAZZLER LIVE
MAYBE I'VE BEEN PICKED TO HOST A LATE-NIGHT TALK SHOW.
Message
MAYBE GOD CALLED AND WANTS TO FIX SOME OF THE EGREGIOUS MISTAKES HE MADE IN REGARDS TO MY--
SLAM
WHERE IS IT?

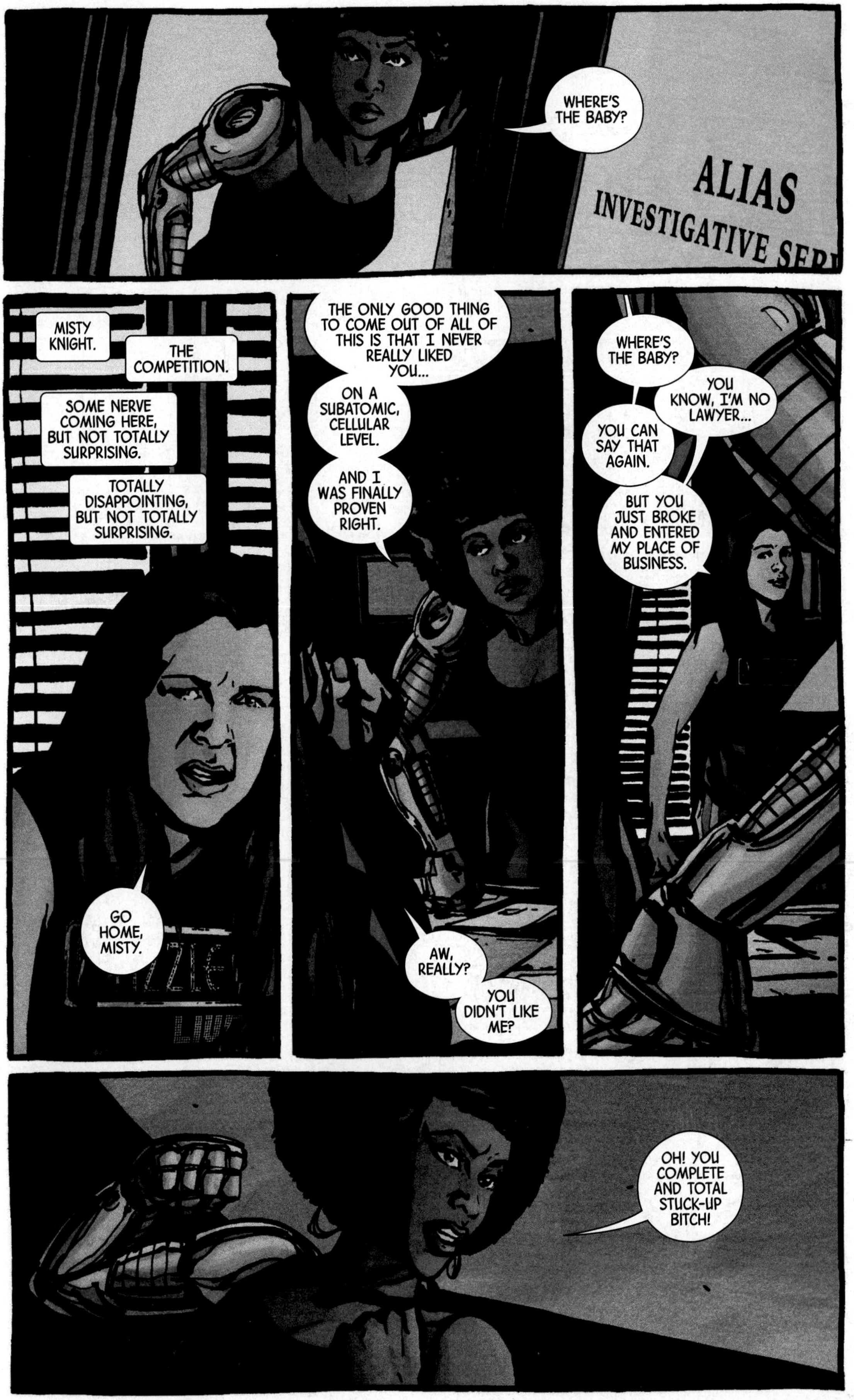
WHERE'S THE BABY?
ALIAS INVESTIGATIVE SER
MISTY KNIGHT.
THE COMPETITION.
SOME NERVE COMING HERE, BUT NOT TOTALLY SURPRISING.
TOTALLY DISAPPOINTING, BUT NOT TOTALLY SURPRISING.
GO HOME, MISTY.
THE ONLY GOOD THING TO COME OUT OF ALL OF THIS IS THAT I NEVER REALLY LIKED YOU...
ON A SUBATOMIC, CELLULAR LEVEL.
AND I WAS FINALLY PROVEN RIGHT.
AW, REALLY?
YOU DIDN'T LIKE ME?
WHERE'S THE BABY?
YOU KNOW, I'M NO LAWYER...
YOU CAN SAY THAT AGAIN.
BUT YOU JUST BROKE AND ENTERED MY PLACE OF BUSINESS.
OH! YOU COMPLETE AND TOTAL STUCK-UP BITCH!

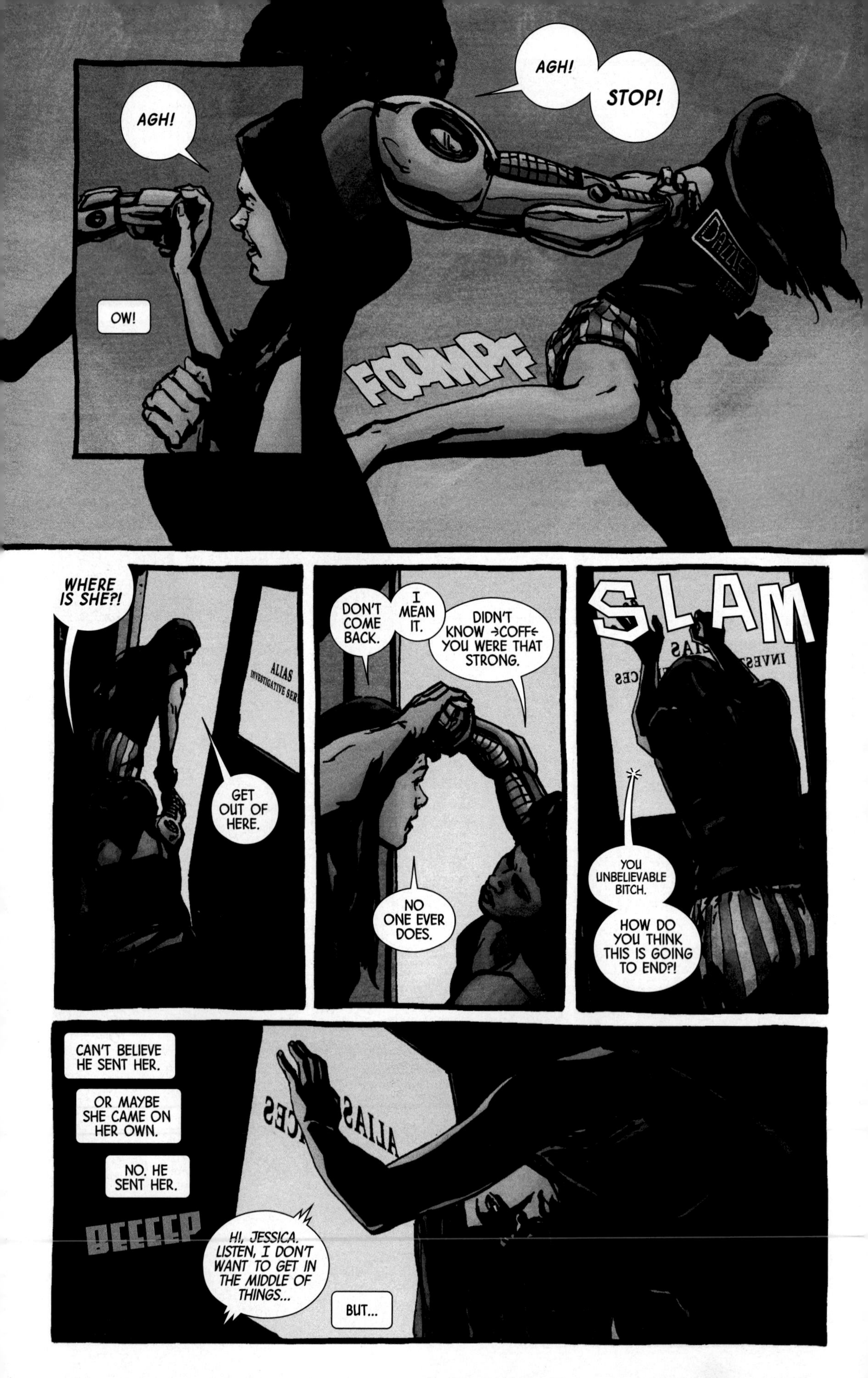
AGH!
OW!
AGH!
STOP!
FOOMPF
WHERE IS SHE?!
GET OUT OF HERE.
ALIAS INVESTIGATIVE SER
DON'T COME BACK.
I MEAN IT.
DIDN'T KNOW →COFF← YOU WERE THAT STRONG.
NO ONE EVER DOES.
SLAM
YOU UNBELIEVABLE BITCH.
HOW DO YOU THINK THIS IS GOING TO END?!
CAN'T BELIEVE HE SENT HER.
OR MAYBE SHE CAME ON HER OWN.
NO. HE SENT HER.
BEEEEP
HI, JESSICA. LISTEN, I DON'T WANT TO GET IN THE MIDDLE OF THINGS...
BUT...

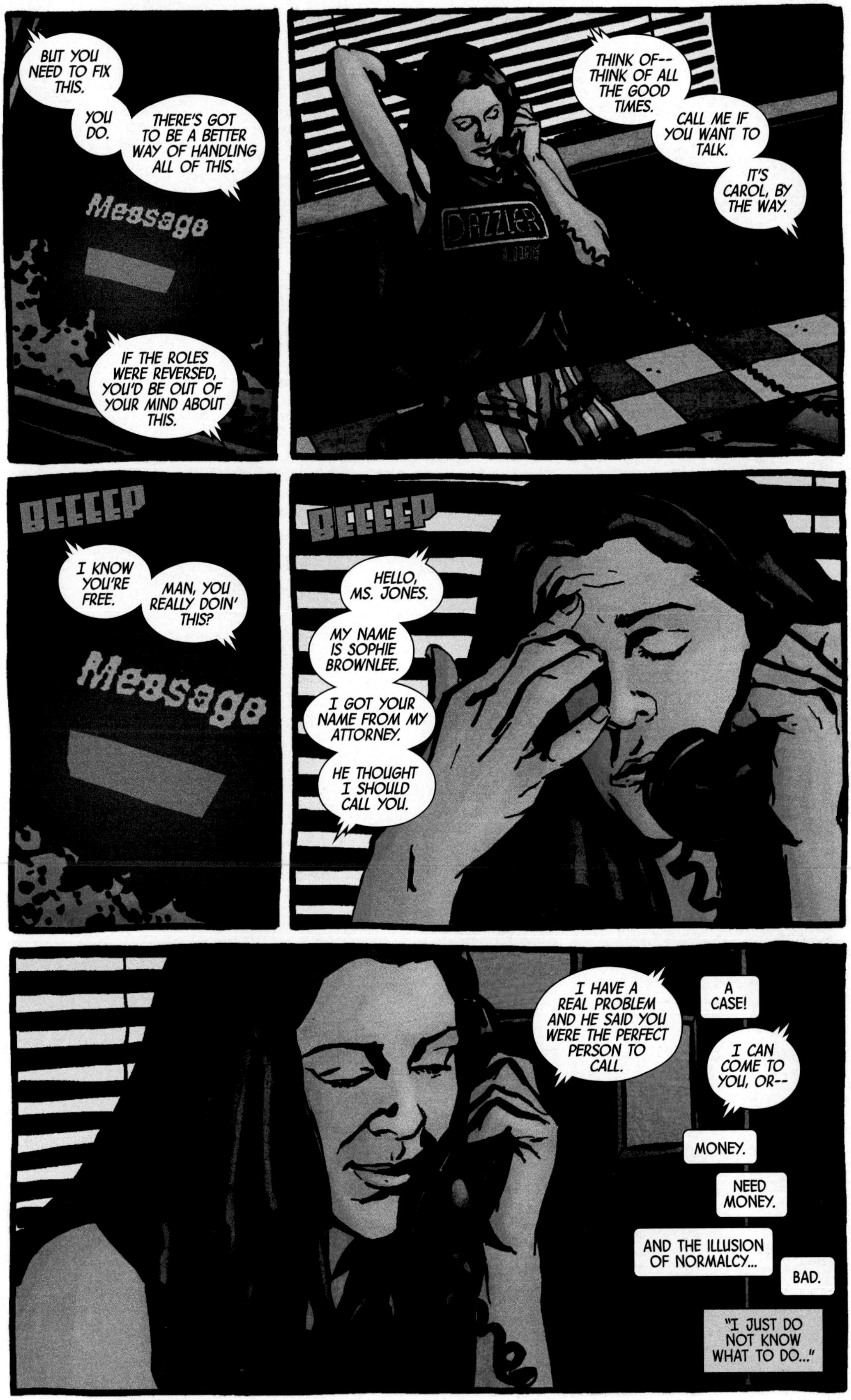
BUT YOU NEED TO FIX THIS.
YOU DO.
THERE'S GOT TO BE A BETTER WAY OF HANDLING ALL OF THIS.
Message
IF THE ROLES WERE REVERSED, YOU'D BE OUT OF YOUR MIND ABOUT THIS.
THINK OF-- THINK OF ALL THE GOOD TIMES.
CALL ME IF YOU WANT TO TALK.
IT'S CAROL, BY THE WAY.
DAZZLER
BEEEEP
I KNOW YOU'RE FREE.
MAN, YOU REALLY DOIN' THIS?
Message
BEEEEP
HELLO, MS. JONES.
MY NAME IS SOPHIE BROWNLEE.
I GOT YOUR NAME FROM MY ATTORNEY.
HE THOUGHT I SHOULD CALL YOU.
I HAVE A REAL PROBLEM AND HE SAID YOU WERE THE PERFECT PERSON TO CALL.
A CASE!
I CAN COME TO YOU, OR--
MONEY.
NEED MONEY.
AND THE ILLUSION OF NORMALCY...
BAD.
"I JUST DO NOT KNOW WHAT TO DO..."

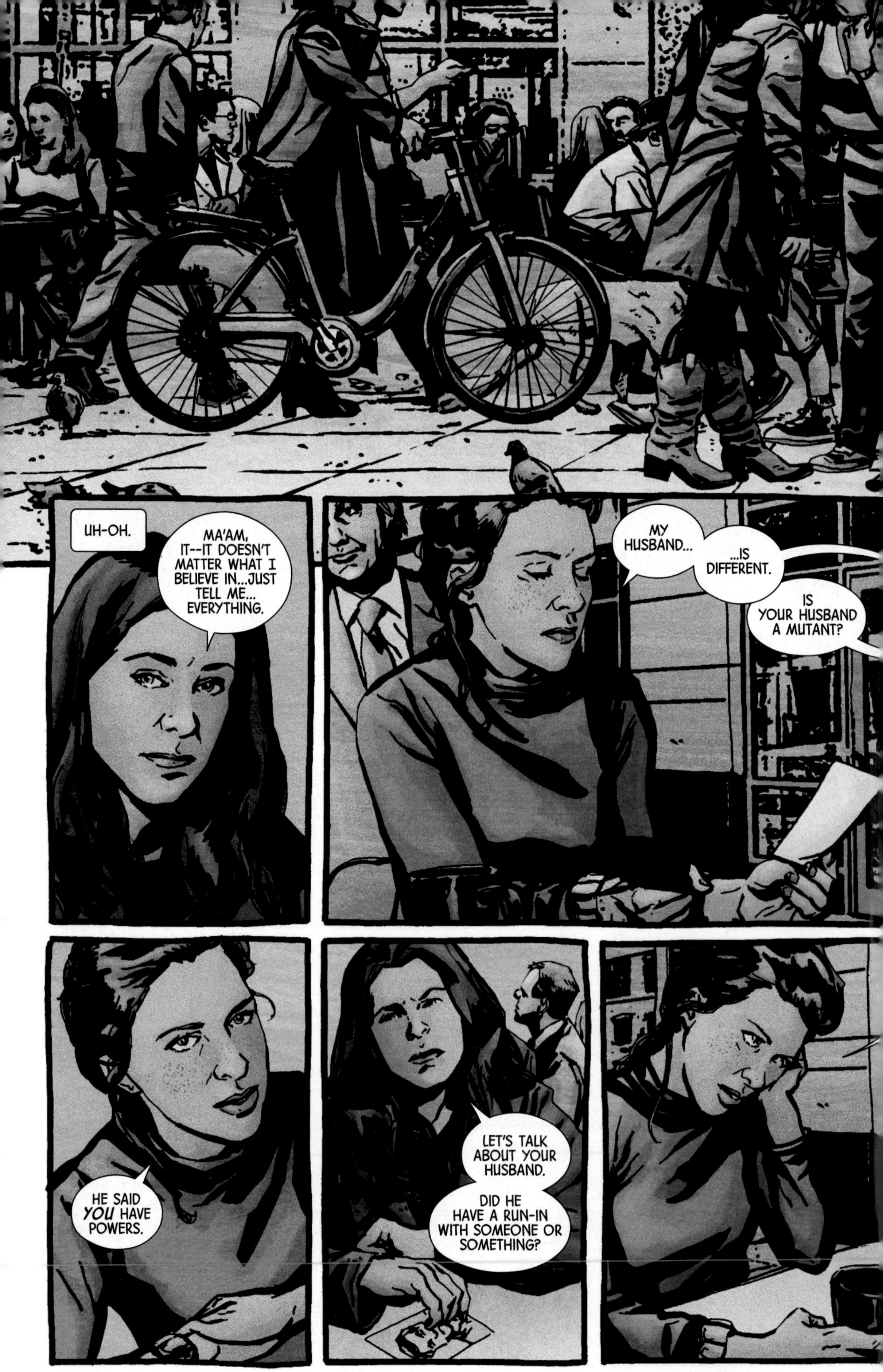
UH-OH.
MA'AM, IT--IT DOESN'T MATTER WHAT I BELIEVE IN...JUST TELL ME... EVERYTHING.
MY HUSBAND...
...IS DIFFERENT.
IS YOUR HUSBAND A MUTANT?
HE SAID *YOU* HAVE POWERS.
LET'S TALK ABOUT YOUR HUSBAND.
DID HE HAVE A RUN-IN WITH SOMEONE OR SOMETHING?

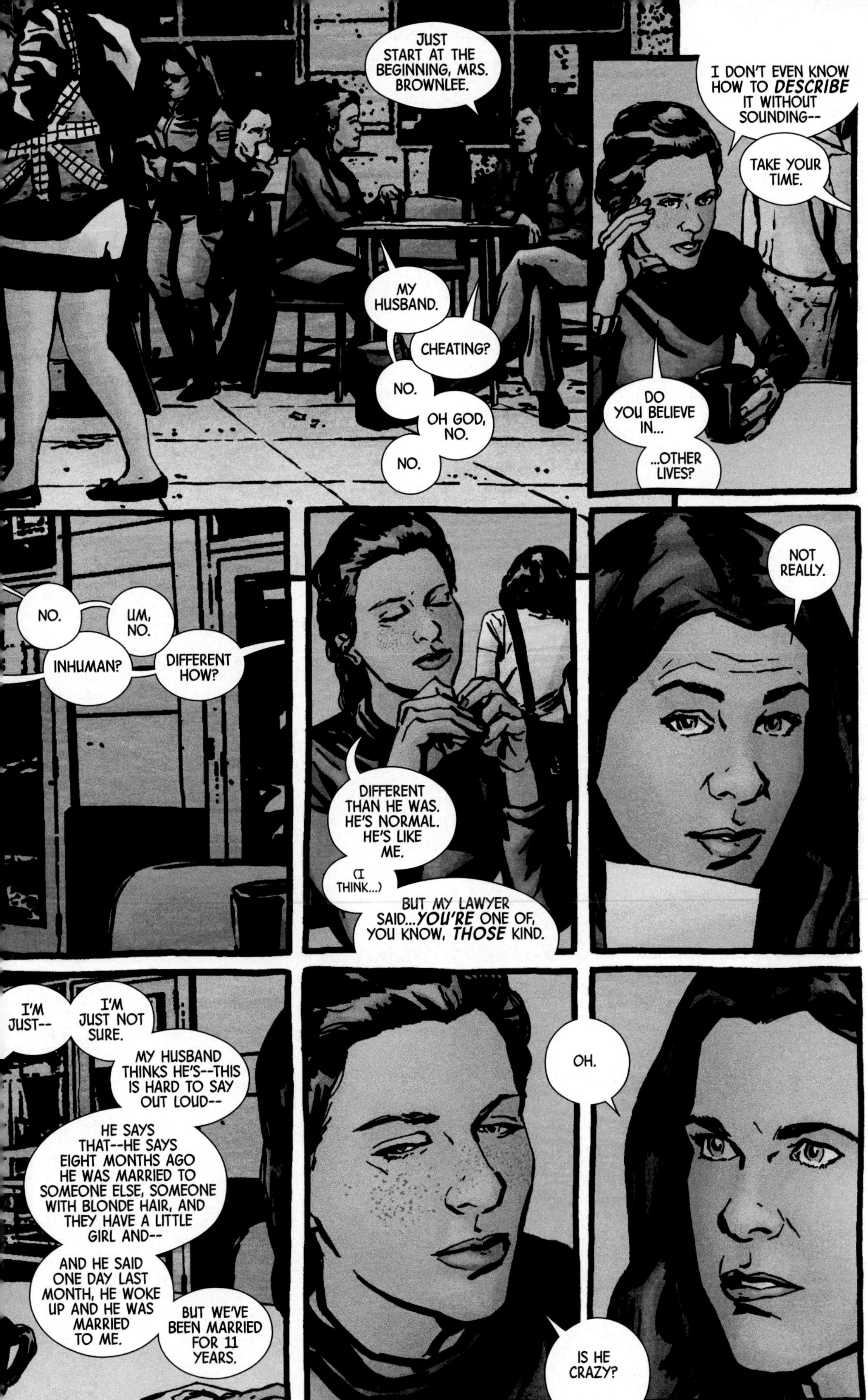
JUST START AT THE BEGINNING, MRS. BROWNLEE.
MY HUSBAND.
CHEATING?
NO.
OH GOD, NO.
NO.
I DON'T EVEN KNOW HOW TO DESCRIBE IT WITHOUT SOUNDING--
TAKE YOUR TIME.
DO YOU BELIEVE IN...
...OTHER LIVES?
NOT REALLY.
NO.
UM, NO.
INHUMAN?
DIFFERENT HOW?
DIFFERENT THAN HE WAS. HE'S NORMAL. HE'S LIKE ME.
(I THINK...)
BUT MY LAWYER SAID...YOU'RE ONE OF, YOU KNOW, THOSE KIND.
I'M JUST--
I'M JUST NOT SURE.
MY HUSBAND THINKS HE'S--THIS IS HARD TO SAY OUT LOUD--
HE SAYS THAT--HE SAYS EIGHT MONTHS AGO HE WAS MARRIED TO SOMEONE ELSE, SOMEONE WITH BLONDE HAIR, AND THEY HAVE A LITTLE GIRL AND--
AND HE SAID ONE DAY LAST MONTH, HE WOKE UP AND HE WAS MARRIED TO ME.
BUT WE'VE BEEN MARRIED FOR 11 YEARS.
OH.
IS HE CRAZY?

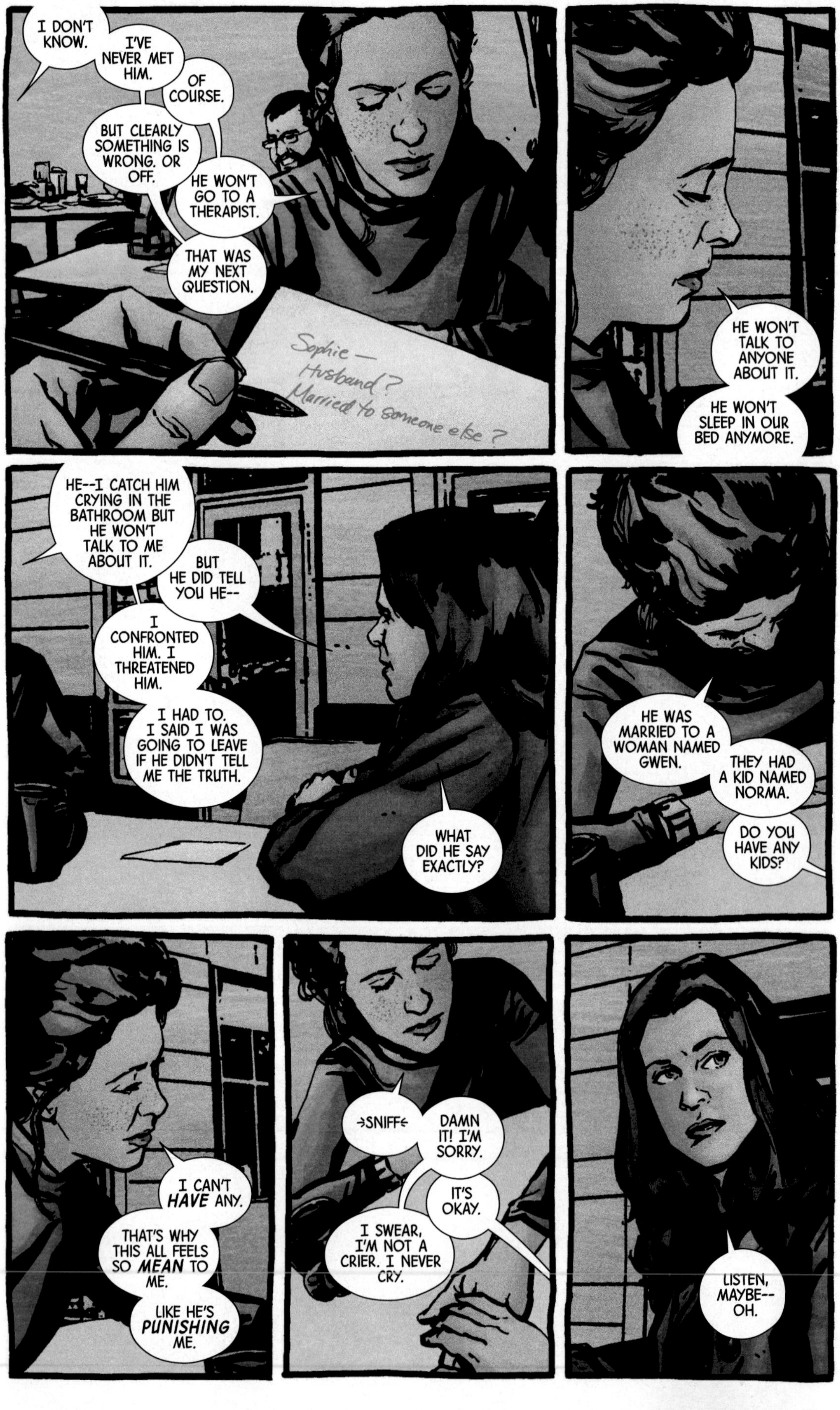
I DON'T KNOW.
I'VE NEVER MET HIM.
OF COURSE.
BUT CLEARLY SOMETHING IS WRONG. OR OFF.
HE WON'T GO TO A THERAPIST.
THAT WAS MY NEXT QUESTION.
Sophie — Husband? Married to someone else?
HE WON'T TALK TO ANYONE ABOUT IT.
HE WON'T SLEEP IN OUR BED ANYMORE.
HE--I CATCH HIM CRYING IN THE BATHROOM BUT HE WON'T TALK TO ME ABOUT IT.
BUT HE DID TELL YOU HE--
I CONFRONTED HIM. I THREATENED HIM.
I HAD TO. I SAID I WAS GOING TO LEAVE IF HE DIDN'T TELL ME THE TRUTH.
WHAT DID HE SAY EXACTLY?
HE WAS MARRIED TO A WOMAN NAMED GWEN.
THEY HAD A KID NAMED NORMA.
DO YOU HAVE ANY KIDS?
I CAN'T *HAVE* ANY.
THAT'S WHY THIS ALL FEELS SO *MEAN* TO ME.
LIKE HE'S *PUNISHING* ME.
SNIFF
DAMN IT! I'M SORRY.
IT'S OKAY.
I SWEAR, I'M NOT A CRIER. I NEVER CRY.
LISTEN, MAYBE-- OH.

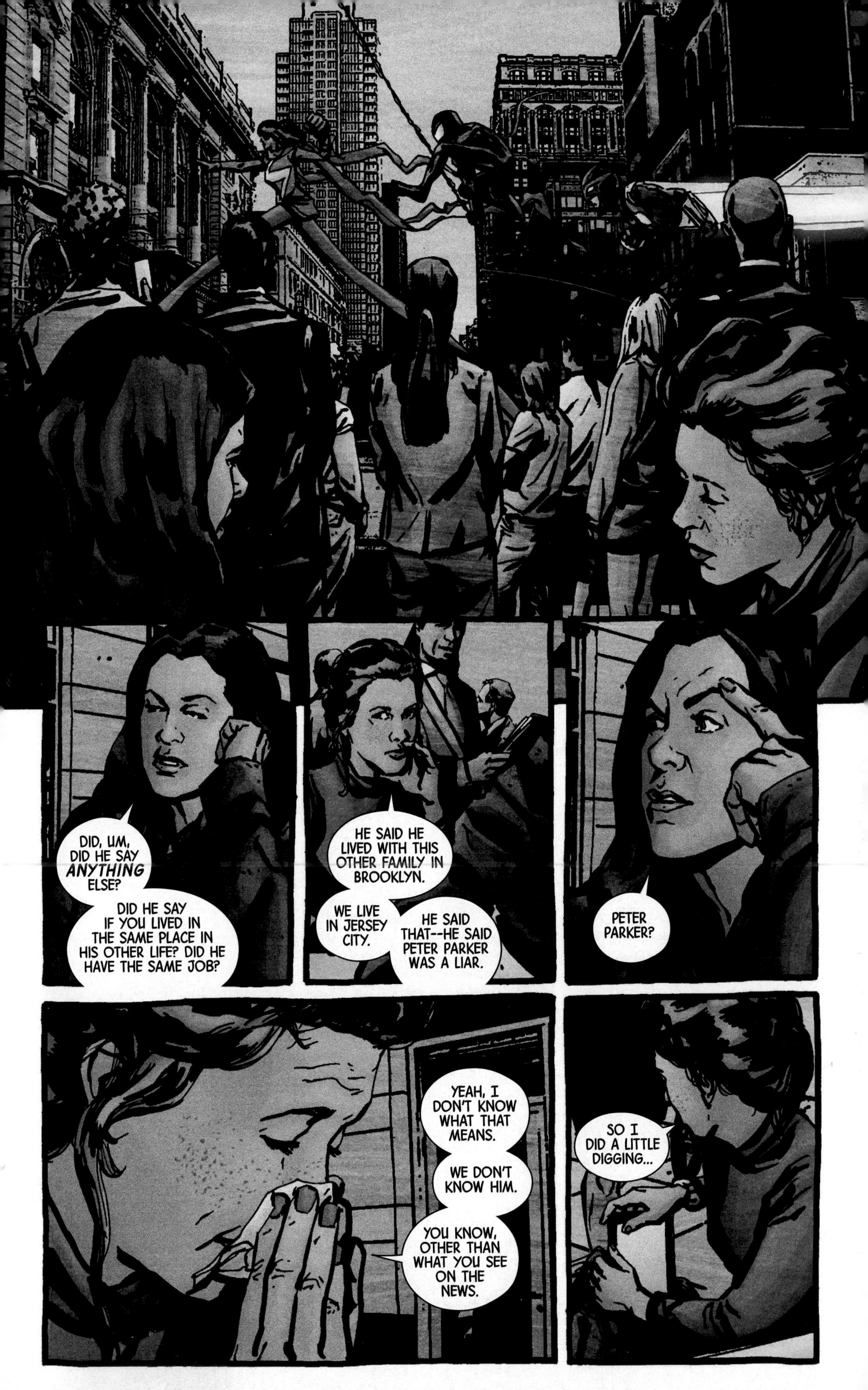
DID, UM, DID HE SAY *ANYTHING* ELSE?
DID HE SAY IF YOU LIVED IN THE SAME PLACE IN HIS OTHER LIFE? DID HE HAVE THE SAME JOB?
HE SAID HE LIVED WITH THIS OTHER FAMILY IN BROOKLYN.
WE LIVE IN JERSEY CITY.
HE SAID THAT--HE SAID PETER PARKER WAS A LIAR.
PETER PARKER?
YEAH, I DON'T KNOW WHAT THAT MEANS.
WE DON'T KNOW HIM.
YOU KNOW, OTHER THAN WHAT YOU SEE ON THE NEWS.
SO I DID A LITTLE DIGGING...

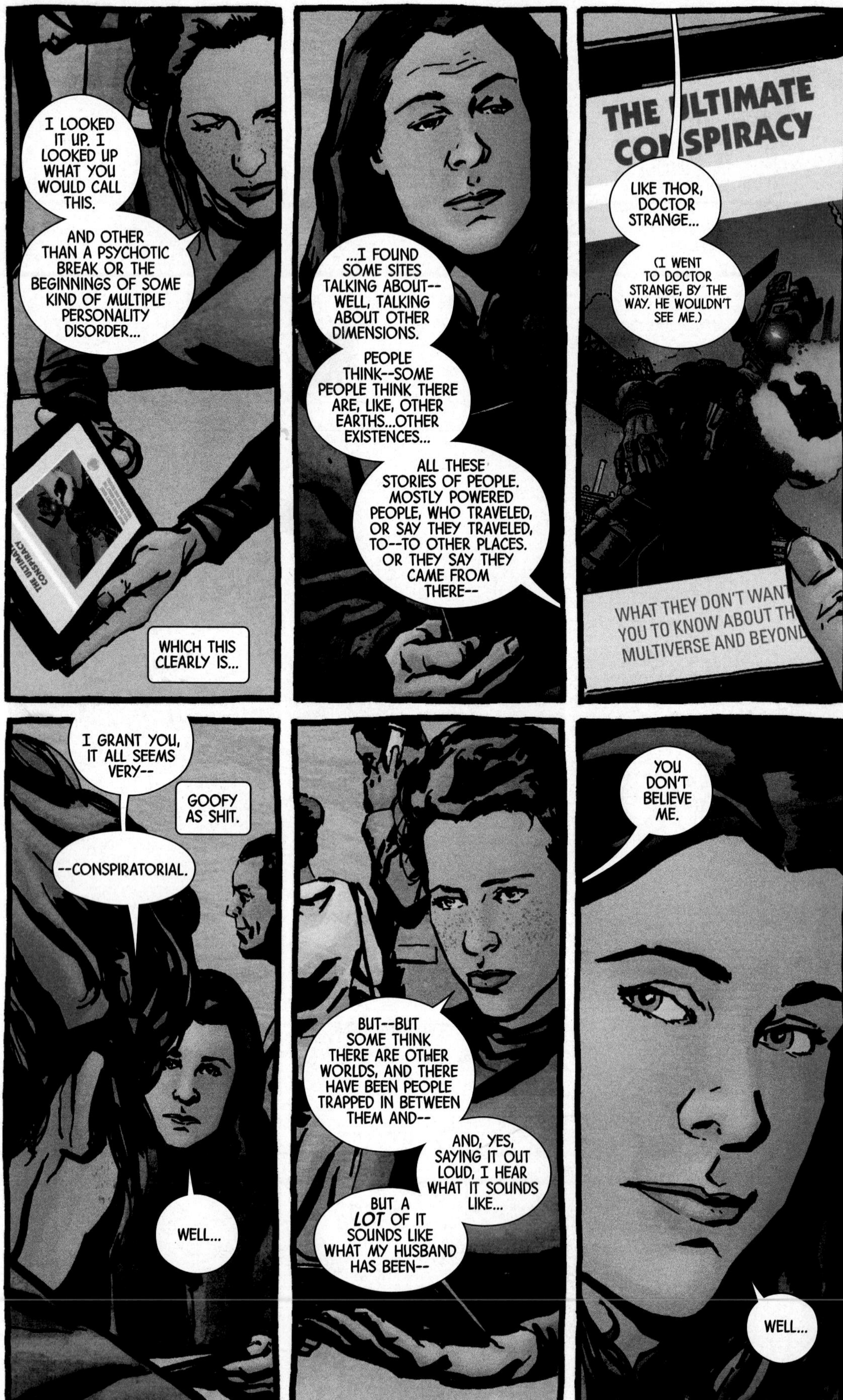
I LOOKED IT UP. I LOOKED UP WHAT YOU WOULD CALL THIS.
AND OTHER THAN A PSYCHOTIC BREAK OR THE BEGINNINGS OF SOME KIND OF MULTIPLE PERSONALITY DISORDER...
THE ULTIMATE CONSPIRACY
WHICH THIS CLEARLY IS...
...I FOUND SOME SITES TALKING ABOUT--WELL, TALKING ABOUT OTHER DIMENSIONS.
PEOPLE THINK--SOME PEOPLE THINK THERE ARE, LIKE, OTHER EARTHS...OTHER EXISTENCES...
ALL THESE STORIES OF PEOPLE. MOSTLY POWERED PEOPLE, WHO TRAVELED, OR SAY THEY TRAVELED, TO--TO OTHER PLACES. OR THEY SAY THEY CAME FROM THERE--
THE ULTIMATE CONSPIRACY
LIKE THOR, DOCTOR STRANGE...
(I WENT TO DOCTOR STRANGE, BY THE WAY. HE WOULDN'T SEE ME.)
WHAT THEY DON'T WANT YOU TO KNOW ABOUT TH MULTIVERSE AND BEYOND
I GRANT YOU, IT ALL SEEMS VERY--
GOOFY AS SHIT.
--CONSPIRATORIAL.
WELL...
BUT--BUT SOME THINK THERE ARE OTHER WORLDS, AND THERE HAVE BEEN PEOPLE TRAPPED IN BETWEEN THEM AND--
AND, YES, SAYING IT OUT LOUD, I HEAR WHAT IT SOUNDS LIKE...
BUT A LOT OF IT SOUNDS LIKE WHAT MY HUSBAND HAS BEEN--
YOU DON'T BELIEVE ME.
WELL...

IT SOUNDS CRAZY, RIGHT?

I MEAN, ONE DAY EVERYTHING IS FINE...

THE NEXT DAY HE COMES HOME LATE FROM WORK AND-- HE'S PACING AROUND...

WHERE DOES HE WORK?

HE'S A SALES REP FOR A RECORD COMPANY. JAZZ AND BLUES...

HAS HE HAD A TRAUMA?

LIKE HE GOT HIT ON THE HEAD? NO.

ANYTHING.

LIKE A FENDER BENDER EVEN.

DID HE GET CAUGHT IN ONE OF THOSE SUPER HERO FIGHTS? WAS HE TRAPPED BY ANYTHING?

I HONESTLY DON'T KNOW.

DO YOU THINK HE'S CRAZY? DO YOU THINK I AM?

I DON'T THINK YOU'RE CRAZY.

I THINK YOU'RE TRYING TO UNDERSTAND SOMETHING THAT DOESN'T MAKE SENSE, AND THERE'S NOTHING CRAZY ABOUT THAT.

ARE YOU MARRIED?

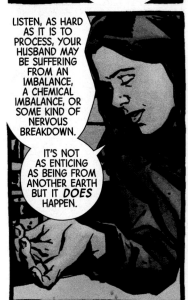

LISTEN, AS HARD AS IT IS TO PROCESS, YOUR HUSBAND MAY BE SUFFERING FROM AN IMBALANCE, A CHEMICAL IMBALANCE, OR SOME KIND OF NERVOUS BREAKDOWN.

IT'S NOT AS ENTICING AS BEING FROM ANOTHER EARTH BUT IT DOES HAPPEN.

GODS, INHUMANS, THORS, HULKS, EVERYONE CRASHING INTO EACH OTHER.

DOCTOR DOOMS.

WHERE ARE THE FANTASTIC FOUR?

NO ONE EVEN TALKS ABOUT THEM ANYMORE.

IS IT NOT POSSIBLE THAT MY HUSBAND IS SANE AND THE WORLD IS CRAZY?

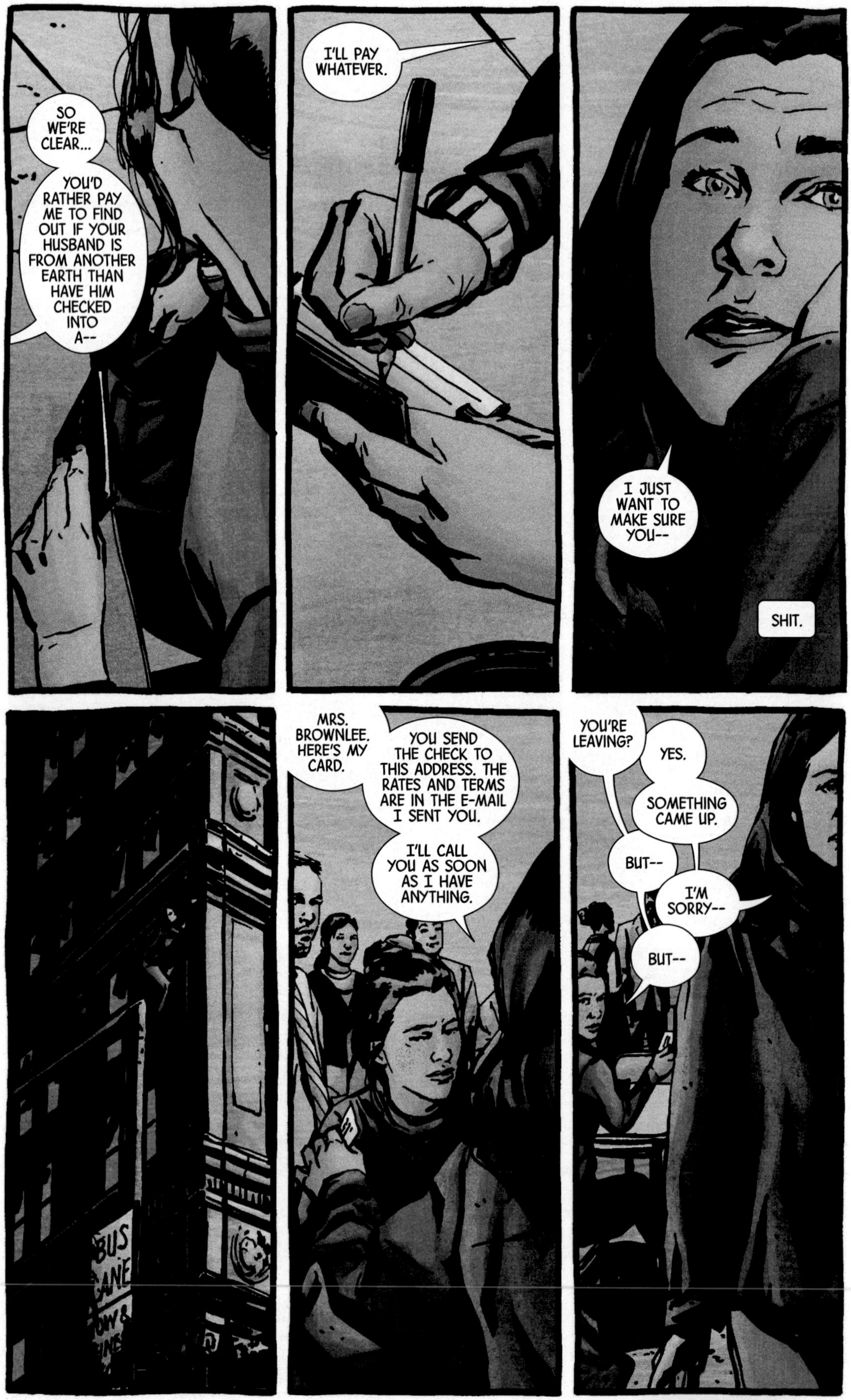
SO WE'RE CLEAR...
YOU'D RATHER PAY ME TO FIND OUT IF YOUR HUSBAND IS FROM ANOTHER EARTH THAN HAVE HIM CHECKED INTO A--
I'LL PAY WHATEVER.
I JUST WANT TO MAKE SURE YOU--
SHIT.
BUS
MRS. BROWNLEE. HERE'S MY CARD.
YOU SEND THE CHECK TO THIS ADDRESS. THE RATES AND TERMS ARE IN THE E-MAIL I SENT YOU.
I'LL CALL YOU AS SOON AS I HAVE ANYTHING.
YOU'RE LEAVING?
YES.
SOMETHING CAME UP.
BUT--
I'M SORRY--
BUT--

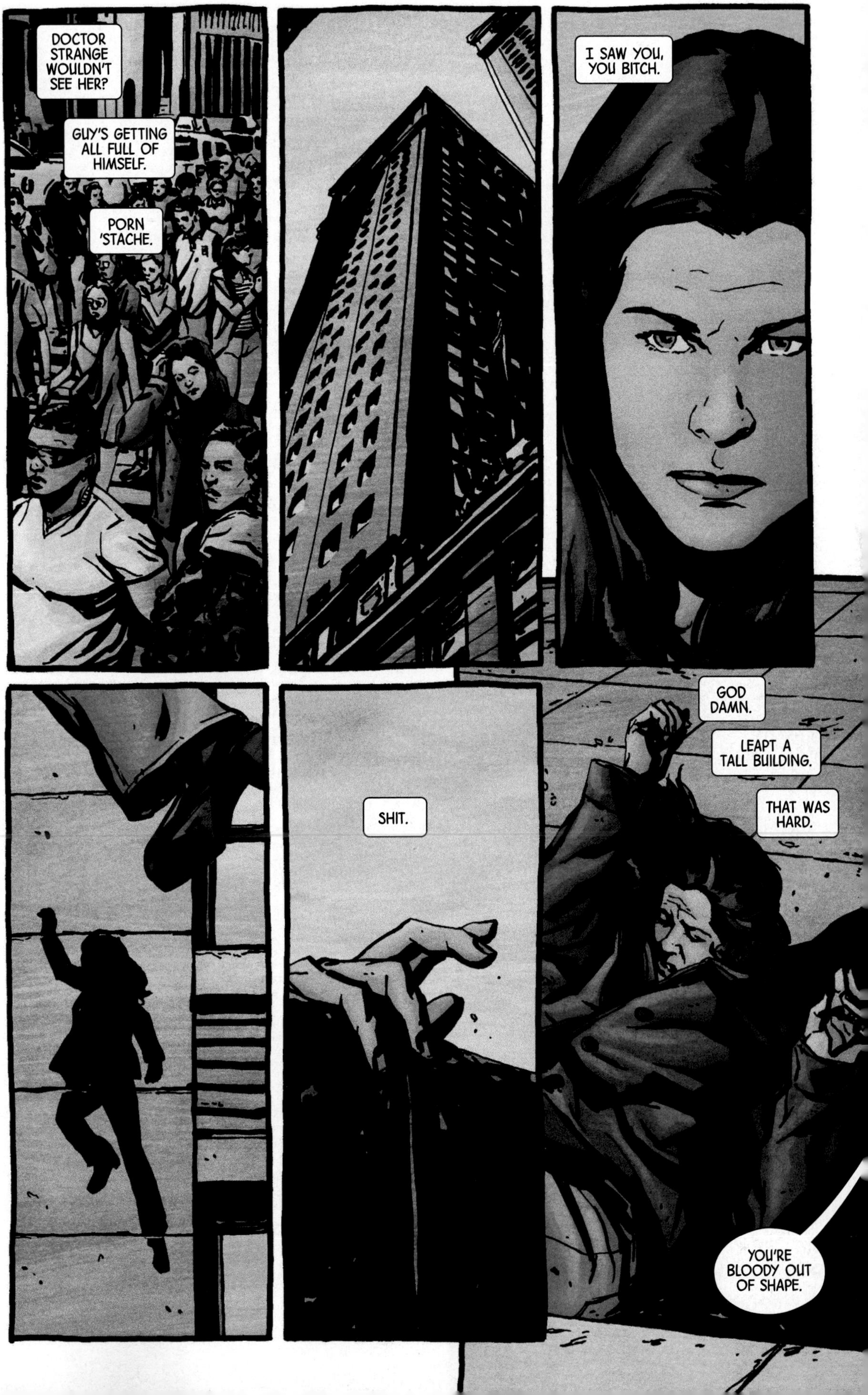
DOCTOR STRANGE WOULDN'T SEE HER?
GUY'S GETTING ALL FULL OF HIMSELF.
PORN 'STACHE.
I SAW YOU, YOU BITCH.
SHIT.
GOD DAMN.
LEAPT A TALL BUILDING.
THAT WAS HARD.
YOU'RE BLOODY OUT OF SHAPE.

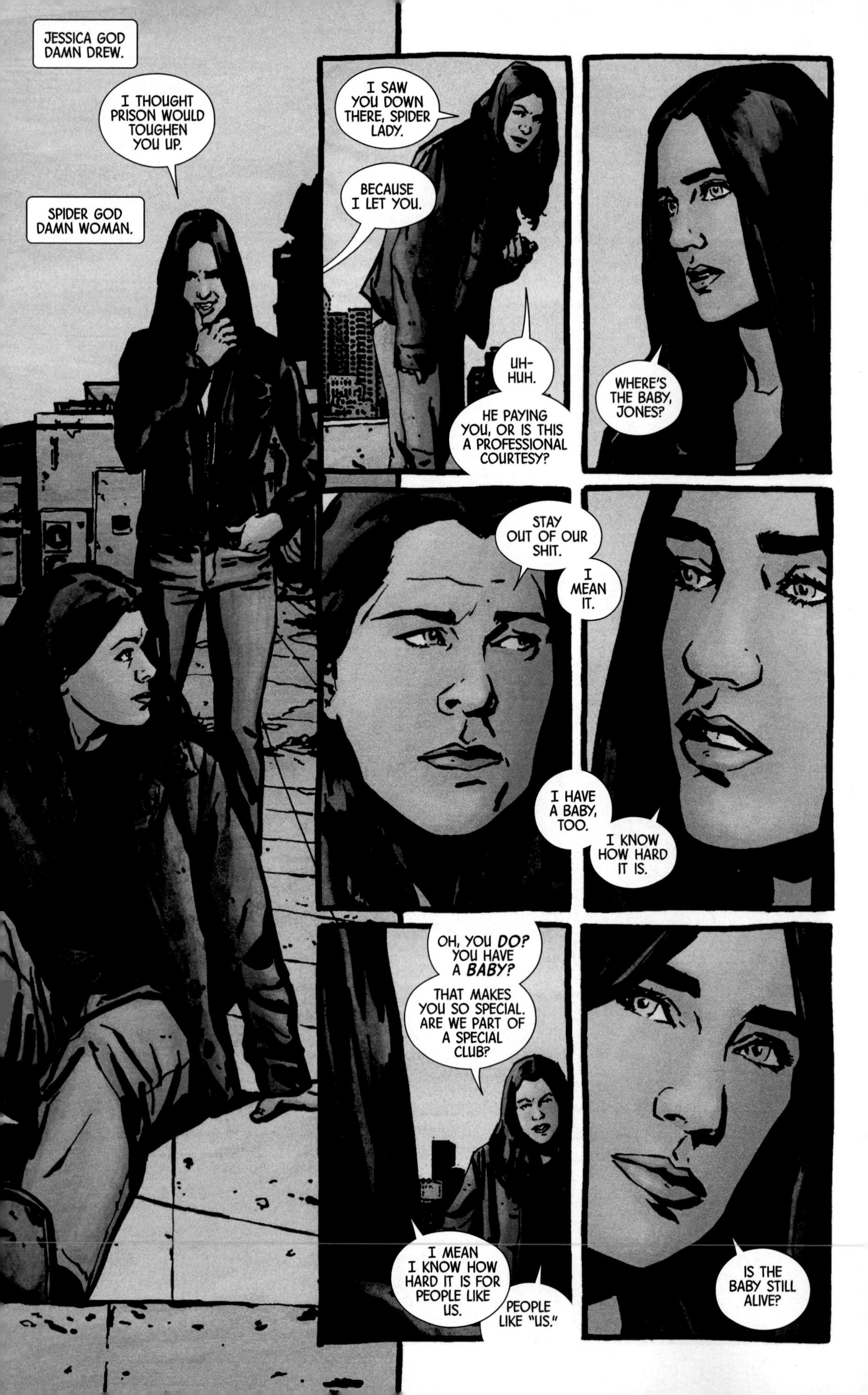
JESSICA GOD DAMN DREW.
I THOUGHT PRISON WOULD TOUGHEN YOU UP.
SPIDER GOD DAMN WOMAN.
I SAW YOU DOWN THERE, SPIDER LADY.
BECAUSE I LET YOU.
UH-HUH.
HE PAYING YOU, OR IS THIS A PROFESSIONAL COURTESY?
WHERE'S THE BABY, JONES?
STAY OUT OF OUR SHIT.
I MEAN IT.
I HAVE A BABY, TOO.
I KNOW HOW HARD IT IS.
OH, YOU DO? YOU HAVE A BABY?
THAT MAKES YOU SO SPECIAL. ARE WE PART OF A SPECIAL CLUB?
I MEAN I KNOW HOW HARD IT IS FOR PEOPLE LIKE US.
PEOPLE LIKE "US."
IS THE BABY STILL ALIVE?

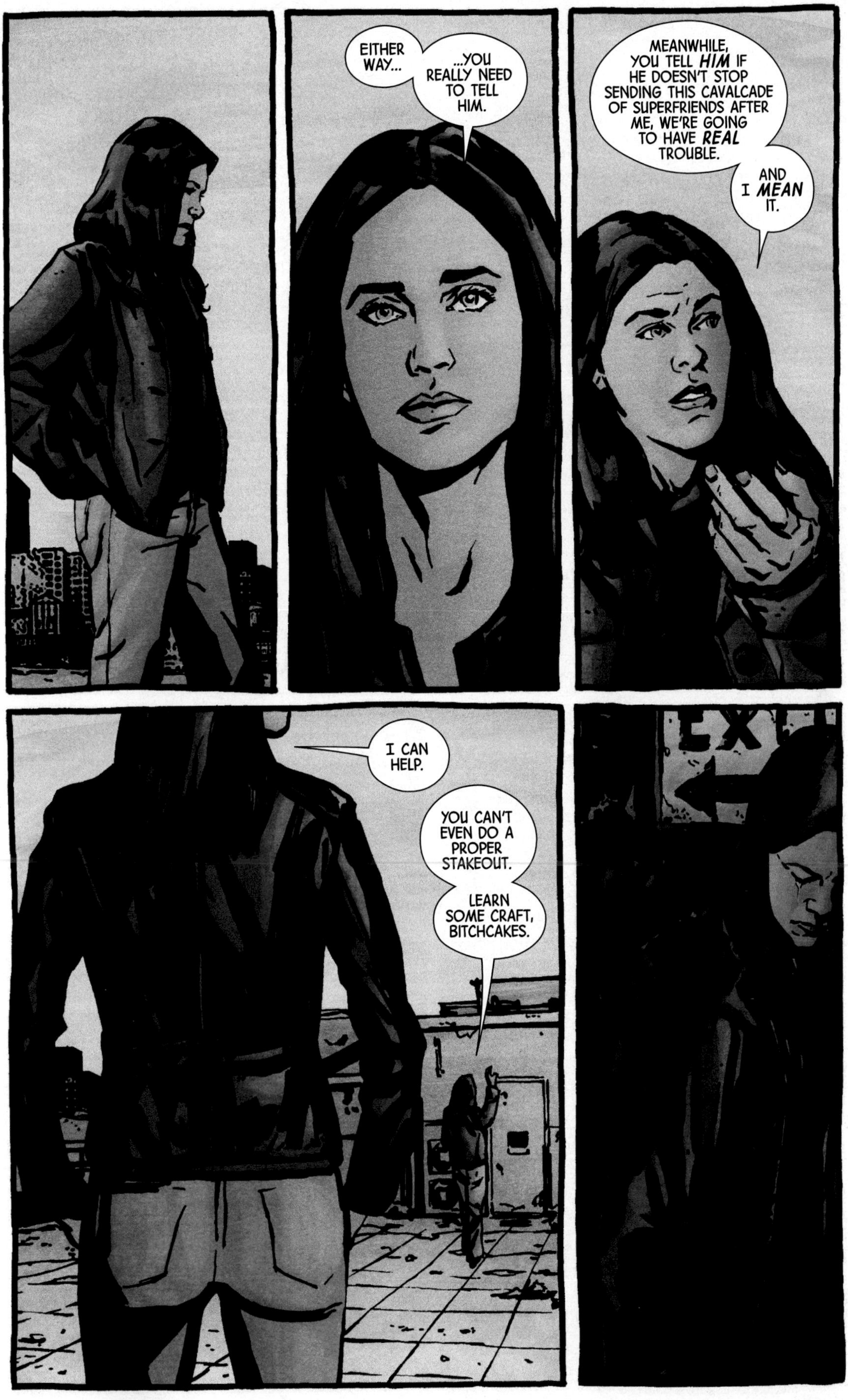
EITHER WAY...
...YOU REALLY NEED TO TELL HIM.
MEANWHILE, YOU TELL HIM IF HE DOESN'T STOP SENDING THIS CAVALCADE OF SUPERFRIENDS AFTER ME, WE'RE GOING TO HAVE REAL TROUBLE.
AND I MEAN IT.
I CAN HELP.
YOU CAN'T EVEN DO A PROPER STAKEOUT.
LEARN SOME CRAFT, BITCHCAKES.
EXI

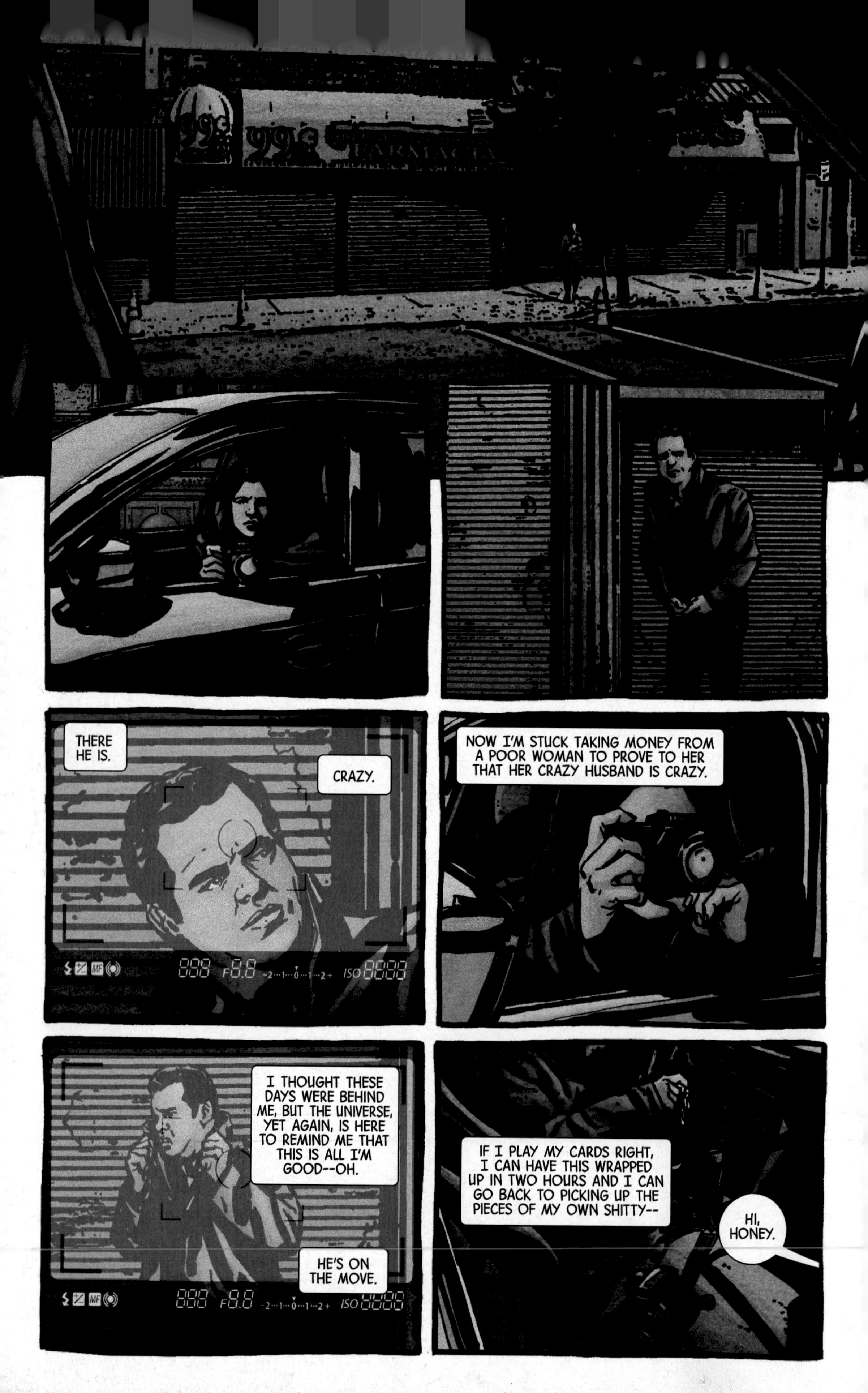
THERE HE IS.
CRAZY.
NOW I'M STUCK TAKING MONEY FROM A POOR WOMAN TO PROVE TO HER THAT HER CRAZY HUSBAND IS CRAZY.
I THOUGHT THESE DAYS WERE BEHIND ME, BUT THE UNIVERSE, YET AGAIN, IS HERE TO REMIND ME THAT THIS IS ALL I'M GOOD--OH.
HE'S ON THE MOVE.
IF I PLAY MY CARDS RIGHT, I CAN HAVE THIS WRAPPED UP IN TWO HOURS AND I CAN GO BACK TO PICKING UP THE PIECES OF MY OWN SHITTY--
HI, HONEY.

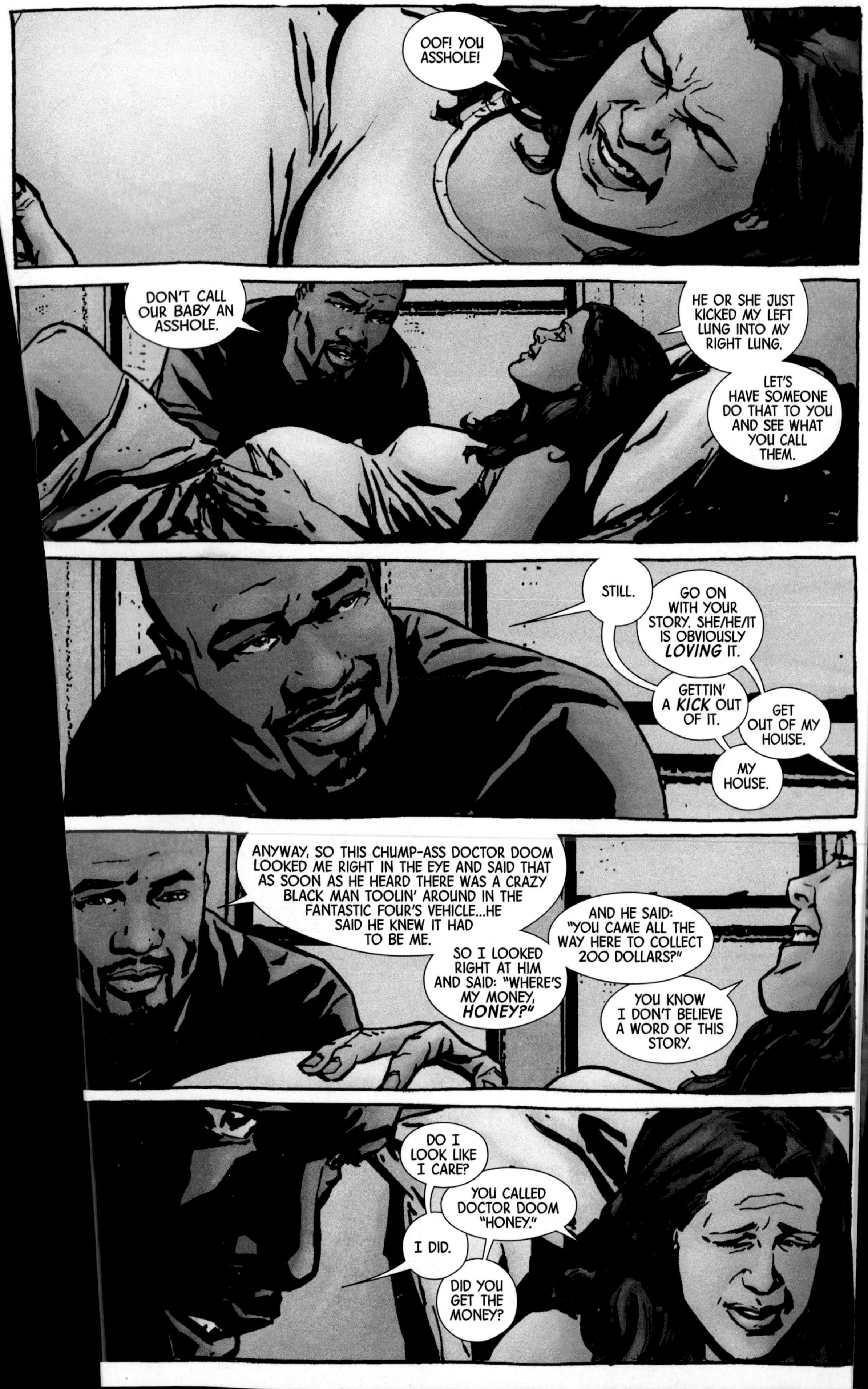
OOF! YOU ASSHOLE!
DON'T CALL OUR BABY AN ASSHOLE.
HE OR SHE JUST KICKED MY LEFT LUNG INTO MY RIGHT LUNG.
LET'S HAVE SOMEONE DO THAT TO YOU AND SEE WHAT YOU CALL THEM.
STILL.
GO ON WITH YOUR STORY. SHE/HE/IT IS OBVIOUSLY LOVING IT.
GETTIN' A KICK OUT OF IT.
GET OUT OF MY HOUSE.
MY HOUSE.
ANYWAY, SO THIS CHUMP-ASS DOCTOR DOOM LOOKED ME RIGHT IN THE EYE AND SAID THAT AS SOON AS HE HEARD THERE WAS A CRAZY BLACK MAN TOOLIN' AROUND IN THE FANTASTIC FOUR'S VEHICLE...HE SAID HE KNEW IT HAD TO BE ME.
AND HE SAID: "YOU CAME ALL THE WAY HERE TO COLLECT 200 DOLLARS?"
SO I LOOKED RIGHT AT HIM AND SAID: "WHERE'S MY MONEY, HONEY?"
YOU KNOW I DON'T BELIEVE A WORD OF THIS STORY.
DO I LOOK LIKE I CARE?
YOU CALLED DOCTOR DOOM "HONEY."
I DID.
DID YOU GET THE MONEY?
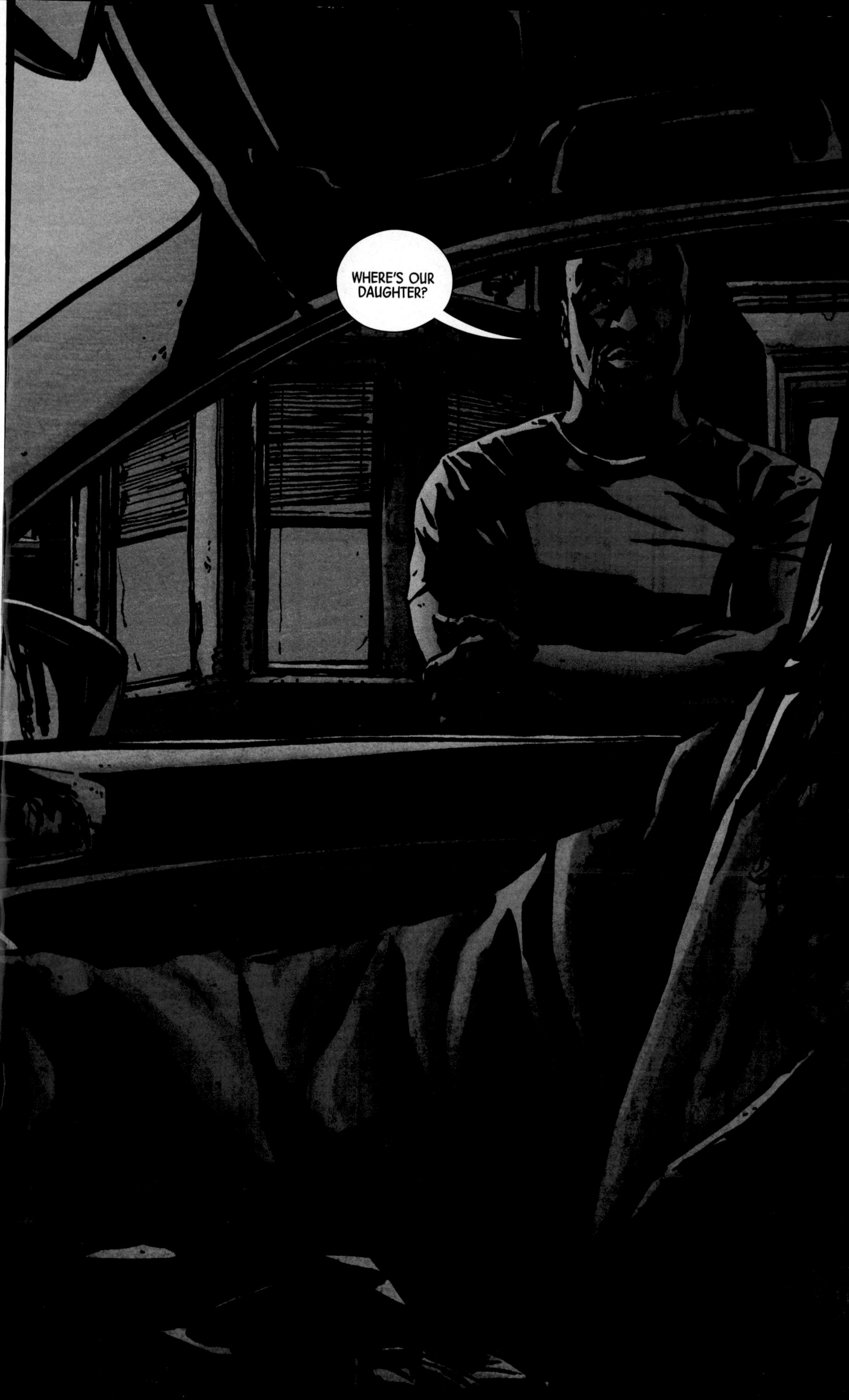
WHERE'S OUR DAUGHTER?

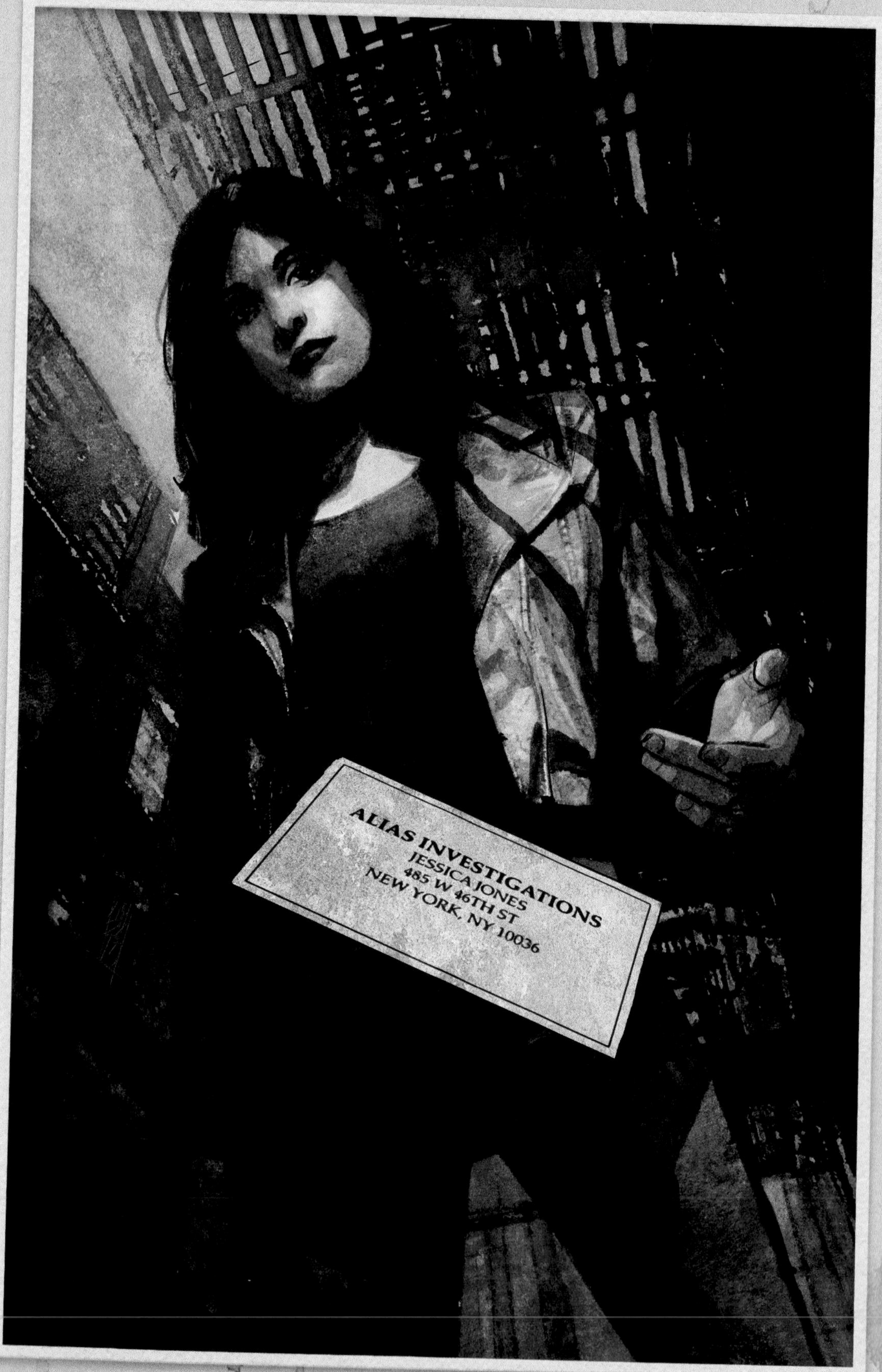
ALIAS INVESTIGATIONS
JESSICA JONES
485 W 46TH ST
NEW YORK, NY 10036

#1 variant by **Alex Maleev**

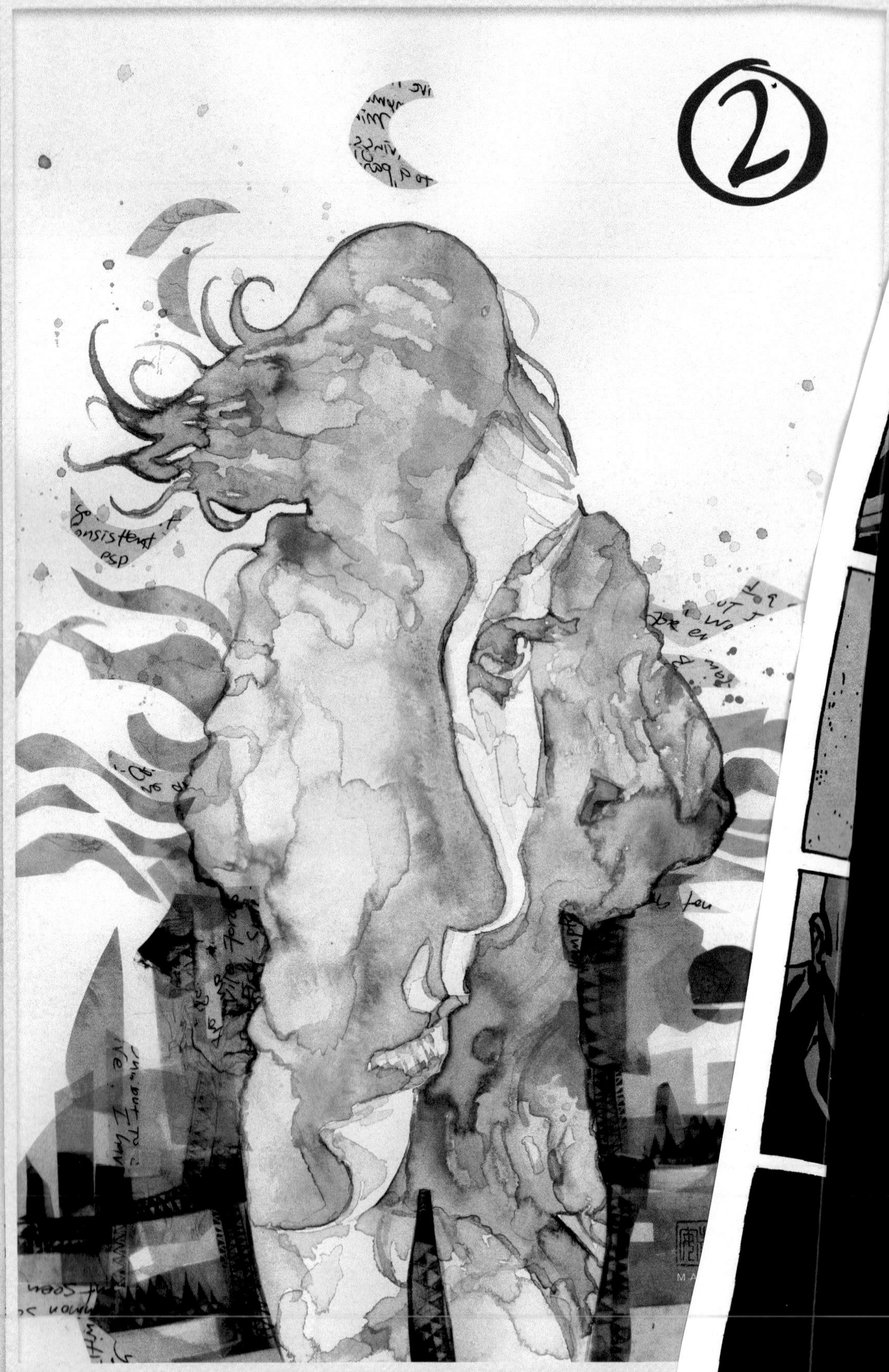
2

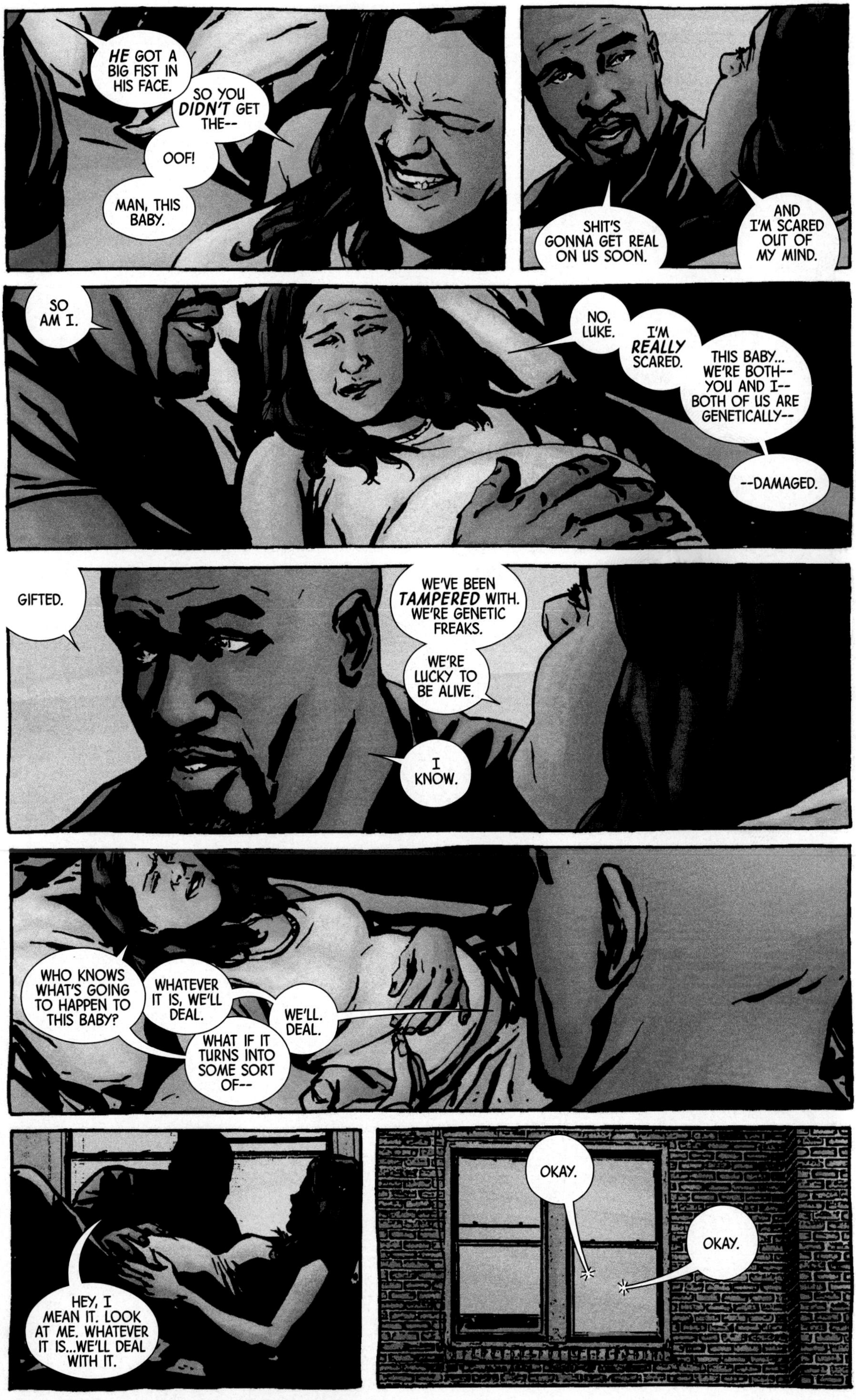
HE GOT A BIG FIST IN HIS FACE.
SO YOU DIDN'T GET THE--
OOF!
MAN, THIS BABY.
SHIT'S GONNA GET REAL ON US SOON.
AND I'M SCARED OUT OF MY MIND.
SO AM I.
NO, LUKE.
I'M REALLY SCARED.
THIS BABY... WE'RE BOTH-- YOU AND I-- BOTH OF US ARE GENETICALLY--
--DAMAGED.
GIFTED.
WE'VE BEEN TAMPERED WITH. WE'RE GENETIC FREAKS.
WE'RE LUCKY TO BE ALIVE.
I KNOW.
WHO KNOWS WHAT'S GOING TO HAPPEN TO THIS BABY?
WHATEVER IT IS, WE'LL DEAL.
WHAT IF IT TURNS INTO SOME SORT OF--
WE'LL. DEAL.
HEY, I MEAN IT. LOOK AT ME. WHATEVER IT IS...WE'LL DEAL WITH IT.
OKAY.
OKAY.

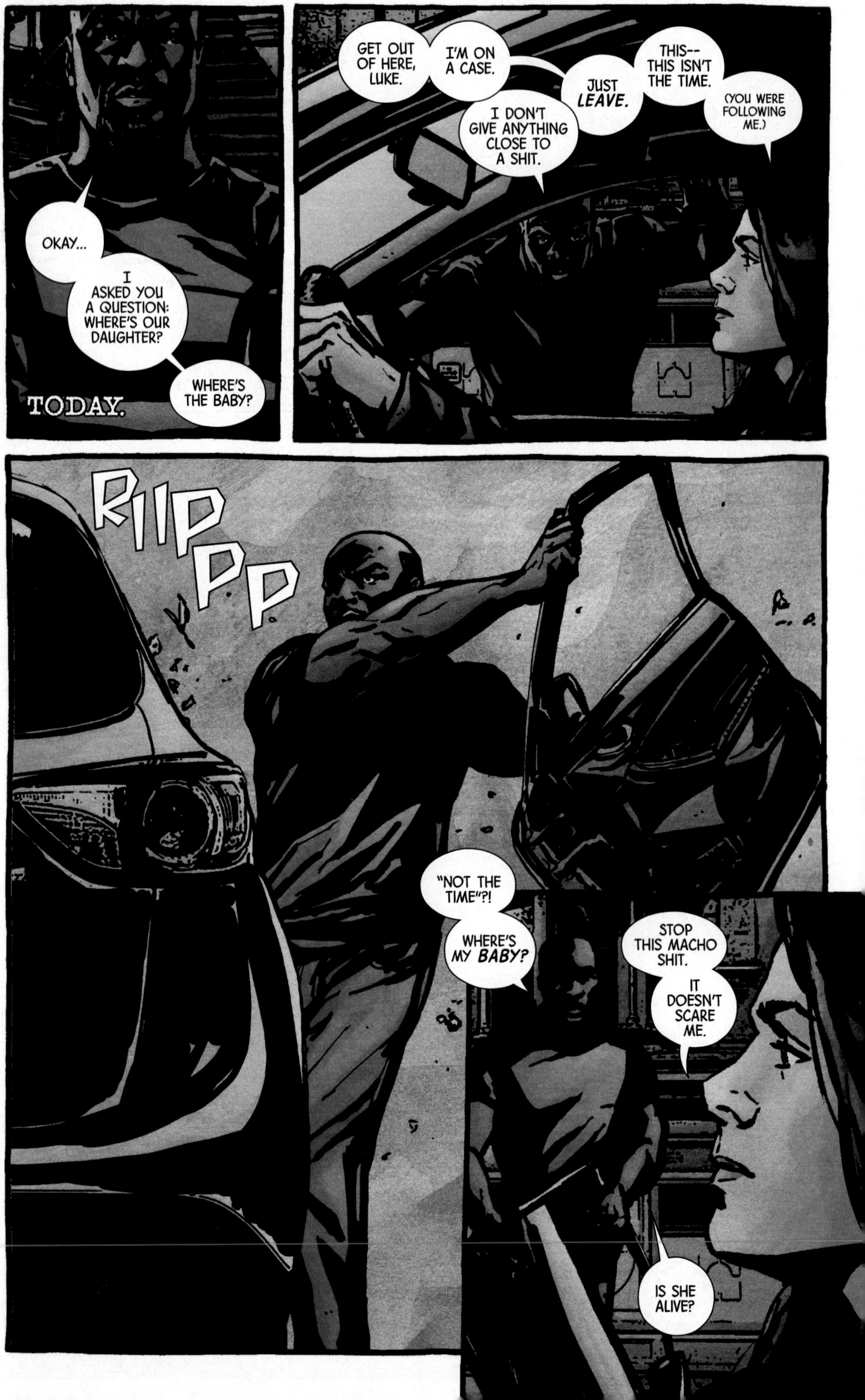
OKAY...
I ASKED YOU A QUESTION: WHERE'S OUR DAUGHTER?
WHERE'S THE BABY?
TODAY.
GET OUT OF HERE, LUKE.
I'M ON A CASE.
I DON'T GIVE ANYTHING CLOSE TO A SHIT.
JUST LEAVE.
THIS-- THIS ISN'T THE TIME.
(YOU WERE FOLLOWING ME.)
RIIPPP
"NOT THE TIME"?!
WHERE'S MY BABY?
STOP THIS MACHO SHIT.
IT DOESN'T SCARE ME.
IS SHE ALIVE?

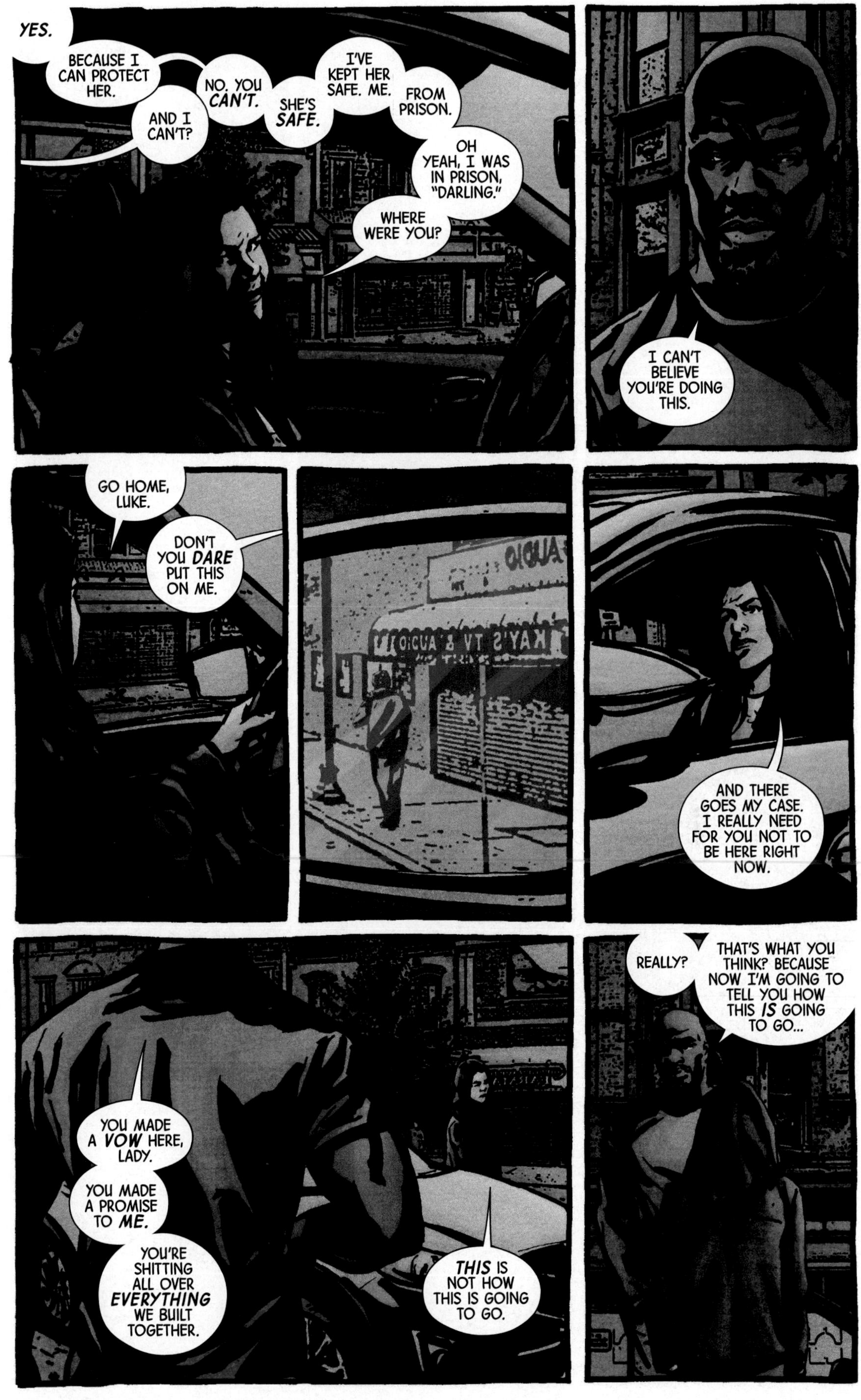

YES.
BECAUSE I CAN PROTECT HER.
AND I CAN'T?
NO. YOU CAN'T.
SHE'S SAFE.
I'VE KEPT HER SAFE. ME.
FROM PRISON.
OH YEAH, I WAS IN PRISON, "DARLING."
WHERE WERE YOU?
I CAN'T BELIEVE YOU'RE DOING THIS.
GO HOME, LUKE.
DON'T YOU DARE PUT THIS ON ME.
KAY'S TV & AUDIO
AND THERE GOES MY CASE. I REALLY NEED FOR YOU NOT TO BE HERE RIGHT NOW.
YOU MADE A VOW HERE, LADY.
YOU MADE A PROMISE TO ME.
YOU'RE SHITTING ALL OVER EVERYTHING WE BUILT TOGETHER.
THIS IS NOT HOW THIS IS GOING TO GO.
REALLY?
THAT'S WHAT YOU THINK? BECAUSE NOW I'M GOING TO TELL YOU HOW THIS IS GOING TO GO...

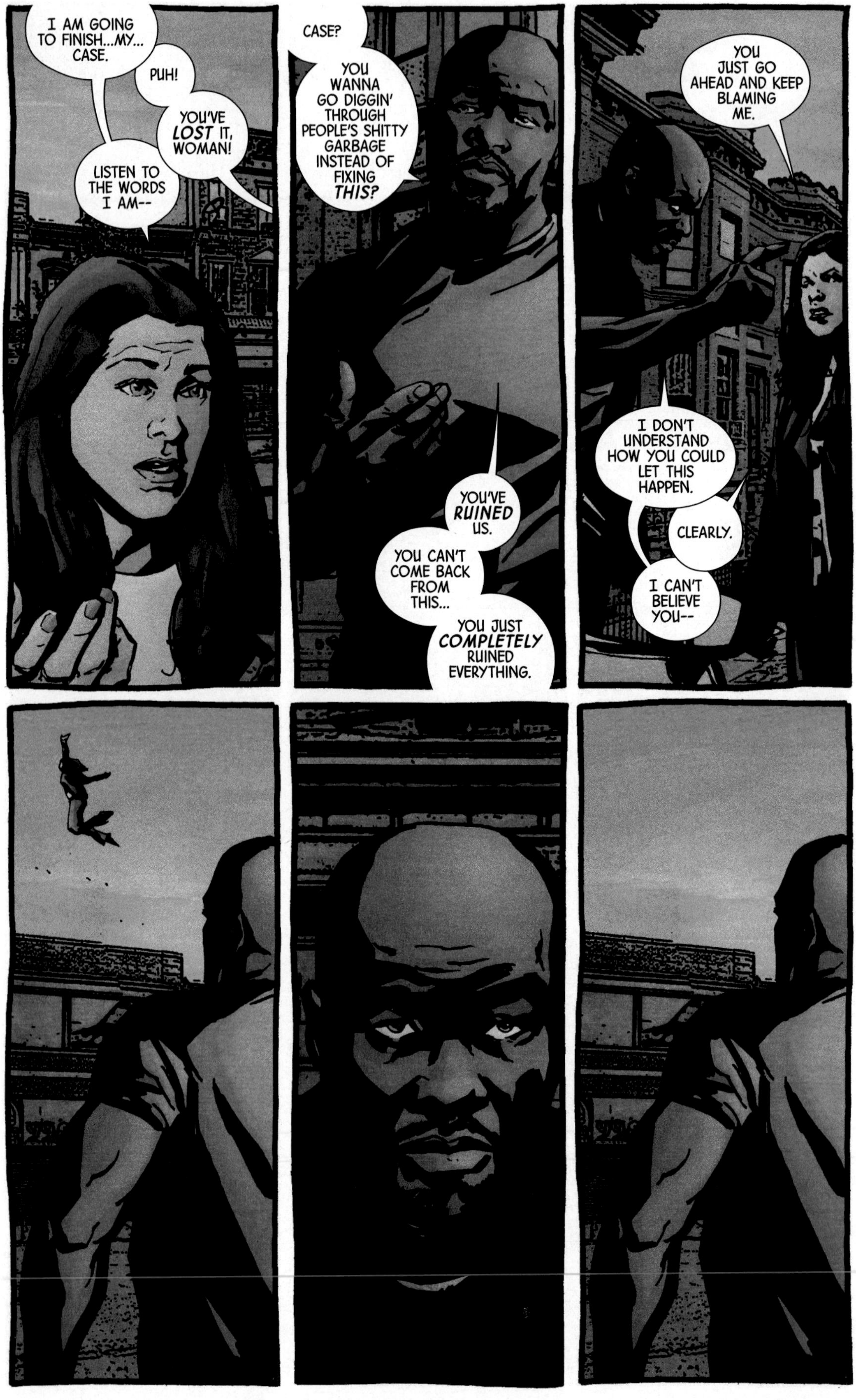
I AM GOING TO FINISH...MY... CASE.
PUH!
YOU'VE *LOST* IT, WOMAN!
LISTEN TO THE WORDS I AM--
CASE?
YOU WANNA GO DIGGIN' THROUGH PEOPLE'S SHITTY GARBAGE INSTEAD OF FIXING *THIS?*
YOU'VE *RUINED* US.
YOU CAN'T COME BACK FROM THIS...
YOU JUST *COMPLETELY* RUINED EVERYTHING.
YOU JUST GO AHEAD AND KEEP BLAMING ME.
I DON'T UNDERSTAND HOW YOU COULD LET THIS HAPPEN.
CLEARLY.
I CAN'T BELIEVE YOU--

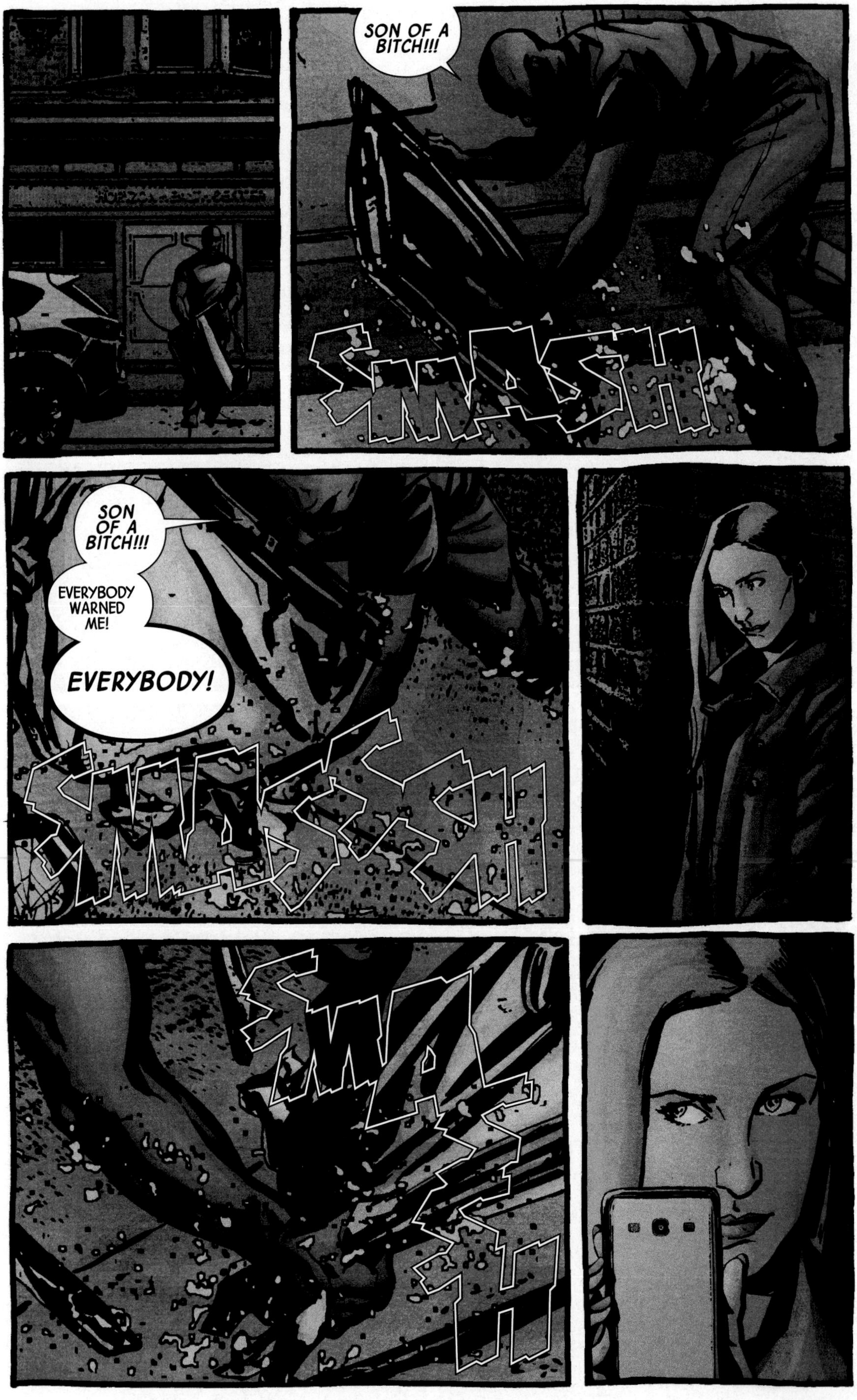
SON OF A BITCH!!!
SMASH
SON OF A BITCH!!!
EVERYBODY WARNED ME!
EVERYBODY!
SMASSH
SMASH

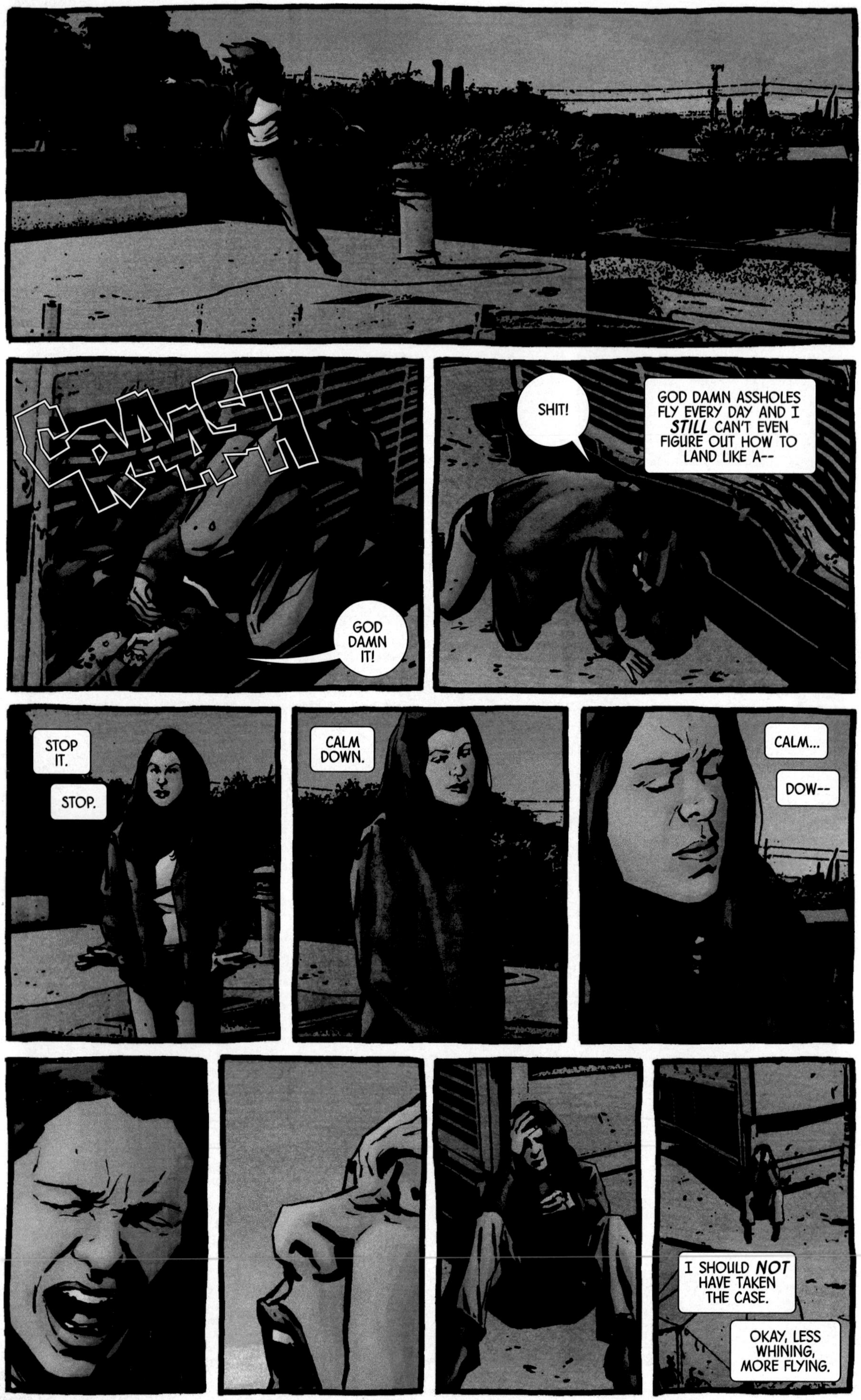
CRAAASH
GOD DAMN IT!
SHIT!
GOD DAMN ASSHOLES FLY EVERY DAY AND I *STILL* CAN'T EVEN FIGURE OUT HOW TO LAND LIKE A--
STOP IT.
STOP.
CALM DOWN.
CALM...
DOW--
I SHOULD *NOT* HAVE TAKEN THE CASE.
OKAY, LESS WHINING, MORE FLYING.

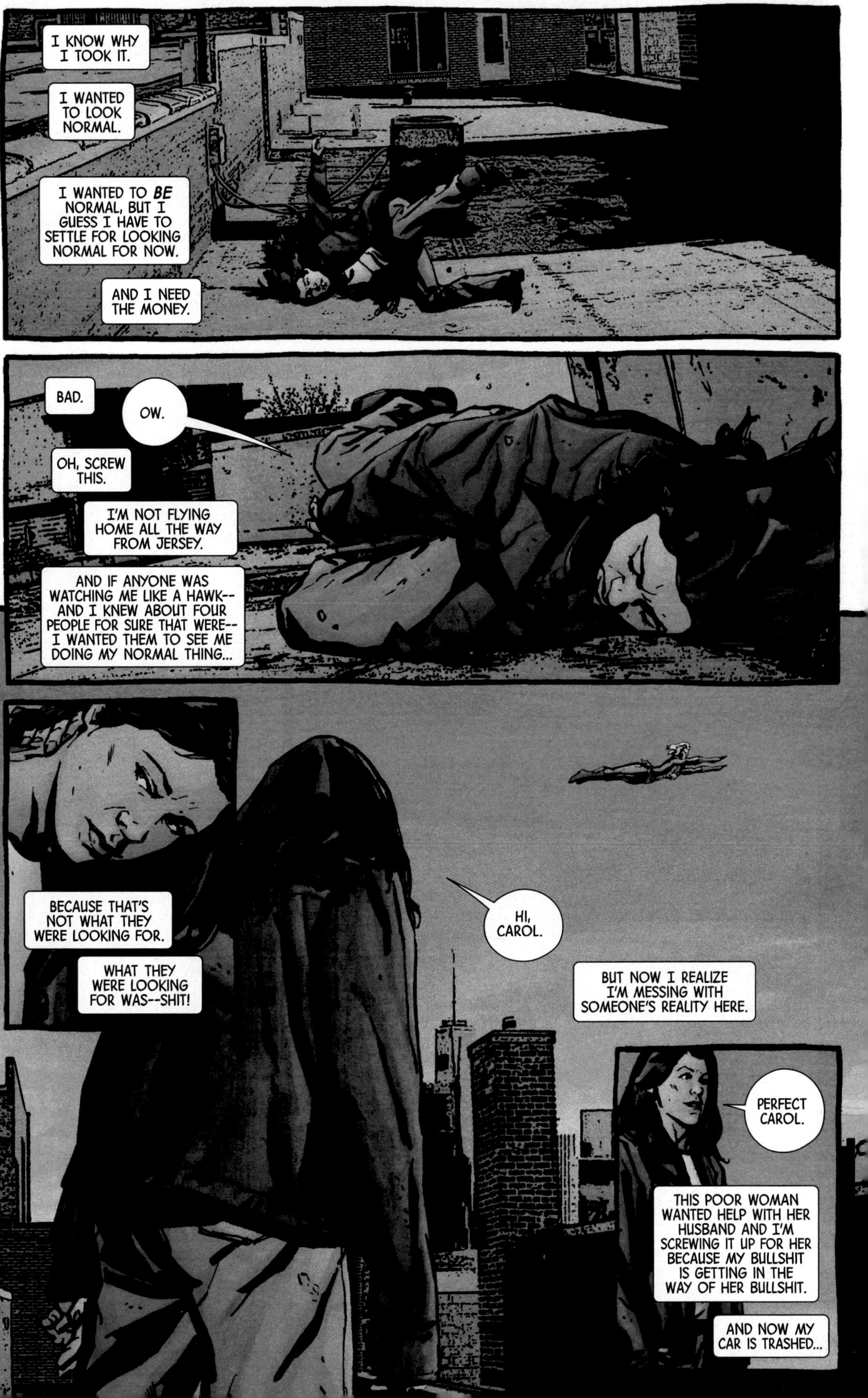
I KNOW WHY I TOOK IT.
I WANTED TO LOOK NORMAL.
I WANTED TO *BE* NORMAL, BUT I GUESS I HAVE TO SETTLE FOR LOOKING NORMAL FOR NOW.
AND I NEED THE MONEY.
BAD.
OW.
OH, SCREW THIS.
I'M NOT FLYING HOME ALL THE WAY FROM JERSEY.
AND IF ANYONE WAS WATCHING ME LIKE A HAWK--AND I KNEW ABOUT FOUR PEOPLE FOR SURE THAT WERE--I WANTED THEM TO SEE ME DOING MY NORMAL THING...
BECAUSE THAT'S NOT WHAT THEY WERE LOOKING FOR.
WHAT THEY WERE LOOKING FOR WAS--SHIT!
HI, CAROL.
BUT NOW I REALIZE I'M MESSING WITH SOMEONE'S REALITY HERE.
PERFECT CAROL.
THIS POOR WOMAN WANTED HELP WITH HER HUSBAND AND I'M SCREWING IT UP FOR HER BECAUSE MY BULLSHIT IS GETTING IN THE WAY OF HER BULLSHIT.
AND NOW MY CAR IS TRASHED...

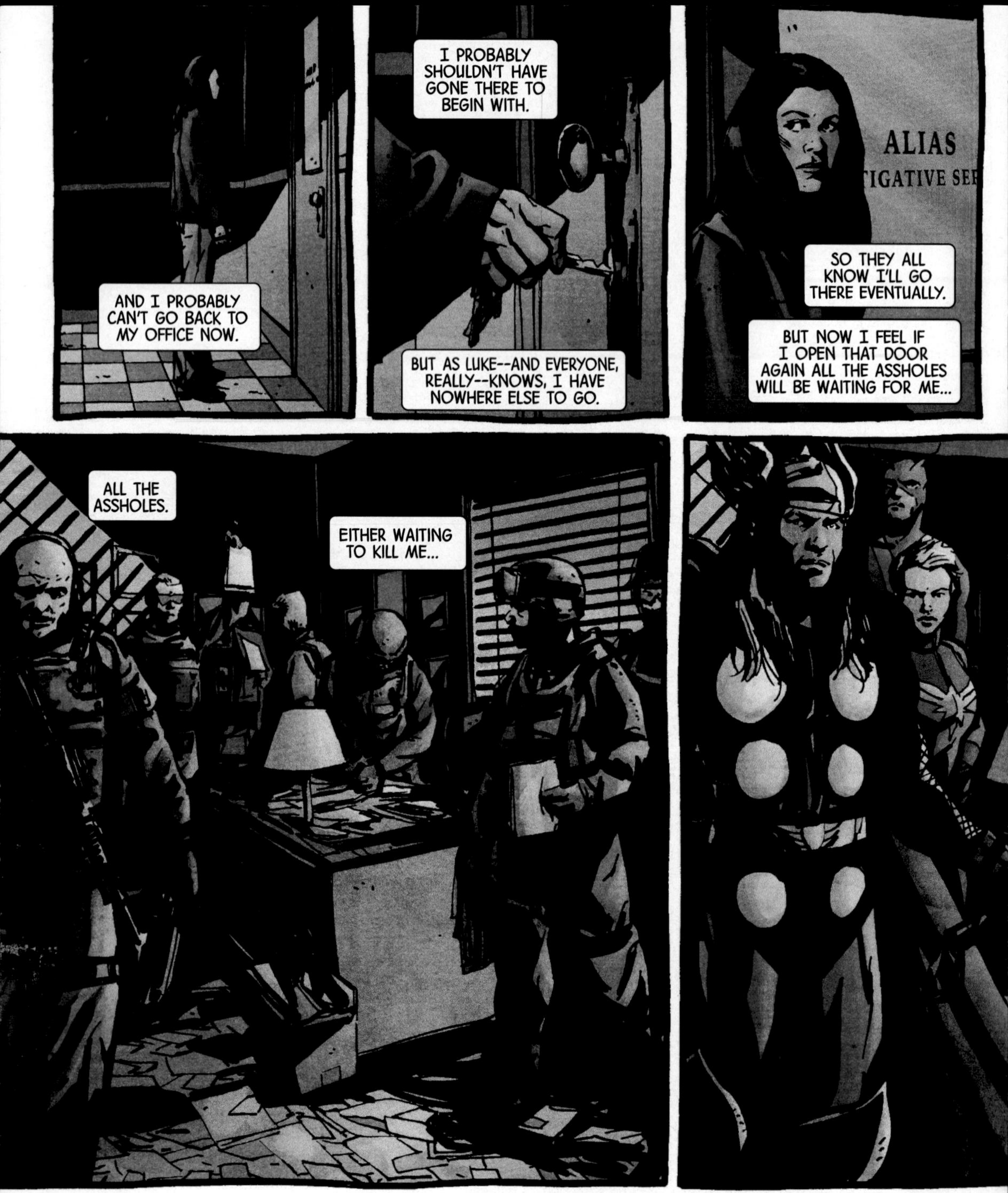
AND I PROBABLY CAN'T GO BACK TO MY OFFICE NOW.
I PROBABLY SHOULDN'T HAVE GONE THERE TO BEGIN WITH.
BUT AS LUKE--AND EVERYONE, REALLY--KNOWS, I HAVE NOWHERE ELSE TO GO.
ALIAS
IGATIVE SE
SO THEY ALL KNOW I'LL GO THERE EVENTUALLY.
BUT NOW I FEEL IF I OPEN THAT DOOR AGAIN ALL THE ASSHOLES WILL BE WAITING FOR ME...
ALL THE ASSHOLES.
EITHER WAITING TO KILL ME...

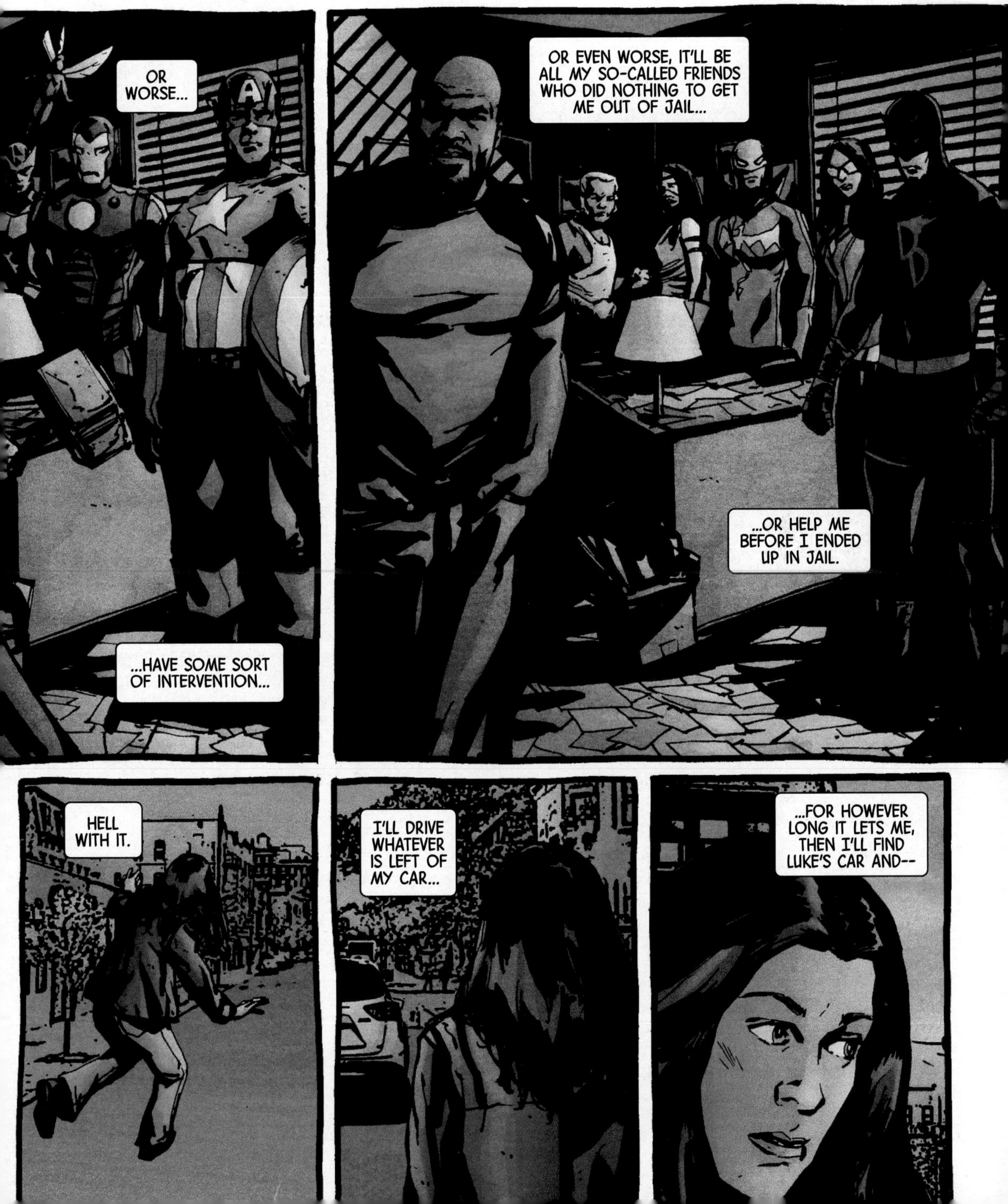
OR WORSE...
...HAVE SOME SORT OF INTERVENTION...
OR EVEN WORSE, IT'LL BE ALL MY SO-CALLED FRIENDS WHO DID NOTHING TO GET ME OUT OF JAIL...
...OR HELP ME BEFORE I ENDED UP IN JAIL.
HELL WITH IT.
I'LL DRIVE WHATEVER IS LEFT OF MY CAR...
...FOR HOWEVER LONG IT LETS ME, THEN I'LL FIND LUKE'S CAR AND--

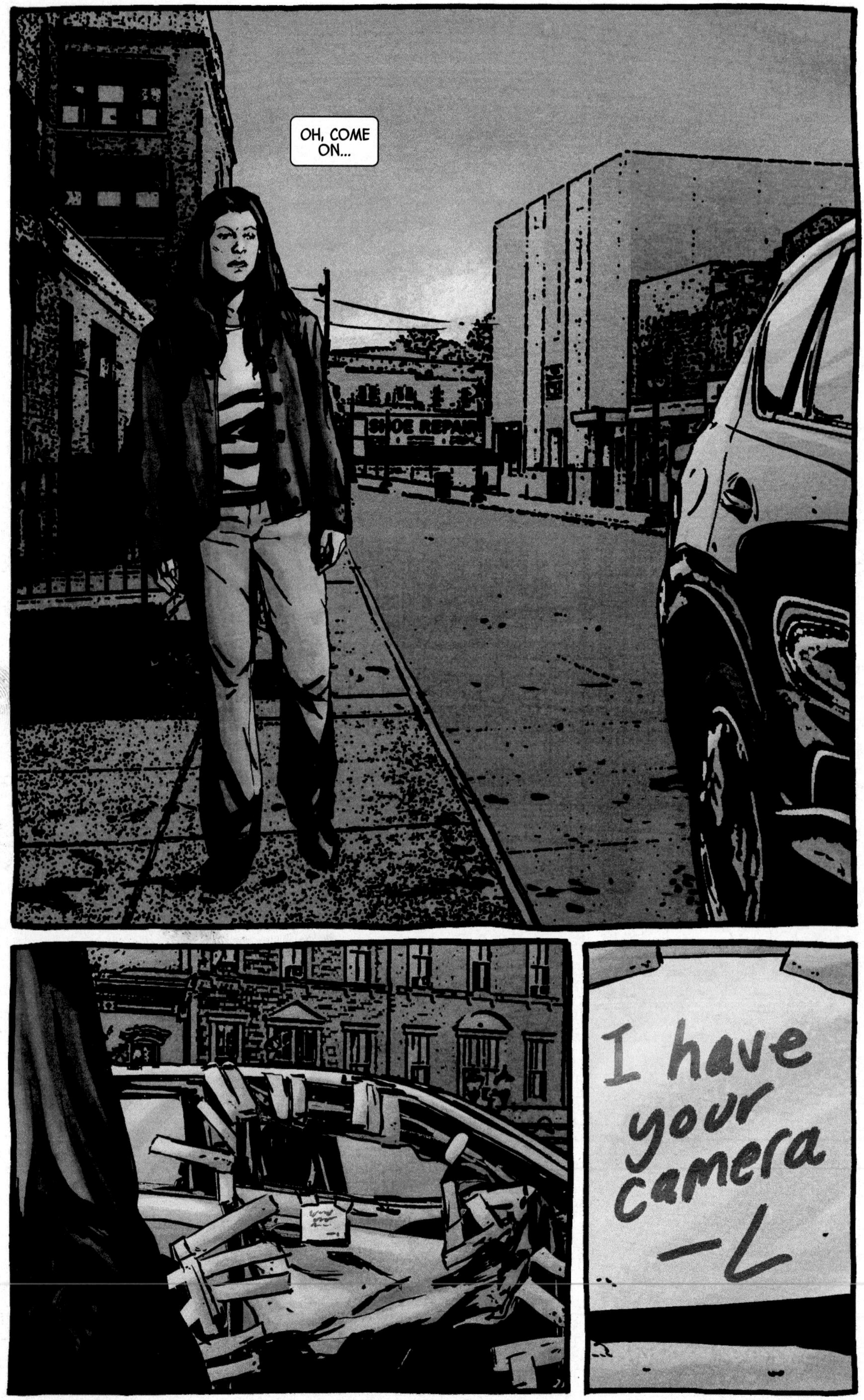

OH, COME ON...
I have your camera
—L

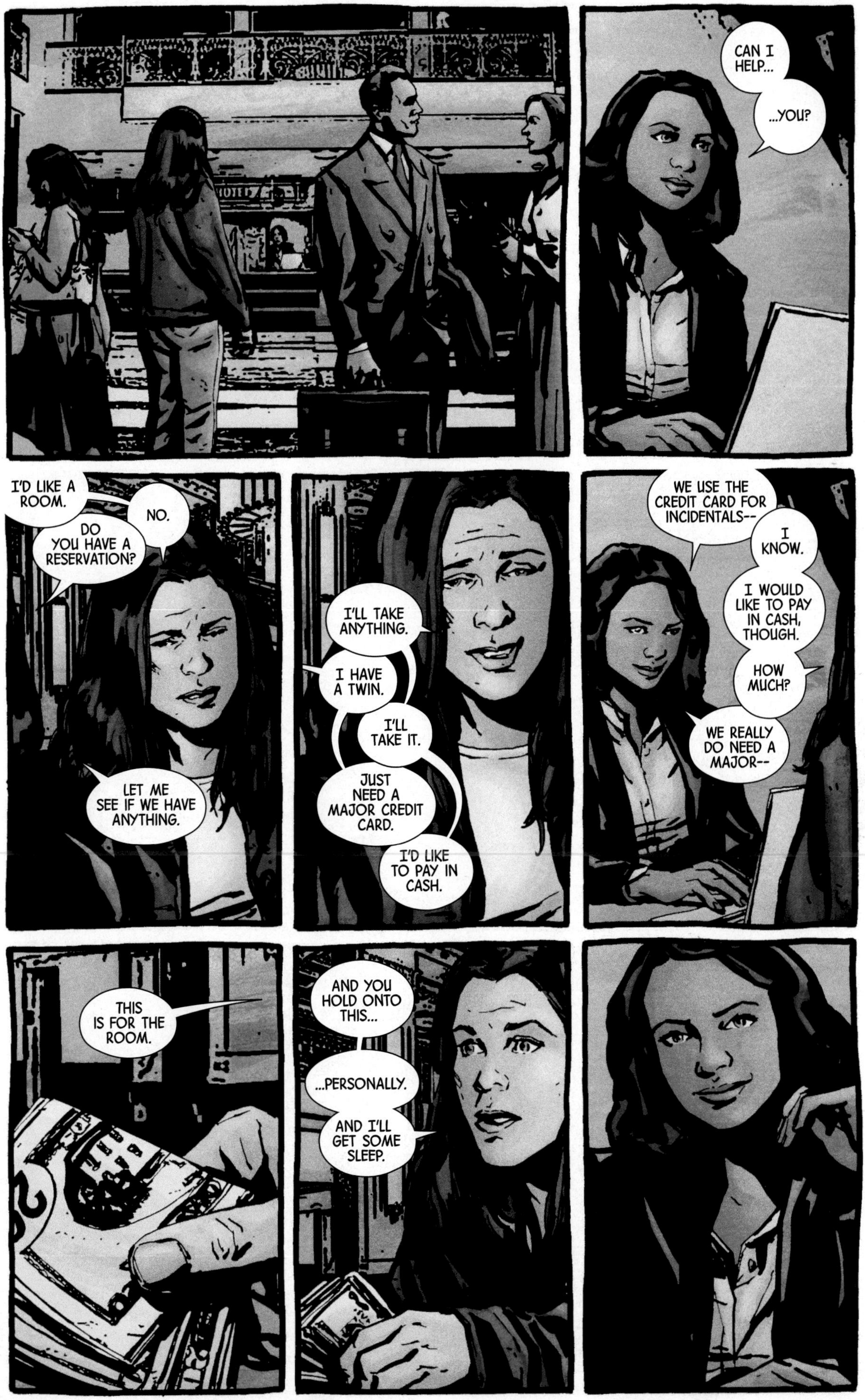
CAN I HELP...
...YOU?
I'D LIKE A ROOM.
DO YOU HAVE A RESERVATION?
NO.
LET ME SEE IF WE HAVE ANYTHING.
I'LL TAKE ANYTHING.
I HAVE A TWIN.
I'LL TAKE IT.
JUST NEED A MAJOR CREDIT CARD.
I'D LIKE TO PAY IN CASH.
WE USE THE CREDIT CARD FOR INCIDENTALS--
I KNOW.
I WOULD LIKE TO PAY IN CASH, THOUGH.
HOW MUCH?
WE REALLY DO NEED A MAJOR--
THIS IS FOR THE ROOM.
AND YOU HOLD ONTO THIS...
...PERSONALLY.
AND I'LL GET SOME SLEEP.

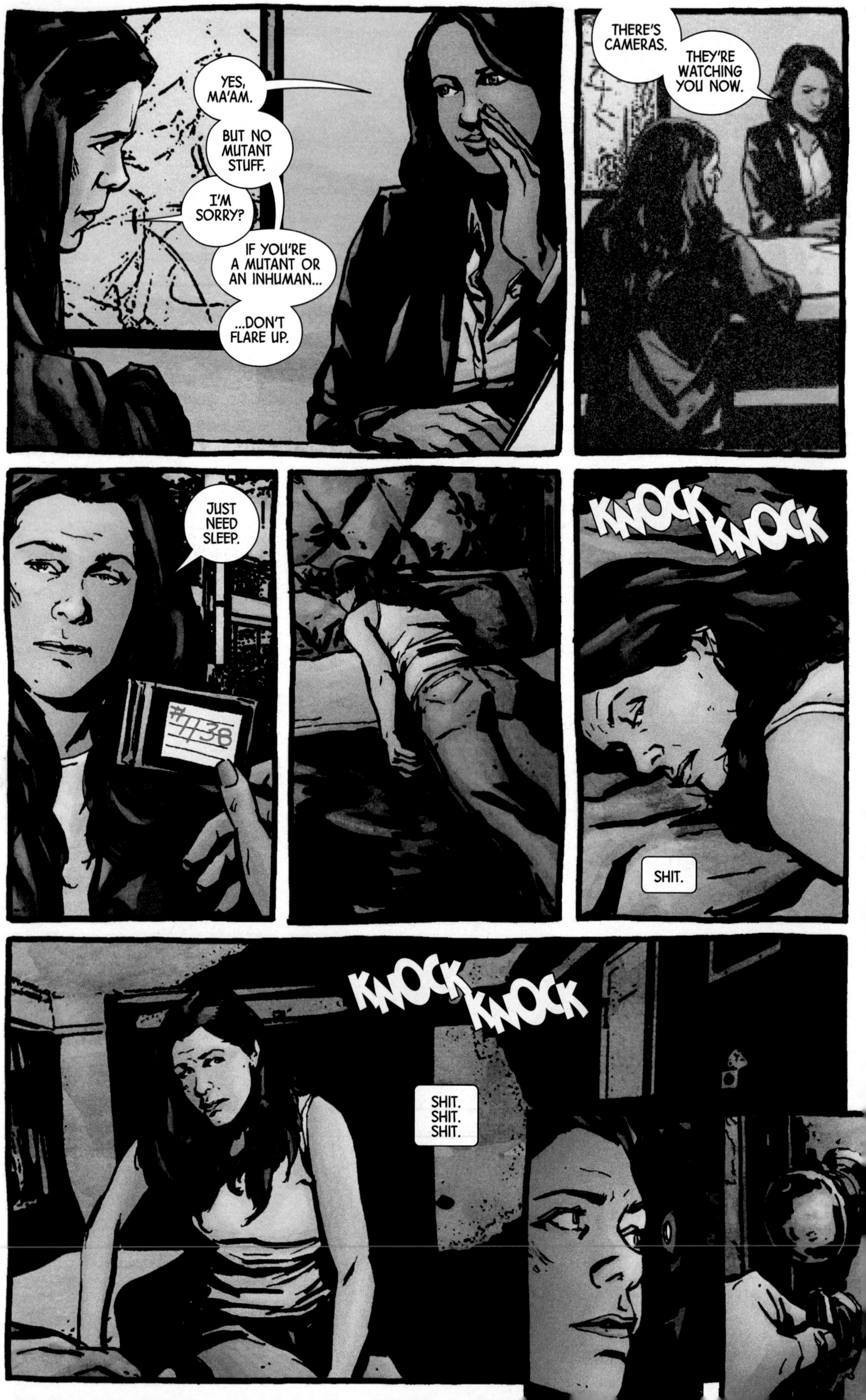

YES, MA'AM.
BUT NO MUTANT STUFF.
I'M SORRY?
IF YOU'RE A MUTANT OR AN INHUMAN...
...DON'T FLARE UP.
THERE'S CAMERAS.
THEY'RE WATCHING YOU NOW.
JUST NEED SLEEP.
#1138
KNOCK KNOCK
SHIT.
KNOCK KNOCK
SHIT. SHIT. SHIT.

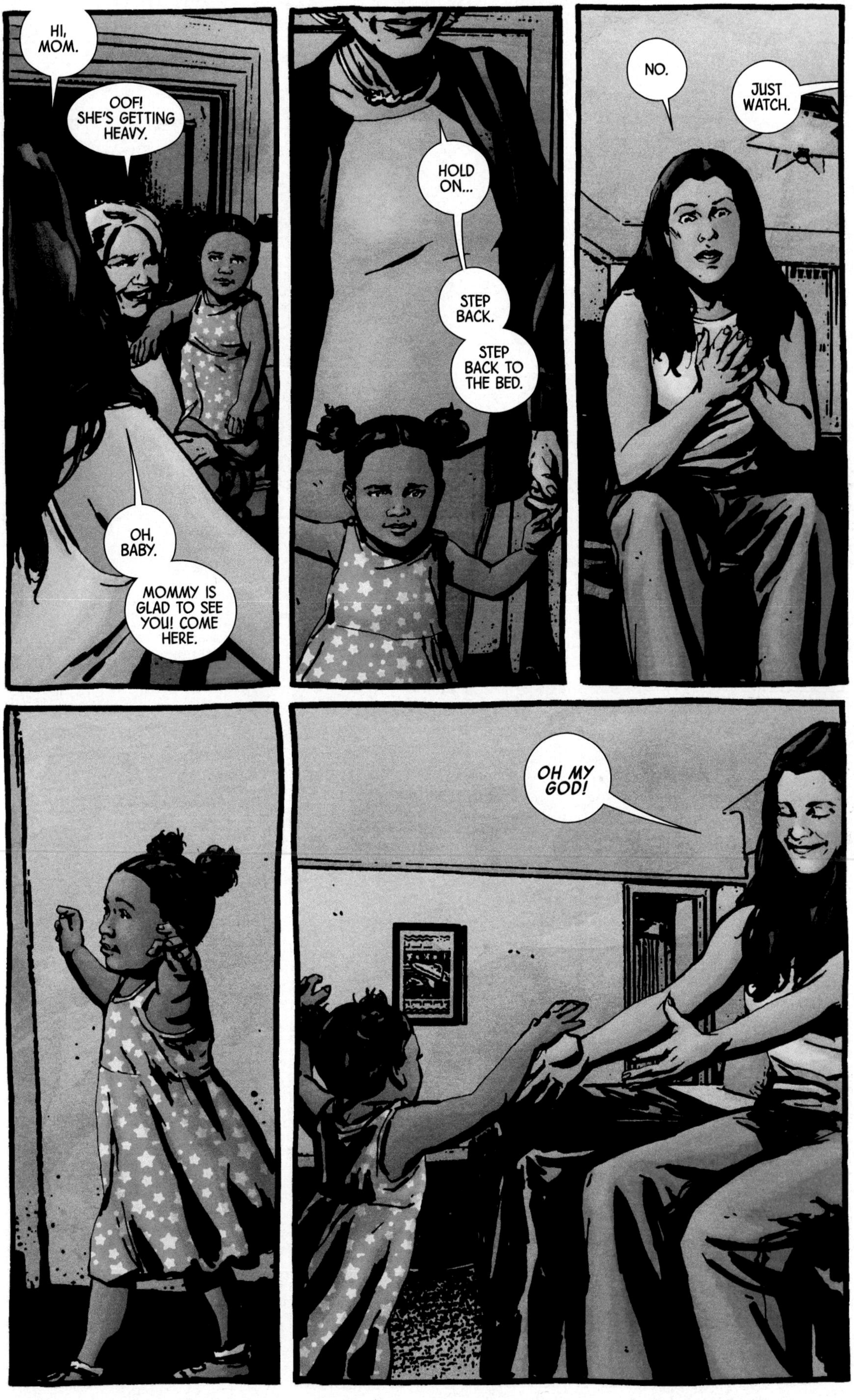
HI, MOM.
OOF! SHE'S GETTING HEAVY.
OH, BABY.
MOMMY IS GLAD TO SEE YOU! COME HERE.
HOLD ON...
STEP BACK.
STEP BACK TO THE BED.
NO.
JUST WATCH.
OH MY GOD!

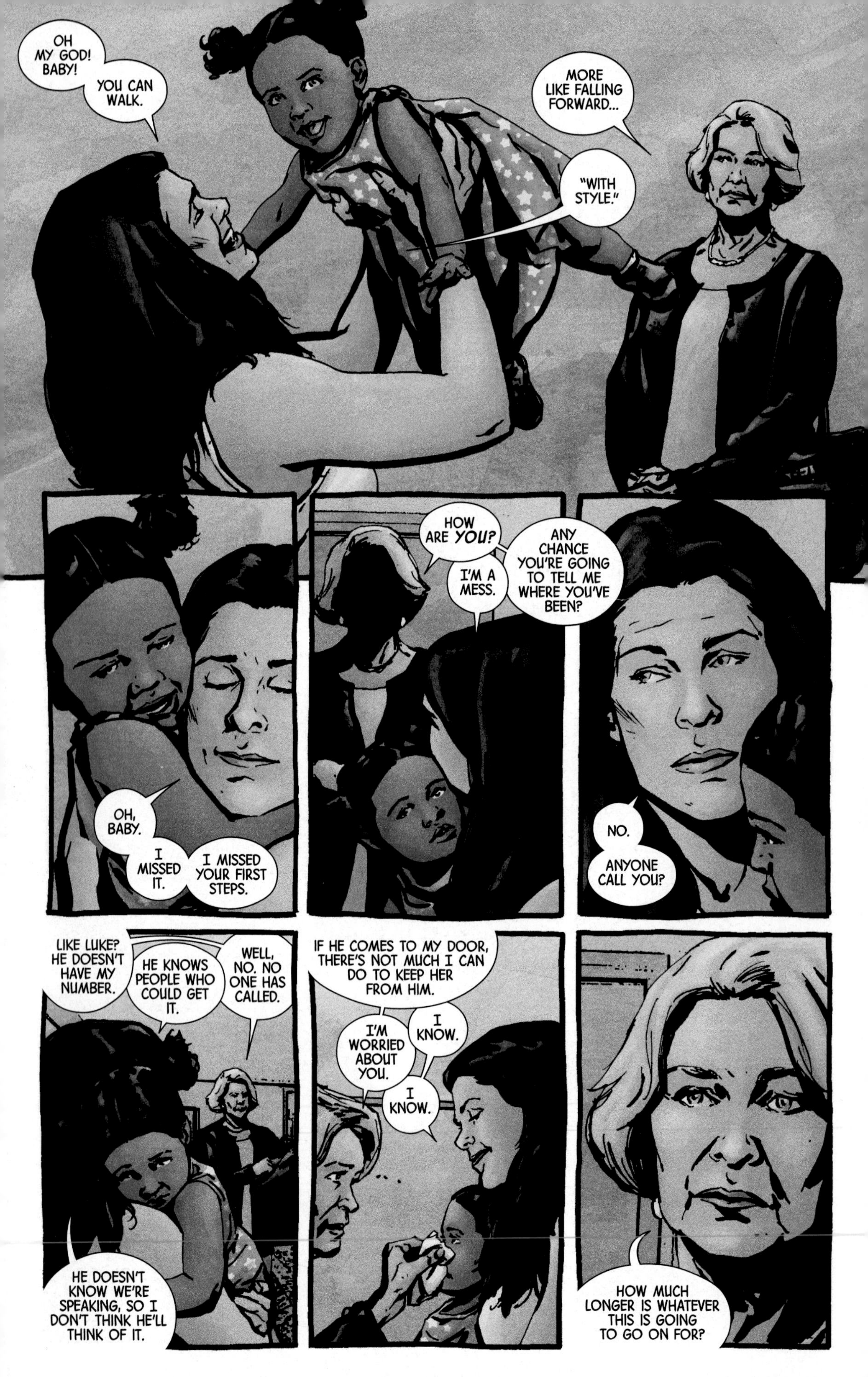
OH MY GOD! BABY!
YOU CAN WALK.
MORE LIKE FALLING FORWARD...
"WITH STYLE."
OH, BABY.
I MISSED IT.
I MISSED YOUR FIRST STEPS.
HOW ARE *YOU*?
I'M A MESS.
ANY CHANCE YOU'RE GOING TO TELL ME WHERE YOU'VE BEEN?
NO.
ANYONE CALL YOU?
LIKE LUKE? HE DOESN'T HAVE MY NUMBER.
HE KNOWS PEOPLE WHO COULD GET IT.
WELL, NO. NO ONE HAS CALLED.
HE DOESN'T KNOW WE'RE SPEAKING, SO I DON'T THINK HE'LL THINK OF IT.
IF HE COMES TO MY DOOR, THERE'S NOT MUCH I CAN DO TO KEEP HER FROM HIM.
I'M WORRIED ABOUT YOU.
I KNOW.
I KNOW.
HOW MUCH LONGER IS WHATEVER THIS IS GOING TO GO ON FOR?

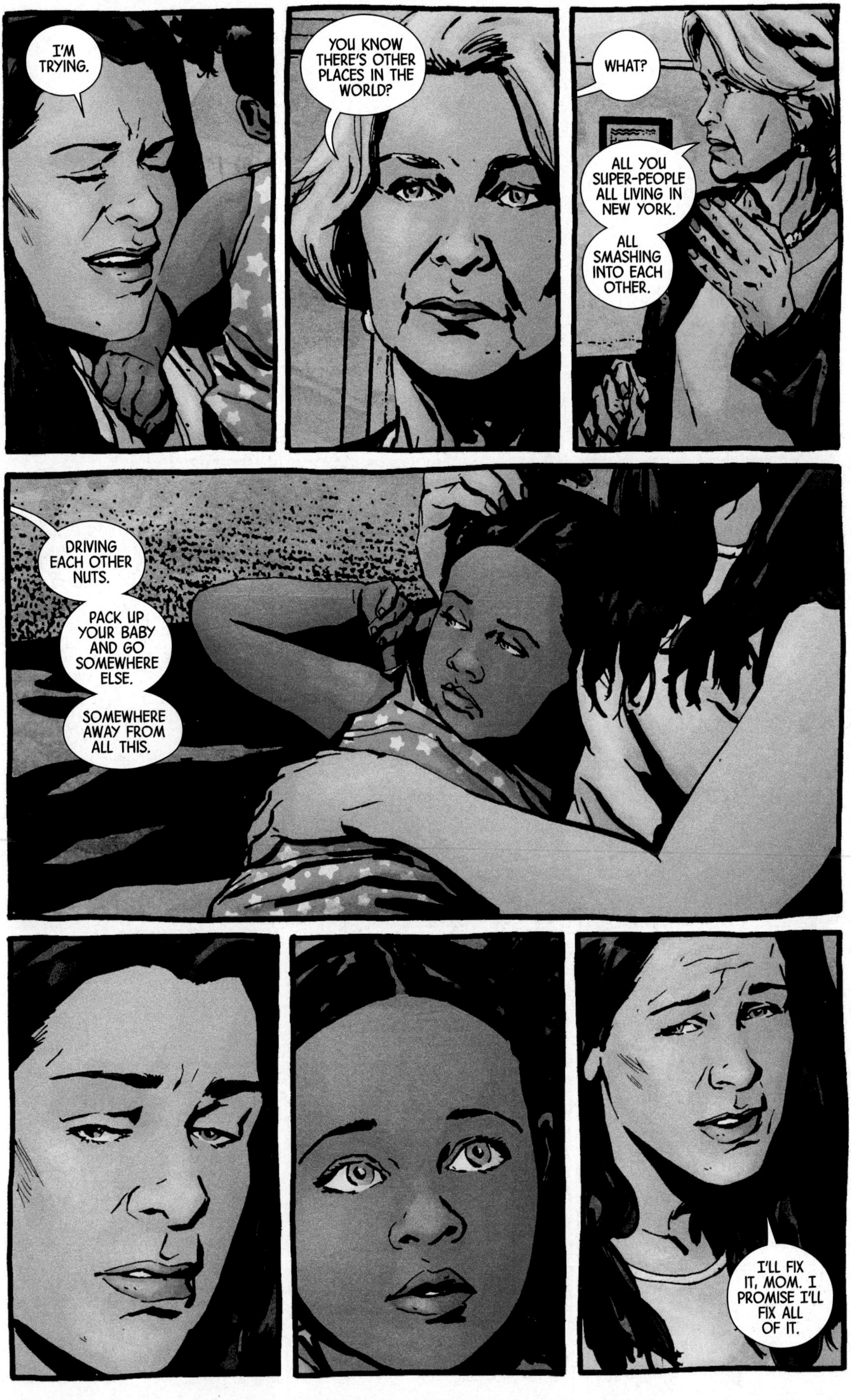
I'M TRYING.
YOU KNOW THERE'S OTHER PLACES IN THE WORLD?
WHAT?
ALL YOU SUPER-PEOPLE ALL LIVING IN NEW YORK.
ALL SMASHING INTO EACH OTHER.
DRIVING EACH OTHER NUTS.
PACK UP YOUR BABY AND GO SOMEWHERE ELSE.
SOMEWHERE AWAY FROM ALL THIS.
I'LL FIX IT, MOM. I PROMISE I'LL FIX ALL OF IT.

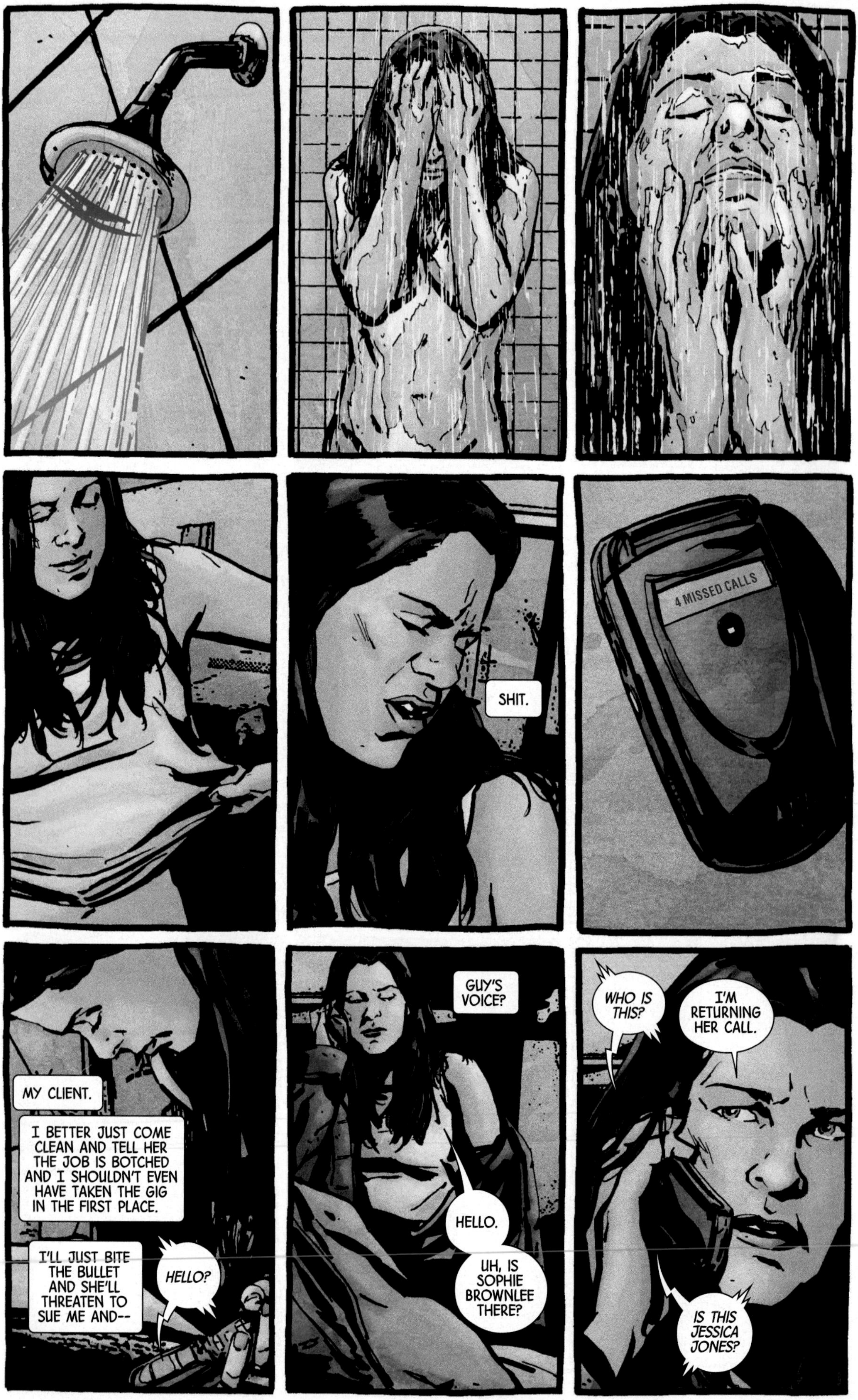
SHIT.
4 MISSED CALLS
MY CLIENT.
I BETTER JUST COME CLEAN AND TELL HER THE JOB IS BOTCHED AND I SHOULDN'T EVEN HAVE TAKEN THE GIG IN THE FIRST PLACE.
I'LL JUST BITE THE BULLET AND SHE'LL THREATEN TO SUE ME AND--
HELLO?
GUY'S VOICE?
HELLO.
UH, IS SOPHIE BROWNLEE THERE?
WHO IS THIS?
I'M RETURNING HER CALL.
IS THIS JESSICA JONES?

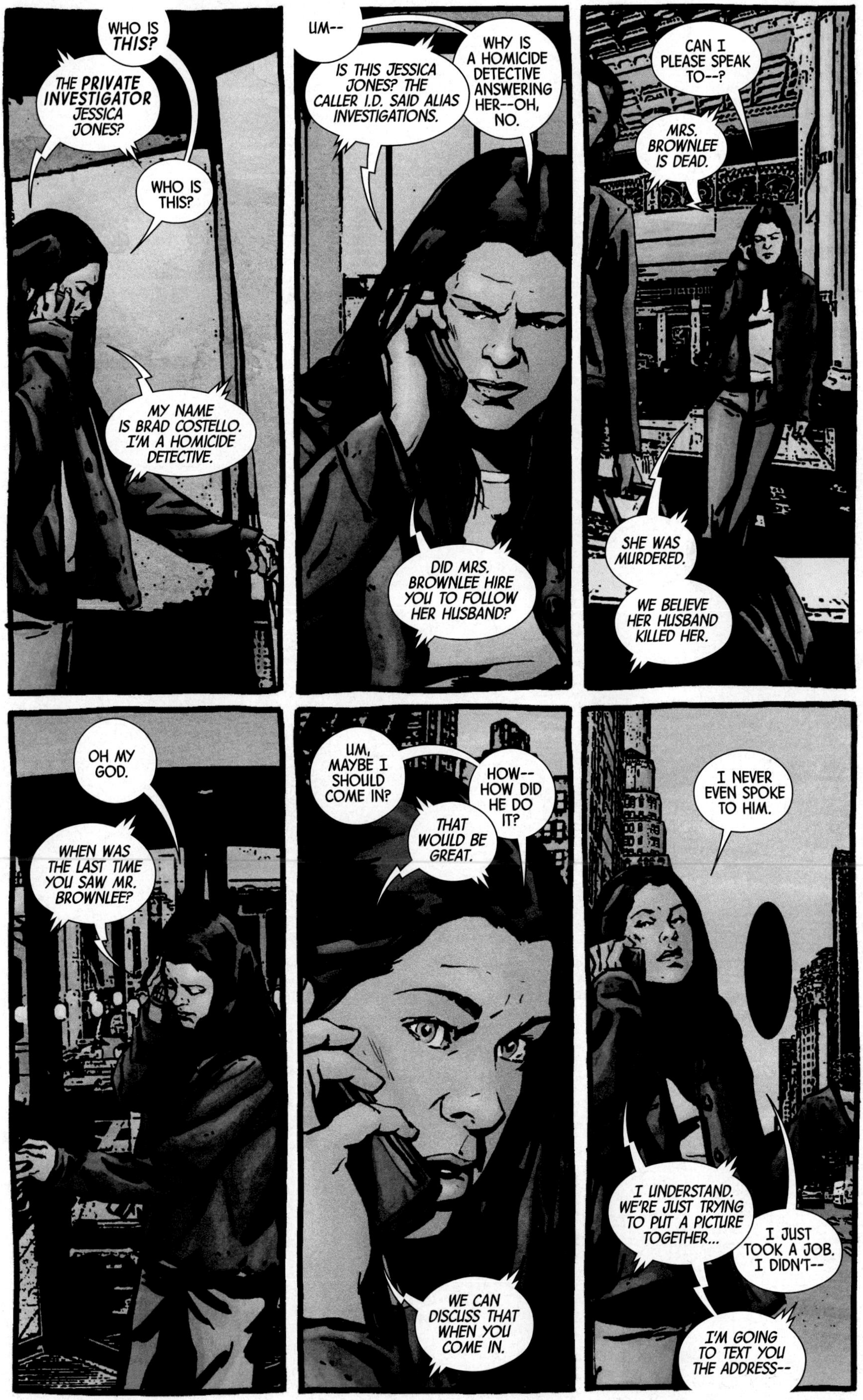
WHO IS THIS?
THE PRIVATE INVESTIGATOR JESSICA JONES?
WHO IS THIS?
MY NAME IS BRAD COSTELLO. I'M A HOMICIDE DETECTIVE.
UM--
IS THIS JESSICA JONES? THE CALLER I.D. SAID ALIAS INVESTIGATIONS.
WHY IS A HOMICIDE DETECTIVE ANSWERING HER--OH, NO.
DID MRS. BROWNLEE HIRE YOU TO FOLLOW HER HUSBAND?
CAN I PLEASE SPEAK TO--?
MRS. BROWNLEE IS DEAD.
SHE WAS MURDERED.
WE BELIEVE HER HUSBAND KILLED HER.
OH MY GOD.
WHEN WAS THE LAST TIME YOU SAW MR. BROWNLEE?
UM, MAYBE I SHOULD COME IN?
HOW--HOW DID HE DO IT?
THAT WOULD BE GREAT.
WE CAN DISCUSS THAT WHEN YOU COME IN.
I NEVER EVEN SPOKE TO HIM.
I UNDERSTAND. WE'RE JUST TRYING TO PUT A PICTURE TOGETHER...
I JUST TOOK A JOB. I DIDN'T--
I'M GOING TO TEXT YOU THE ADDRESS--

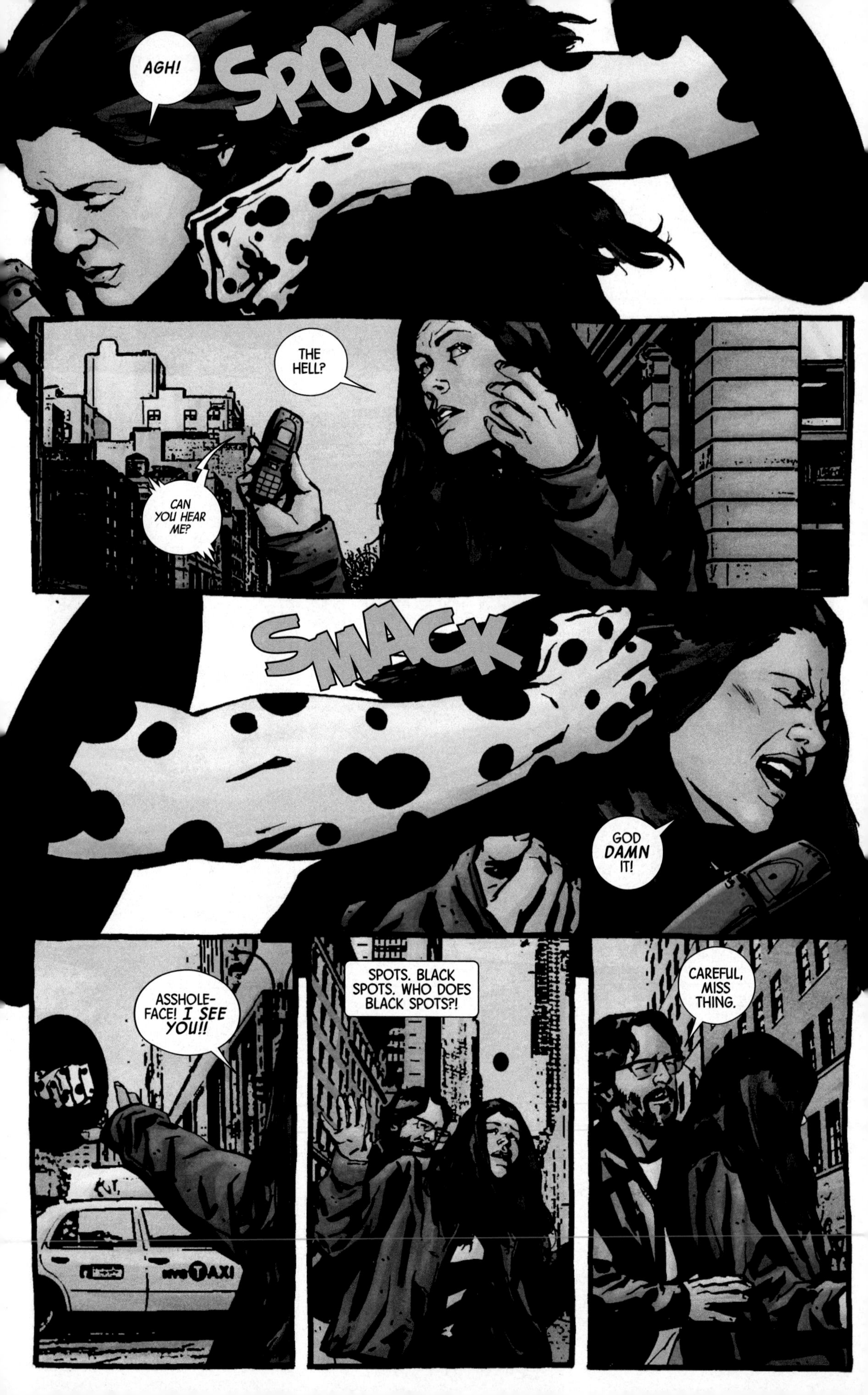
AGH!
SPOK
THE HELL?
CAN YOU HEAR ME?
SMACK
GOD DAMN IT!
ASSHOLE-FACE! I SEE YOU!!
SPOTS. BLACK SPOTS. WHO DOES BLACK SPOTS?!
CAREFUL, MISS THING.

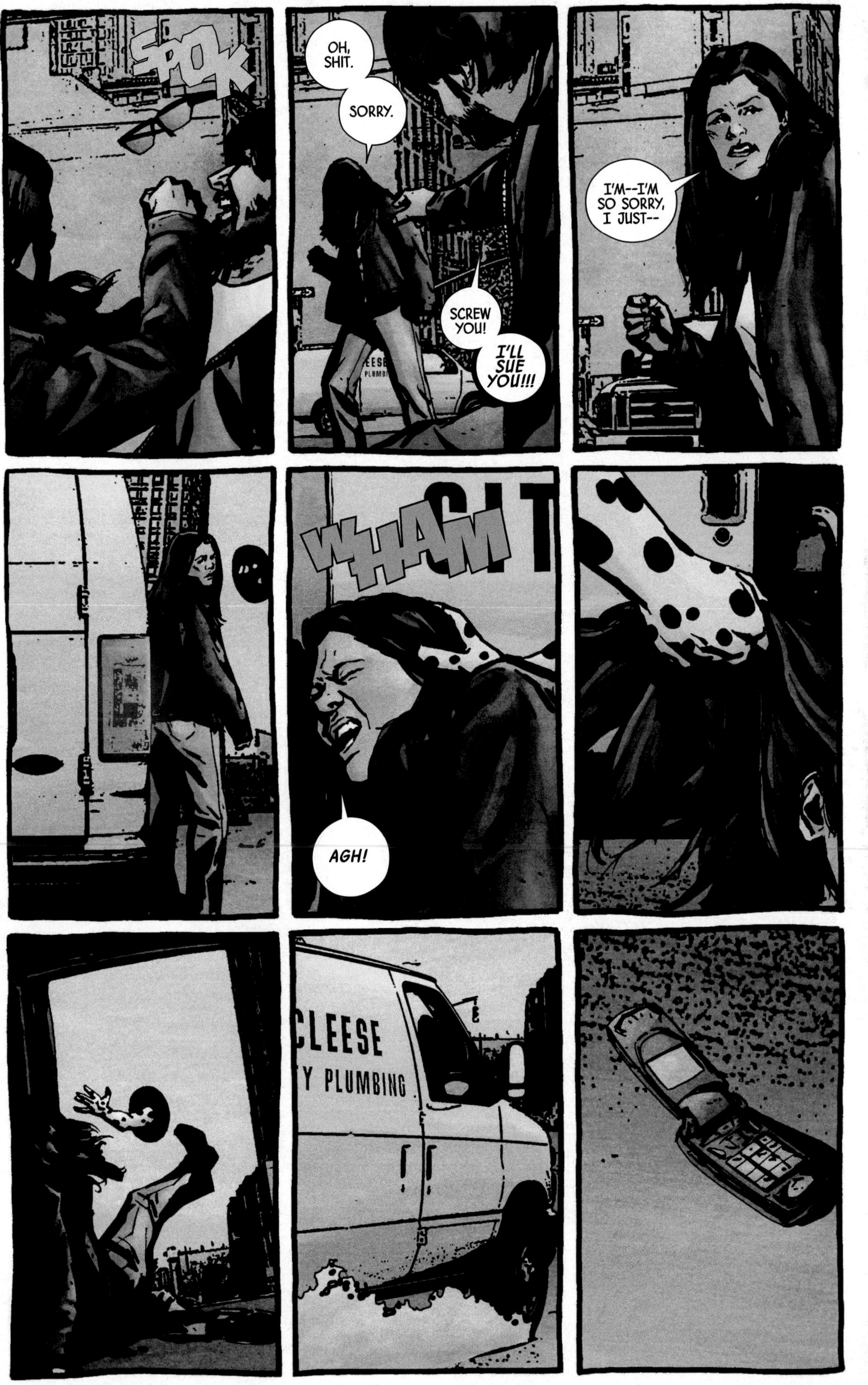
SPOK
OH, SHIT.
SORRY.
SCREW YOU!
I'LL SUE YOU!!!
I'M--I'M SO SORRY, I JUST--
WHAM
AGH!
CLEESE
Y PLUMBING

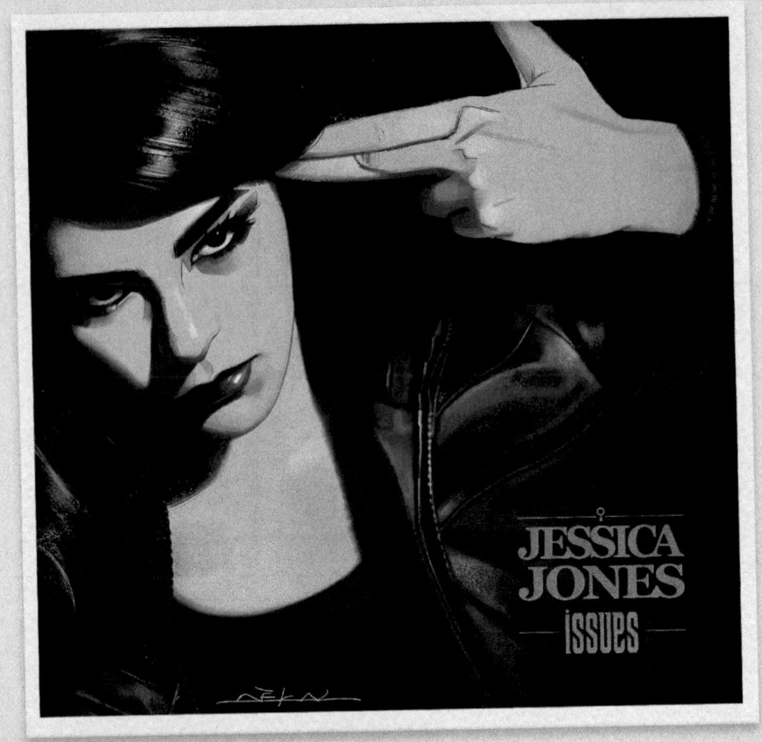
JESSICA
JONES
issues

#1 hip-hop variant by **Jeff Dekal**

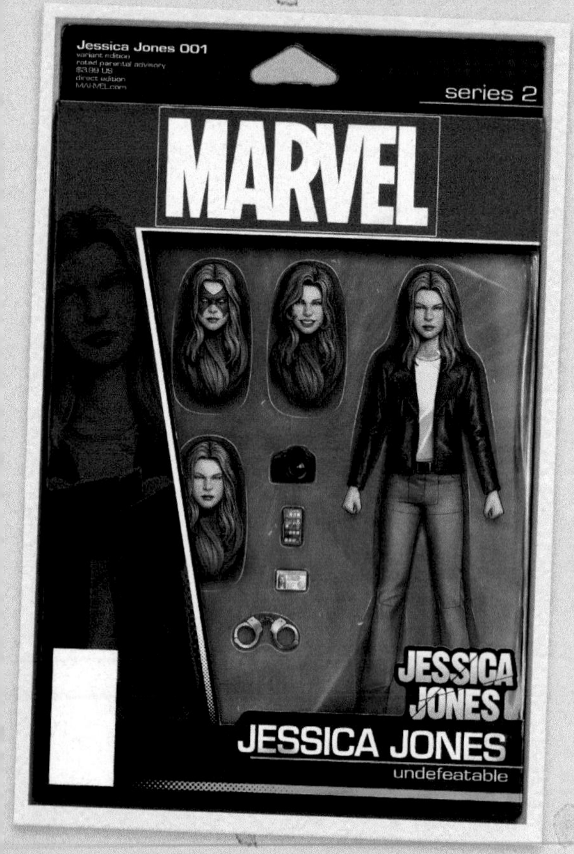
Jessica Jones 001
series 2
MARVEL
JESSICA
JONES
JESSICA JONES
undefeatable

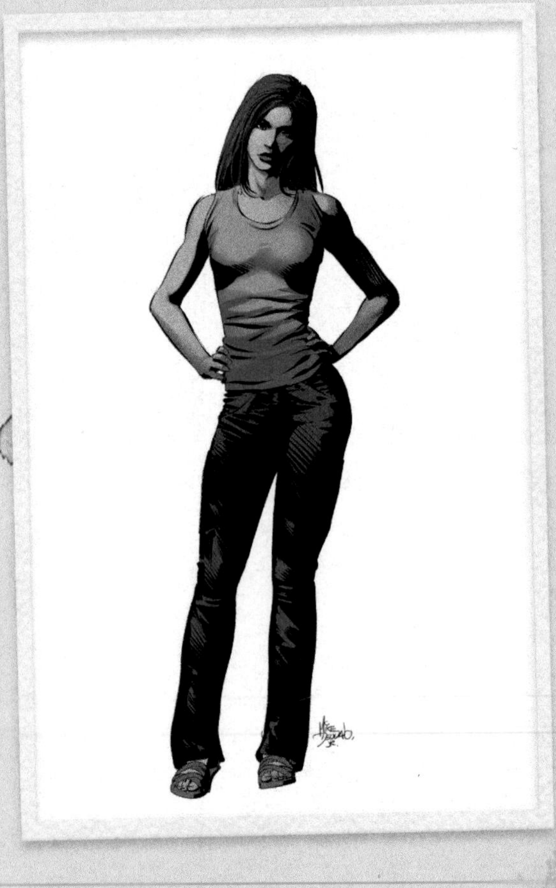

#1 action figure variant by **John Tyler Christopher**

#1 teaser variant by **Mike Deodato** & **Frank Martin**

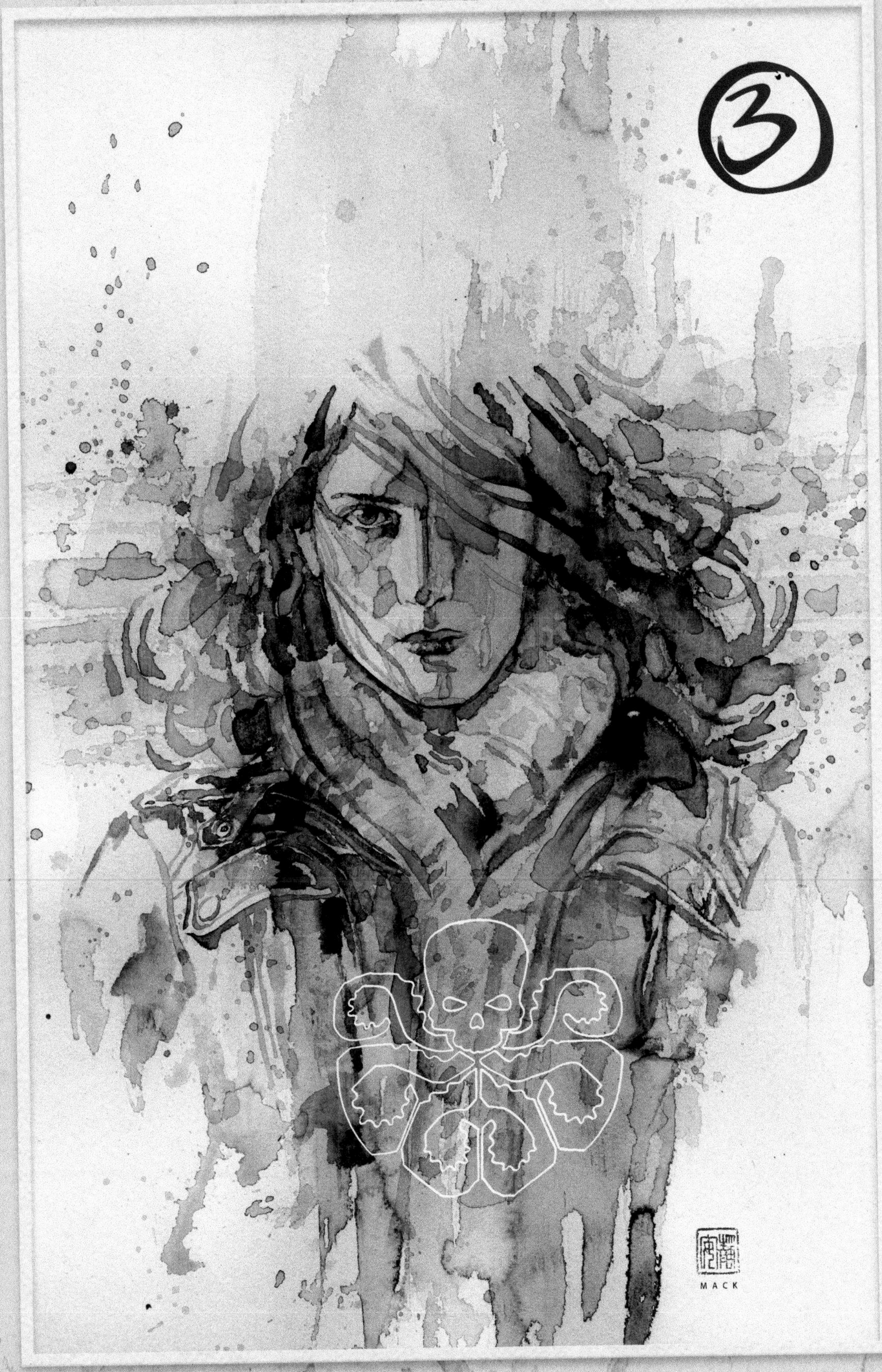
3
MACK

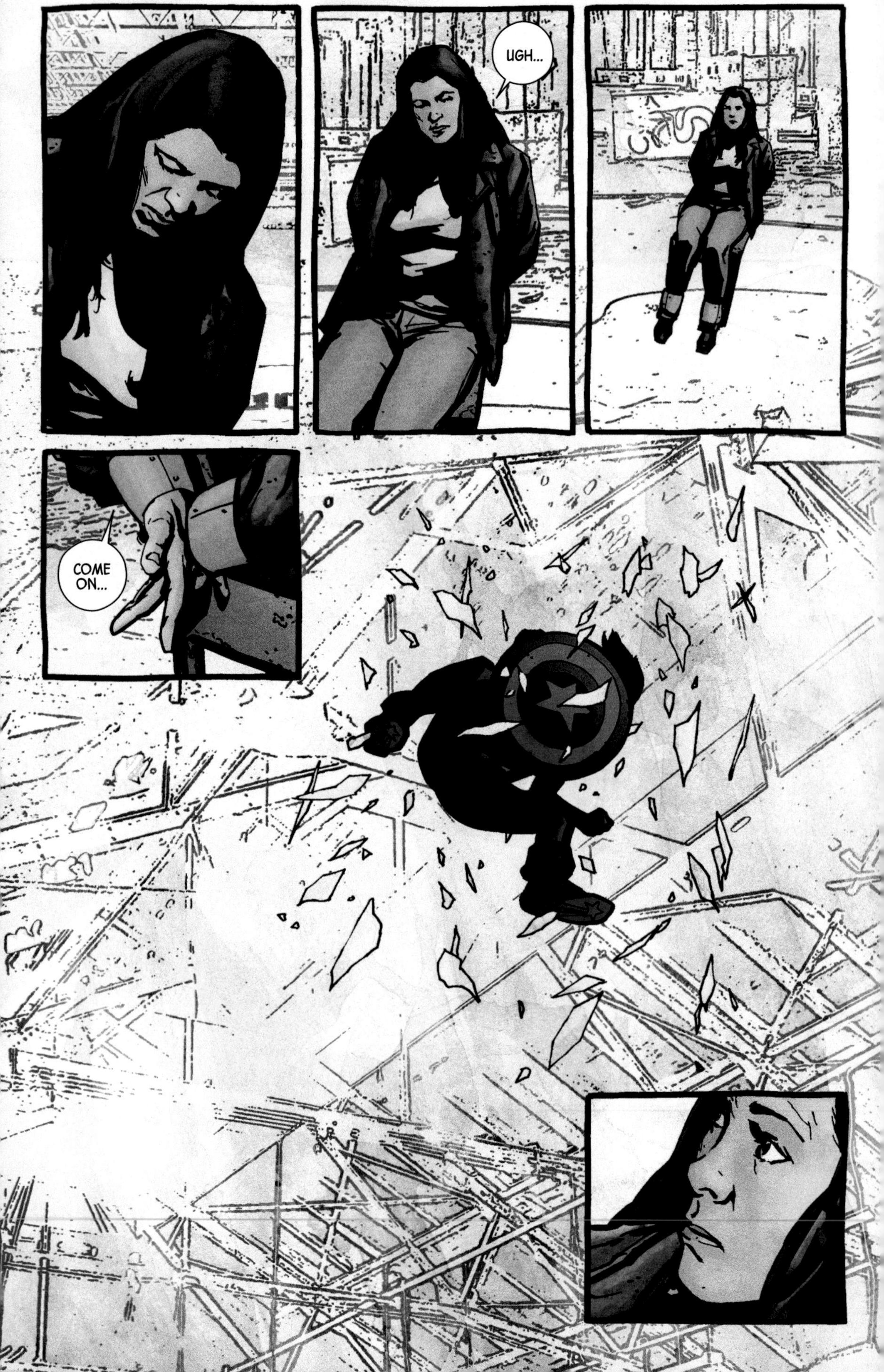
UGH...
COME ON...

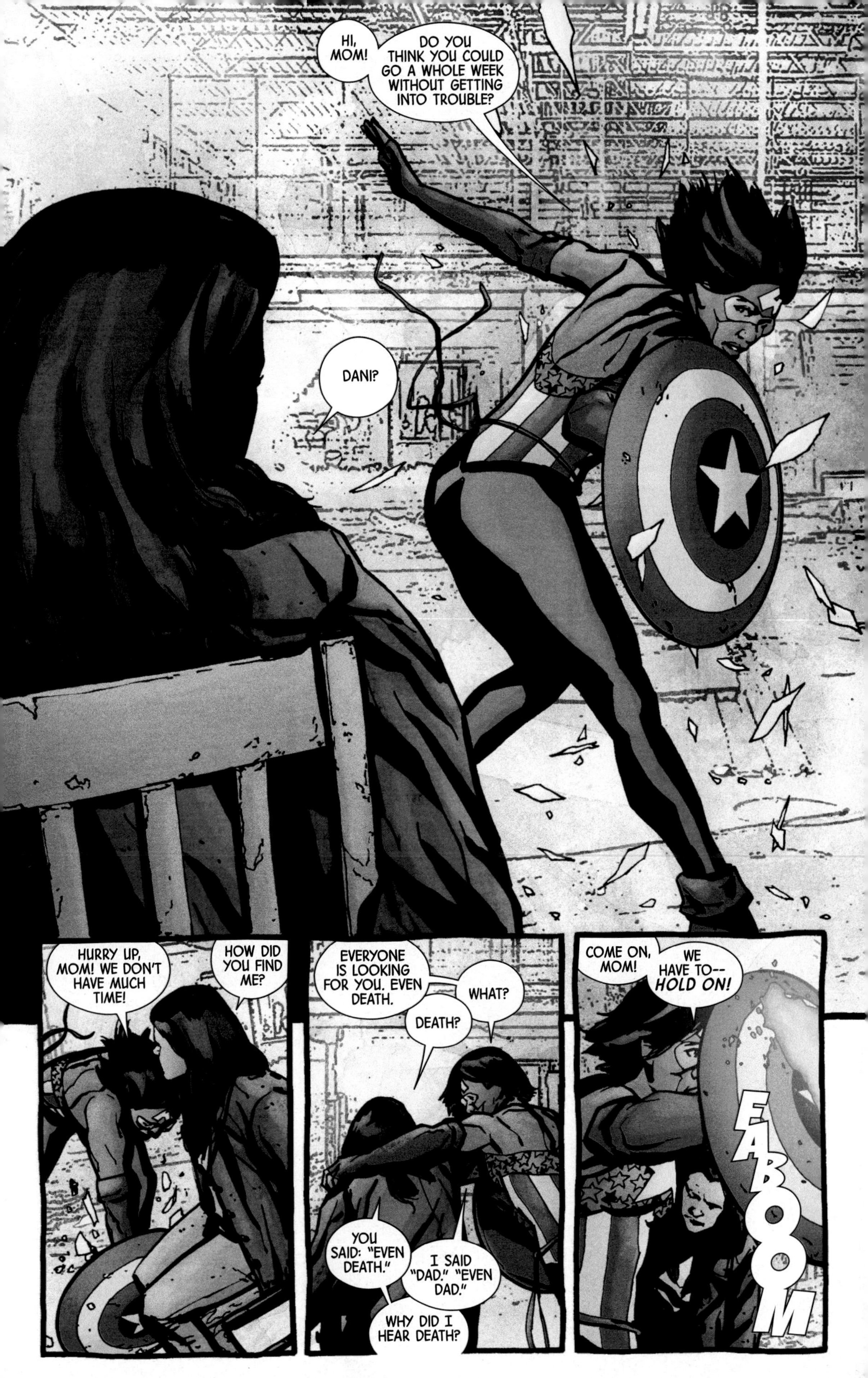
HI, MOM!
DO YOU THINK YOU COULD GO A WHOLE WEEK WITHOUT GETTING INTO TROUBLE?
DANI?
HURRY UP, MOM! WE DON'T HAVE MUCH TIME!
HOW DID YOU FIND ME?
EVERYONE IS LOOKING FOR YOU. EVEN DEATH.
WHAT?
DEATH?
YOU SAID: "EVEN DEATH."
I SAID "DAD." "EVEN DAD."
WHY DID I HEAR DEATH?
COME ON, MOM!
WE HAVE TO-- HOLD ON!
FABOOM

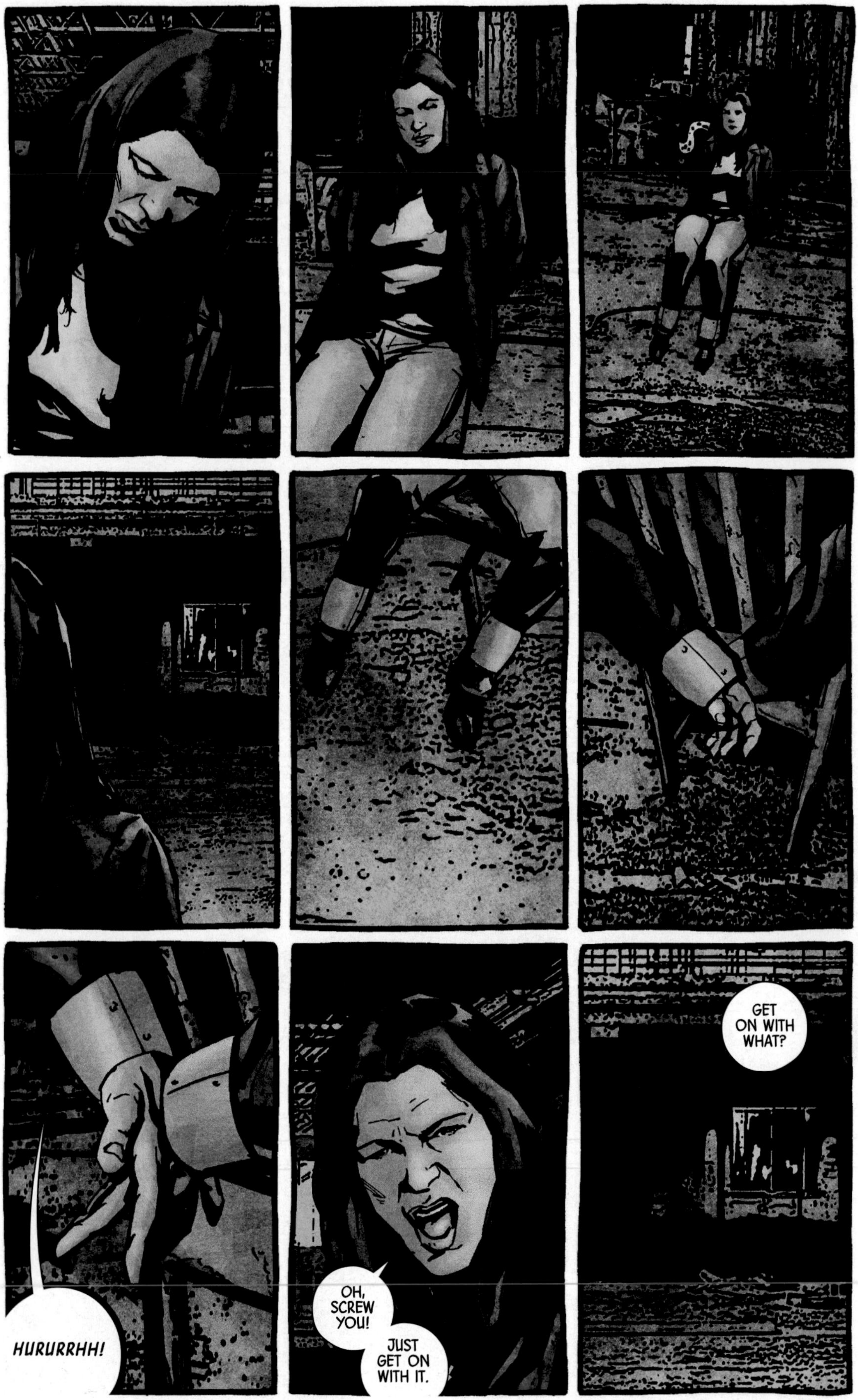
HURURRHH!
OH, SCREW YOU!
JUST GET ON WITH IT.
GET ON WITH WHAT?

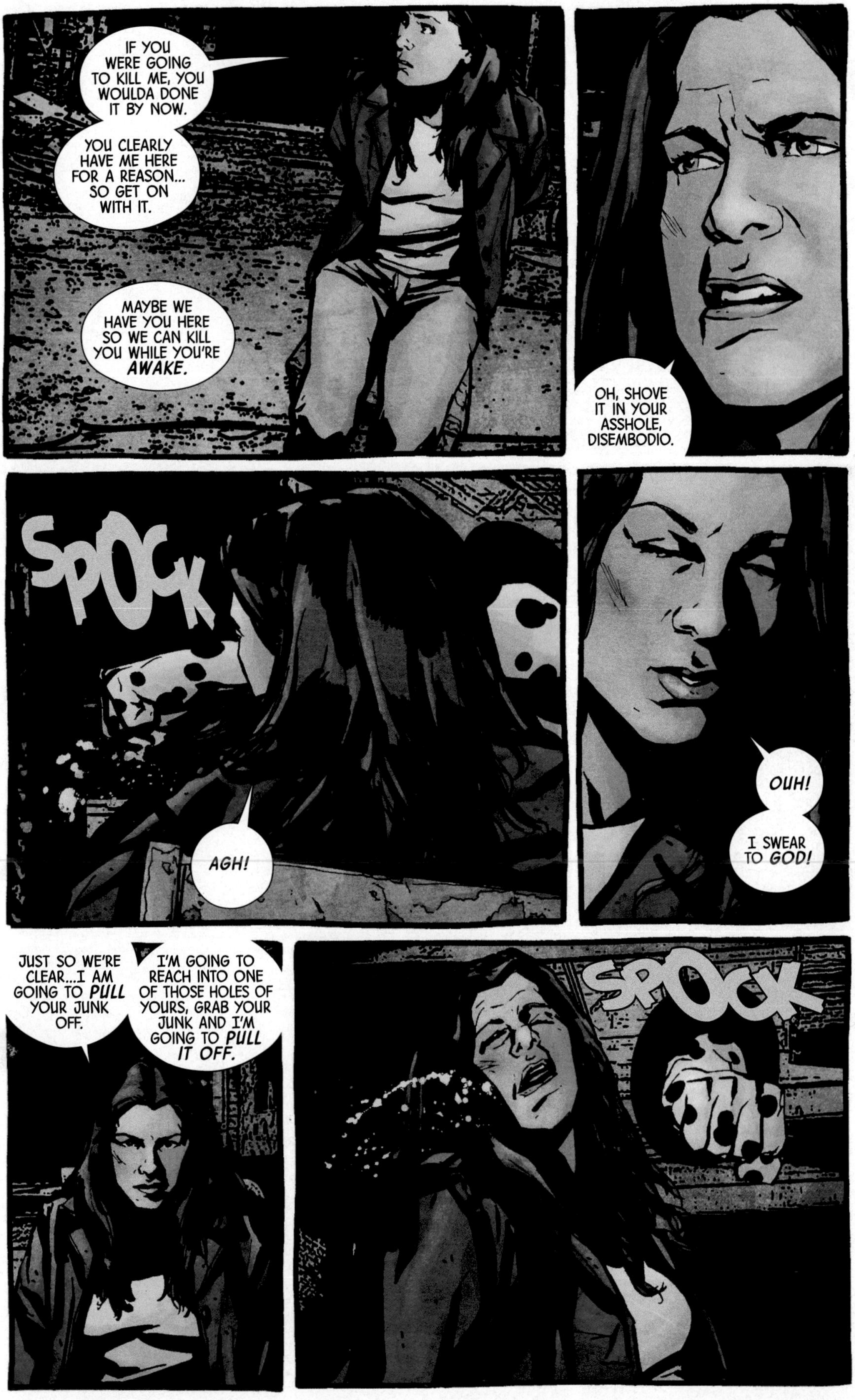
IF YOU WERE GOING TO KILL ME, YOU WOULDA DONE IT BY NOW.
YOU CLEARLY HAVE ME HERE FOR A REASON... SO GET ON WITH IT.
MAYBE WE HAVE YOU HERE SO WE CAN KILL YOU WHILE YOU'RE AWAKE.
OH, SHOVE IT IN YOUR ASSHOLE, DISEMBODIO.
SPOCK
AGH!
OUH!
I SWEAR TO GOD!
JUST SO WE'RE CLEAR...I AM GOING TO PULL YOUR JUNK OFF.
I'M GOING TO REACH INTO ONE OF THOSE HOLES OF YOURS, GRAB YOUR JUNK AND I'M GOING TO PULL IT OFF.
SPOCK

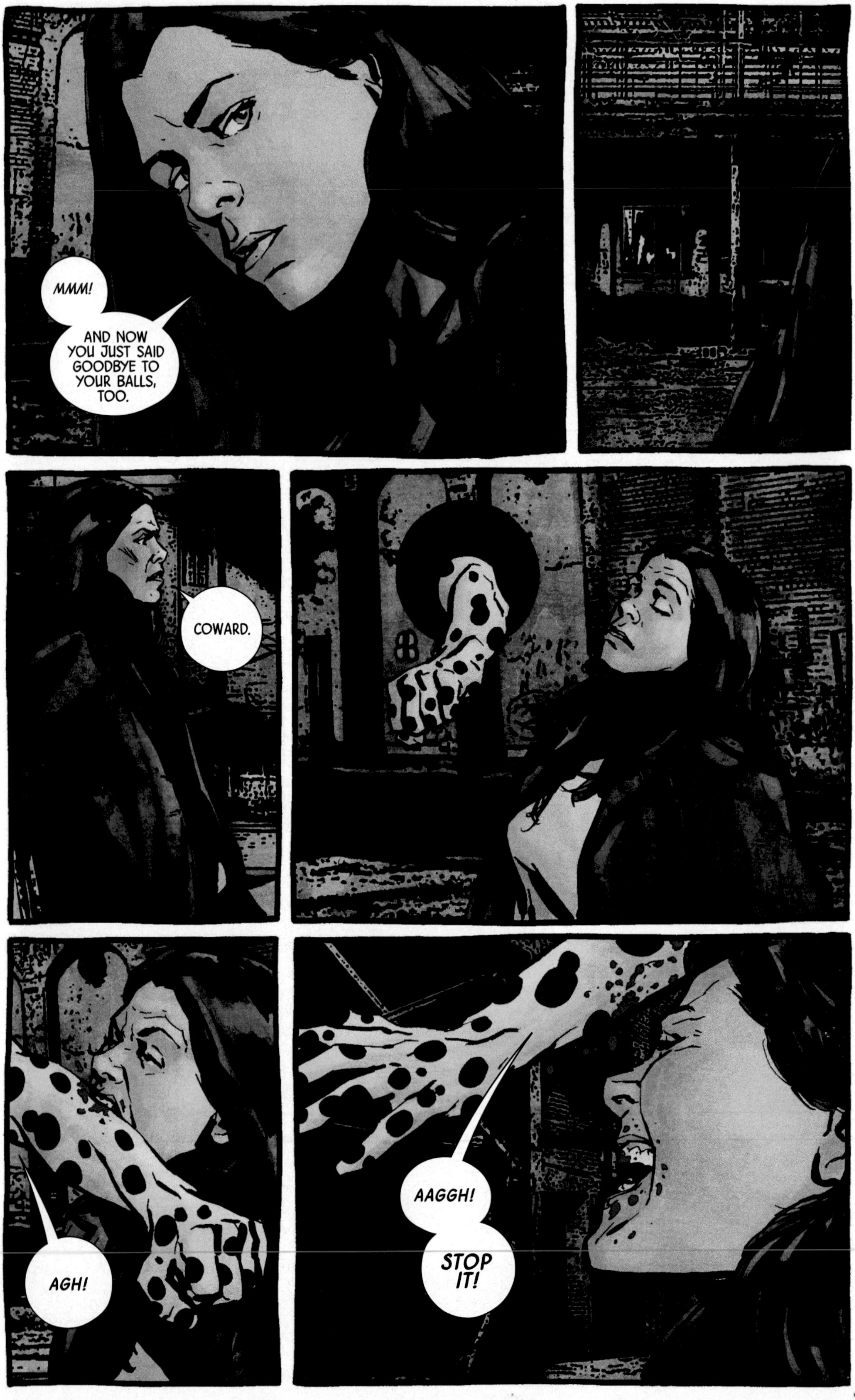
MMM!
AND NOW YOU JUST SAID GOODBYE TO YOUR BALLS, TOO.
COWARD.
AGH!
AAGGH!
STOP IT!

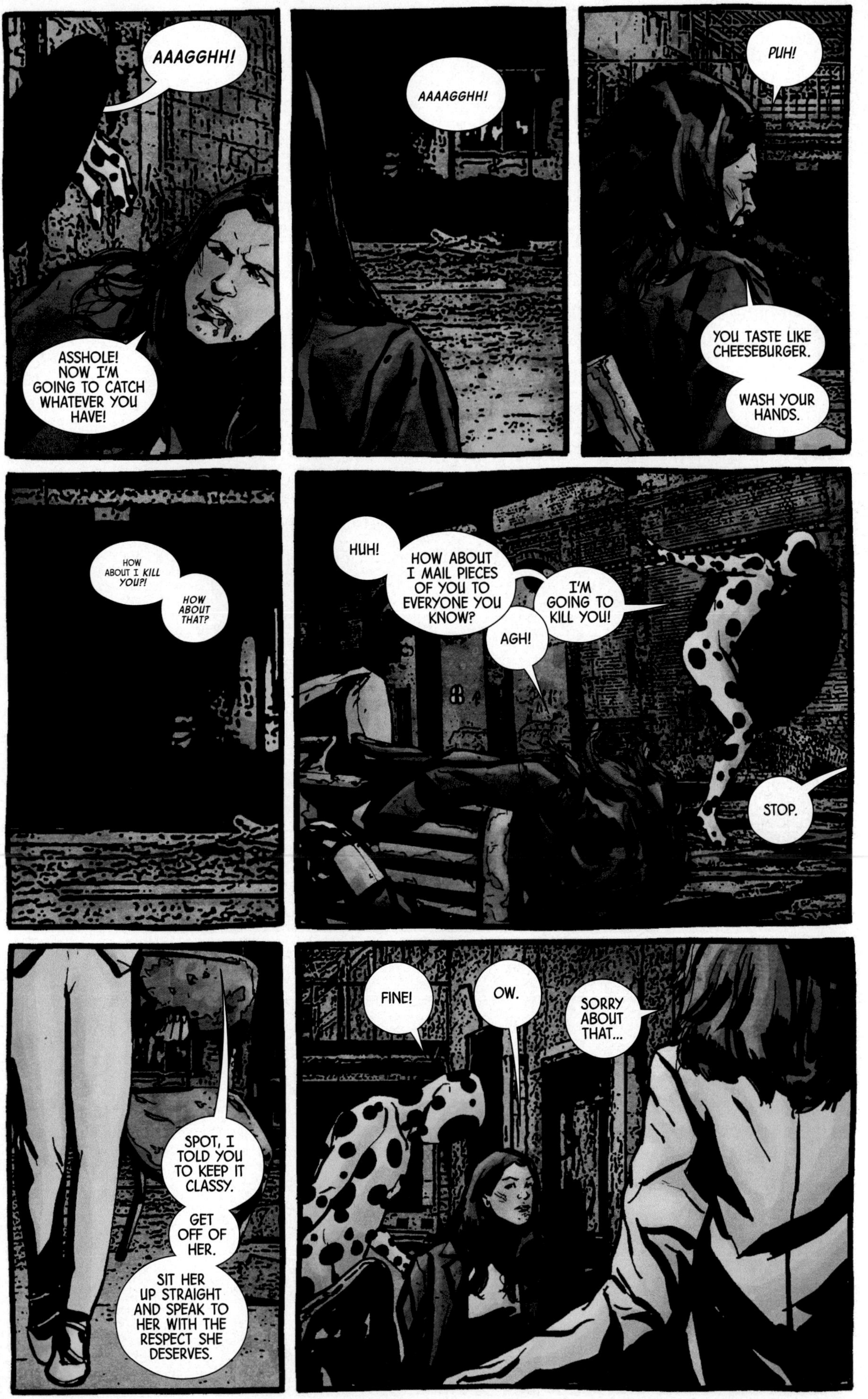
AAAGGHH!
ASSHOLE! NOW I'M GOING TO CATCH WHATEVER YOU HAVE!
AAAAGGHH!
PUH!
YOU TASTE LIKE CHEESEBURGER.
WASH YOUR HANDS.
HOW ABOUT I KILL YOU?!
HOW ABOUT THAT?
HUH!
HOW ABOUT I MAIL PIECES OF YOU TO EVERYONE YOU KNOW?
AGH!
I'M GOING TO KILL YOU!
STOP.
SPOT, I TOLD YOU TO KEEP IT CLASSY.
GET OFF OF HER.
SIT HER UP STRAIGHT AND SPEAK TO HER WITH THE RESPECT SHE DESERVES.
FINE!
OW.
SORRY ABOUT THAT...

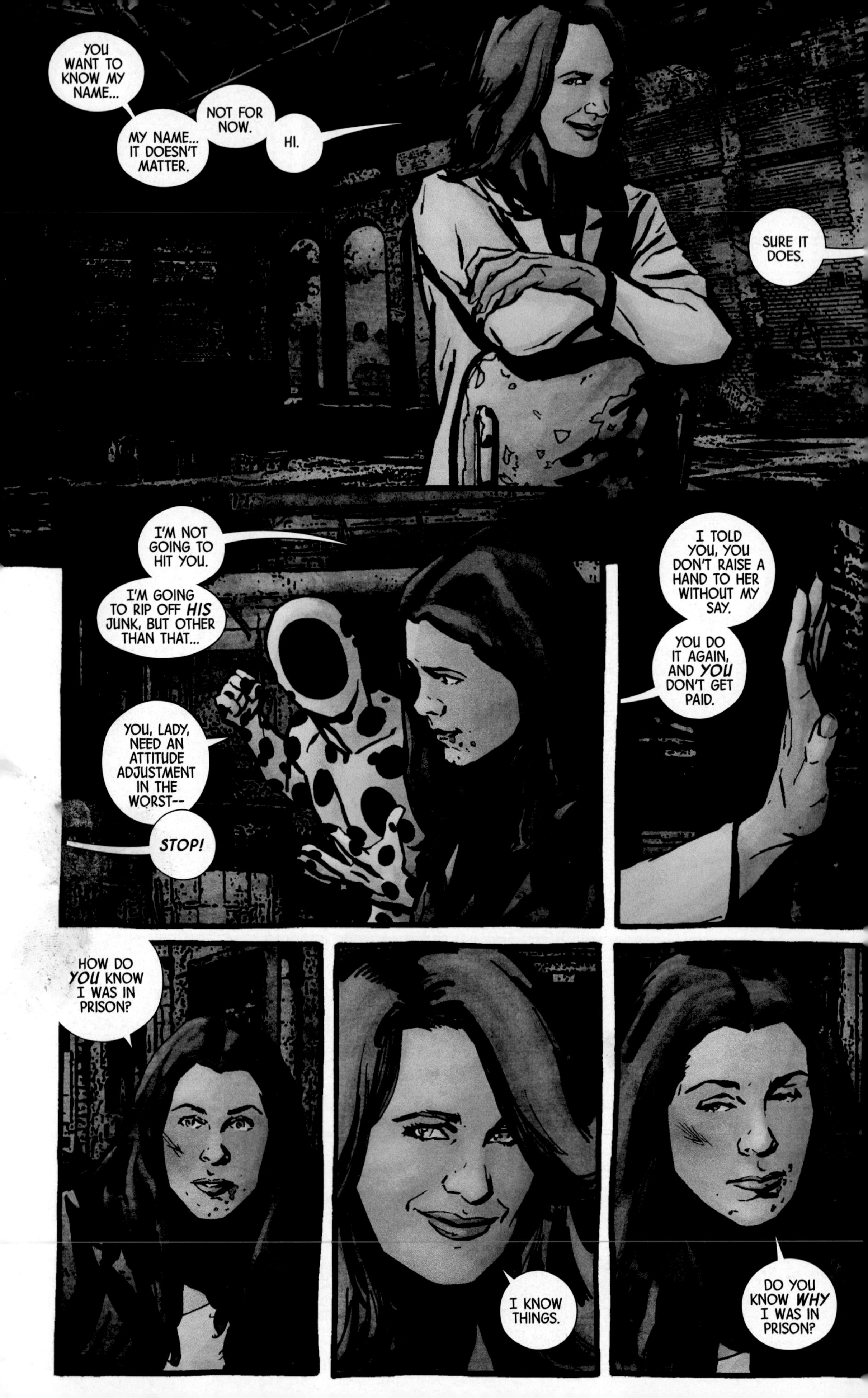
YOU WANT TO KNOW MY NAME...
MY NAME... IT DOESN'T MATTER.
NOT FOR NOW.
HI.
SURE IT DOES.
I'M NOT GOING TO HIT YOU.
I'M GOING TO RIP OFF HIS JUNK, BUT OTHER THAN THAT...
YOU, LADY, NEED AN ATTITUDE ADJUSTMENT IN THE WORST--
STOP!
I TOLD YOU, YOU DON'T RAISE A HAND TO HER WITHOUT MY SAY.
YOU DO IT AGAIN, AND YOU DON'T GET PAID.
HOW DO YOU KNOW I WAS IN PRISON?
I KNOW THINGS.
DO YOU KNOW WHY I WAS IN PRISON?

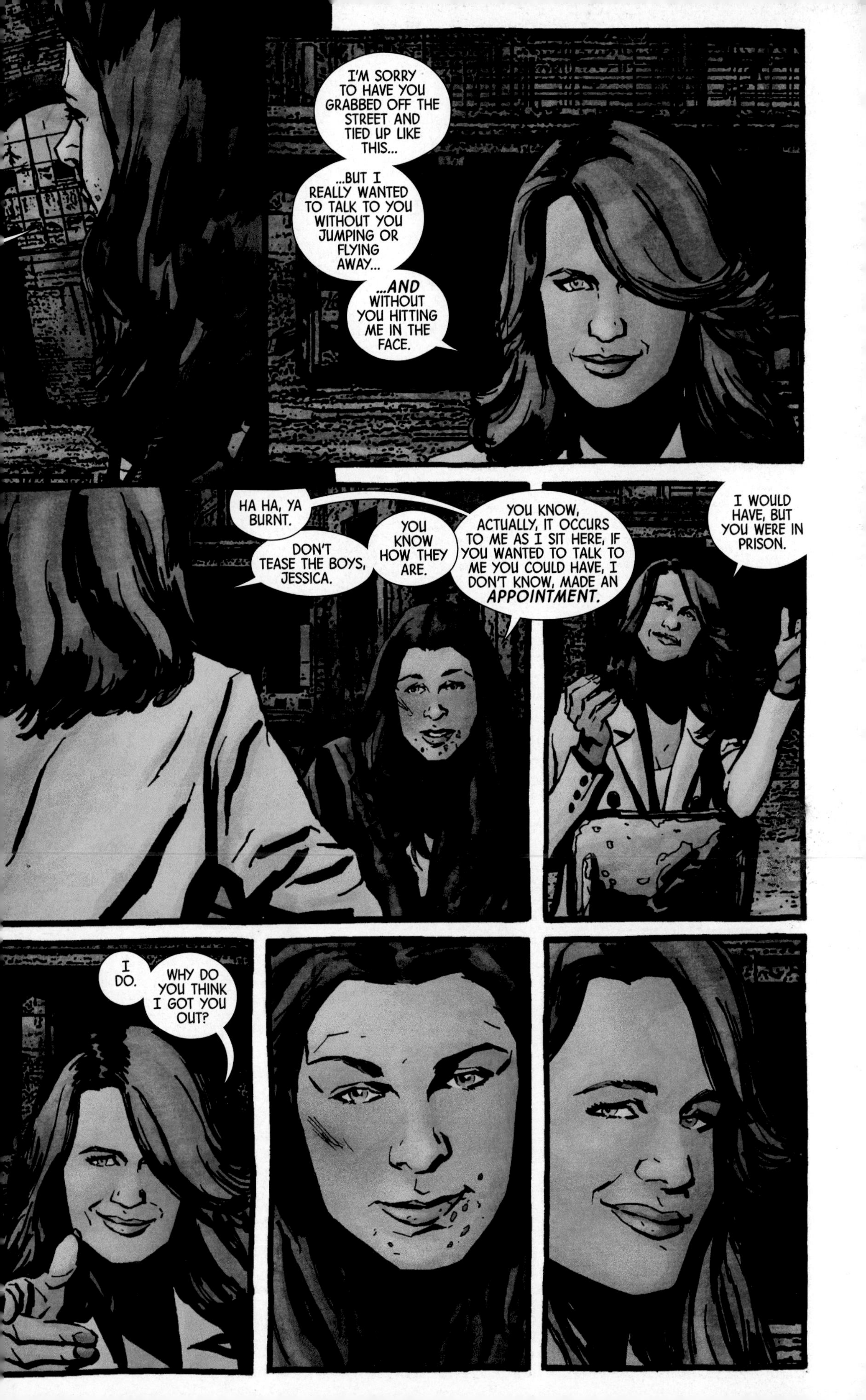
I'M SORRY TO HAVE YOU GRABBED OFF THE STREET AND TIED UP LIKE THIS...
...BUT I REALLY WANTED TO TALK TO YOU WITHOUT YOU JUMPING OR FLYING AWAY...
...AND WITHOUT YOU HITTING ME IN THE FACE.
HA HA, YA BURNT.
DON'T TEASE THE BOYS, JESSICA.
YOU KNOW HOW THEY ARE.
YOU KNOW, ACTUALLY, IT OCCURS TO ME AS I SIT HERE, IF YOU WANTED TO TALK TO ME YOU COULD HAVE, I DON'T KNOW, MADE AN APPOINTMENT.
I WOULD HAVE, BUT YOU WERE IN PRISON.
I DO.
WHY DO YOU THINK I GOT YOU OUT?

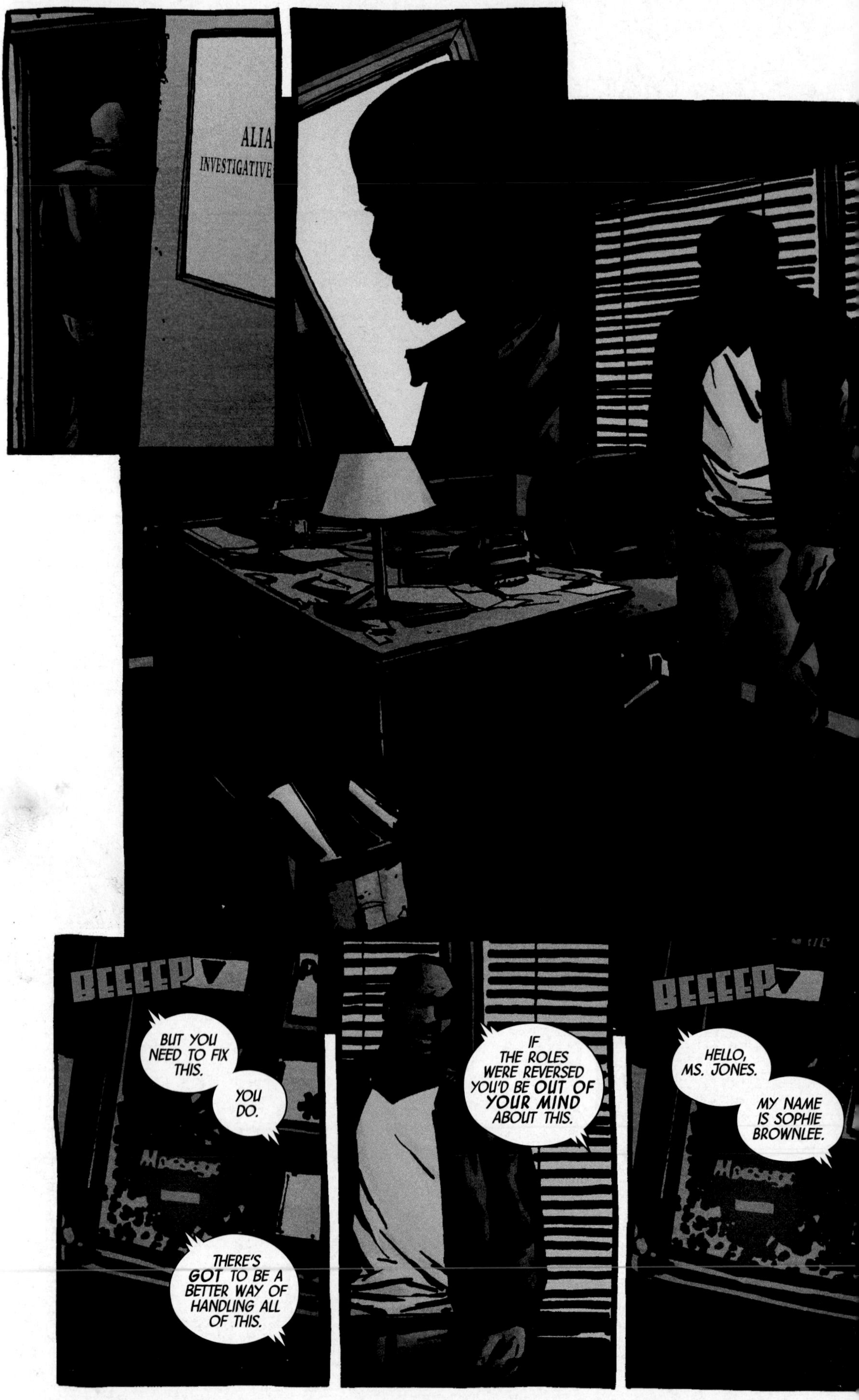
ALIA
INVESTIGATIVE
BEEEEP
BUT YOU NEED TO FIX THIS.
YOU DO.
THERE'S GOT TO BE A BETTER WAY OF HANDLING ALL OF THIS.
IF THE ROLES WERE REVERSED YOU'D BE OUT OF YOUR MIND ABOUT THIS.
BEEEEP
HELLO, MS. JONES.
MY NAME IS SOPHIE BROWNLEE.

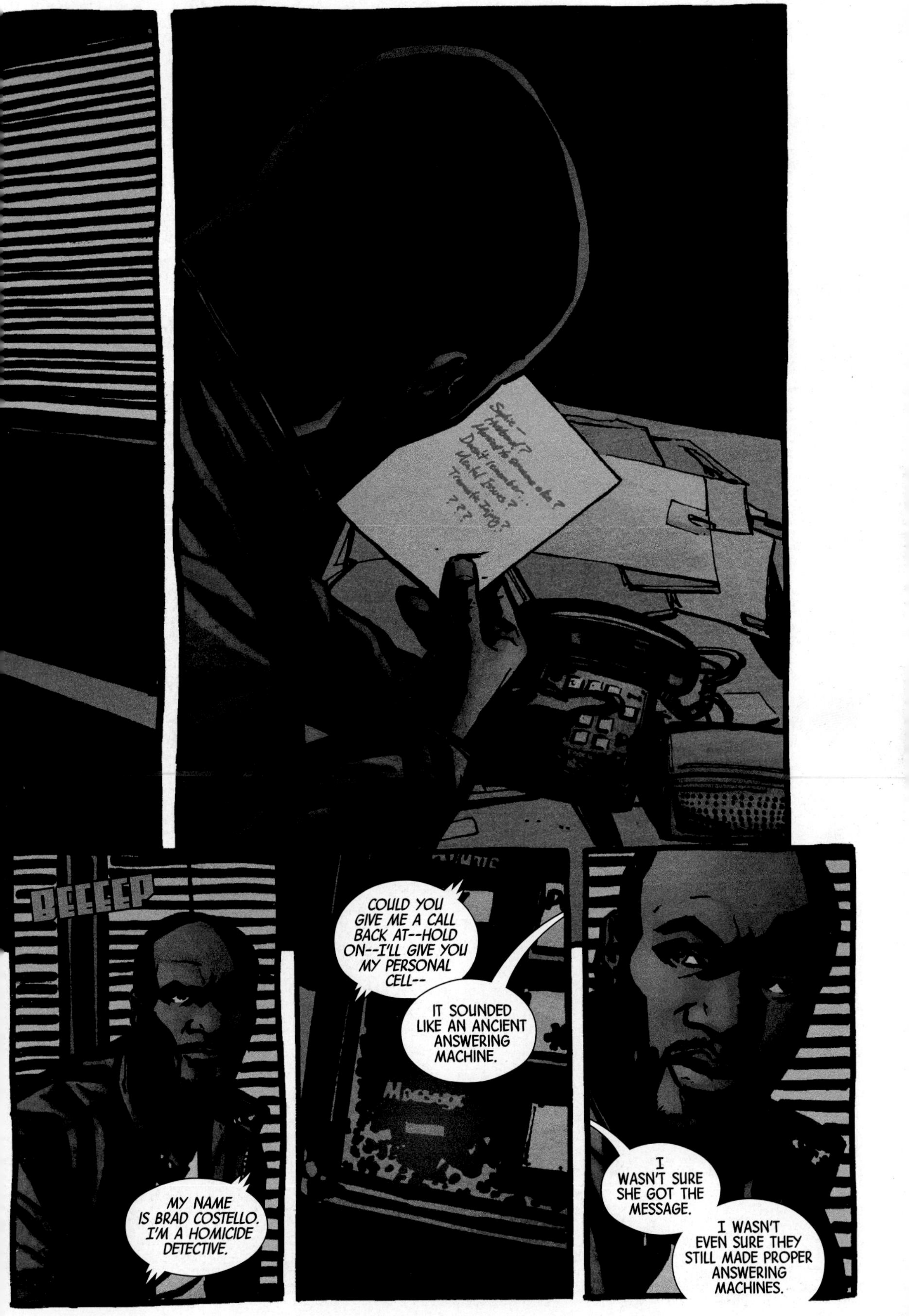
BEEEEP
MY NAME IS BRAD COSTELLO. I'M A HOMICIDE DETECTIVE.
COULD YOU GIVE ME A CALL BACK AT--HOLD ON--I'LL GIVE YOU MY PERSONAL CELL--
IT SOUNDED LIKE AN ANCIENT ANSWERING MACHINE.
I WASN'T SURE SHE GOT THE MESSAGE.
I WASN'T EVEN SURE THEY STILL MADE PROPER ANSWERING MACHINES.

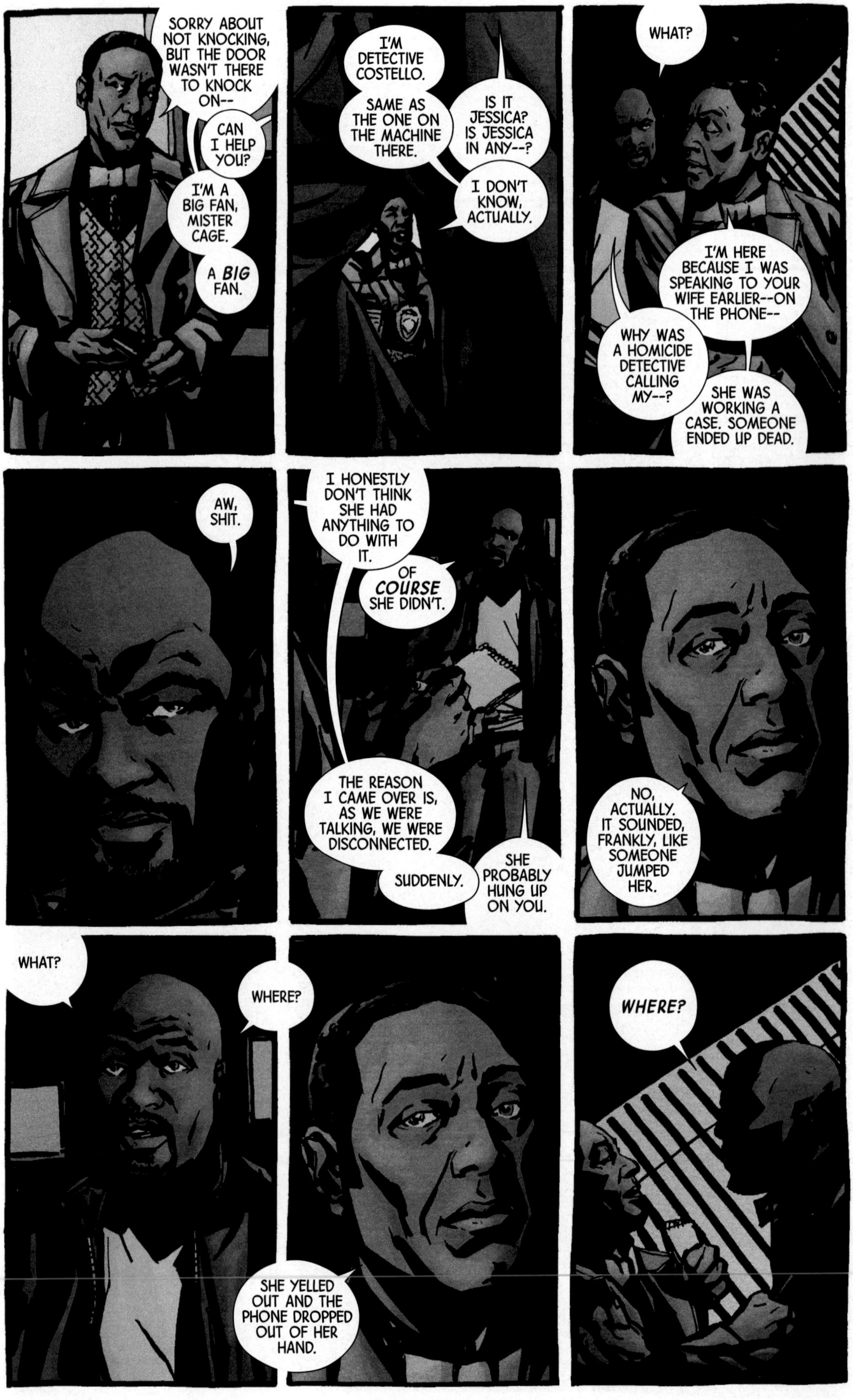
SORRY ABOUT NOT KNOCKING, BUT THE DOOR WASN'T THERE TO KNOCK ON--
CAN I HELP YOU?
I'M A BIG FAN, MISTER CAGE.
A BIG FAN.
I'M DETECTIVE COSTELLO.
SAME AS THE ONE ON THE MACHINE THERE.
IS IT JESSICA? IS JESSICA IN ANY--?
I DON'T KNOW, ACTUALLY.
WHAT?
I'M HERE BECAUSE I WAS SPEAKING TO YOUR WIFE EARLIER--ON THE PHONE--
WHY WAS A HOMICIDE DETECTIVE CALLING MY--?
SHE WAS WORKING A CASE. SOMEONE ENDED UP DEAD.
AW, SHIT.
I HONESTLY DON'T THINK SHE HAD ANYTHING TO DO WITH IT.
OF COURSE SHE DIDN'T.
THE REASON I CAME OVER IS, AS WE WERE TALKING, WE WERE DISCONNECTED.
SUDDENLY.
SHE PROBABLY HUNG UP ON YOU.
NO, ACTUALLY. IT SOUNDED, FRANKLY, LIKE SOMEONE JUMPED HER.
WHAT?
WHERE?
SHE YELLED OUT AND THE PHONE DROPPED OUT OF HER HAND.
WHERE?

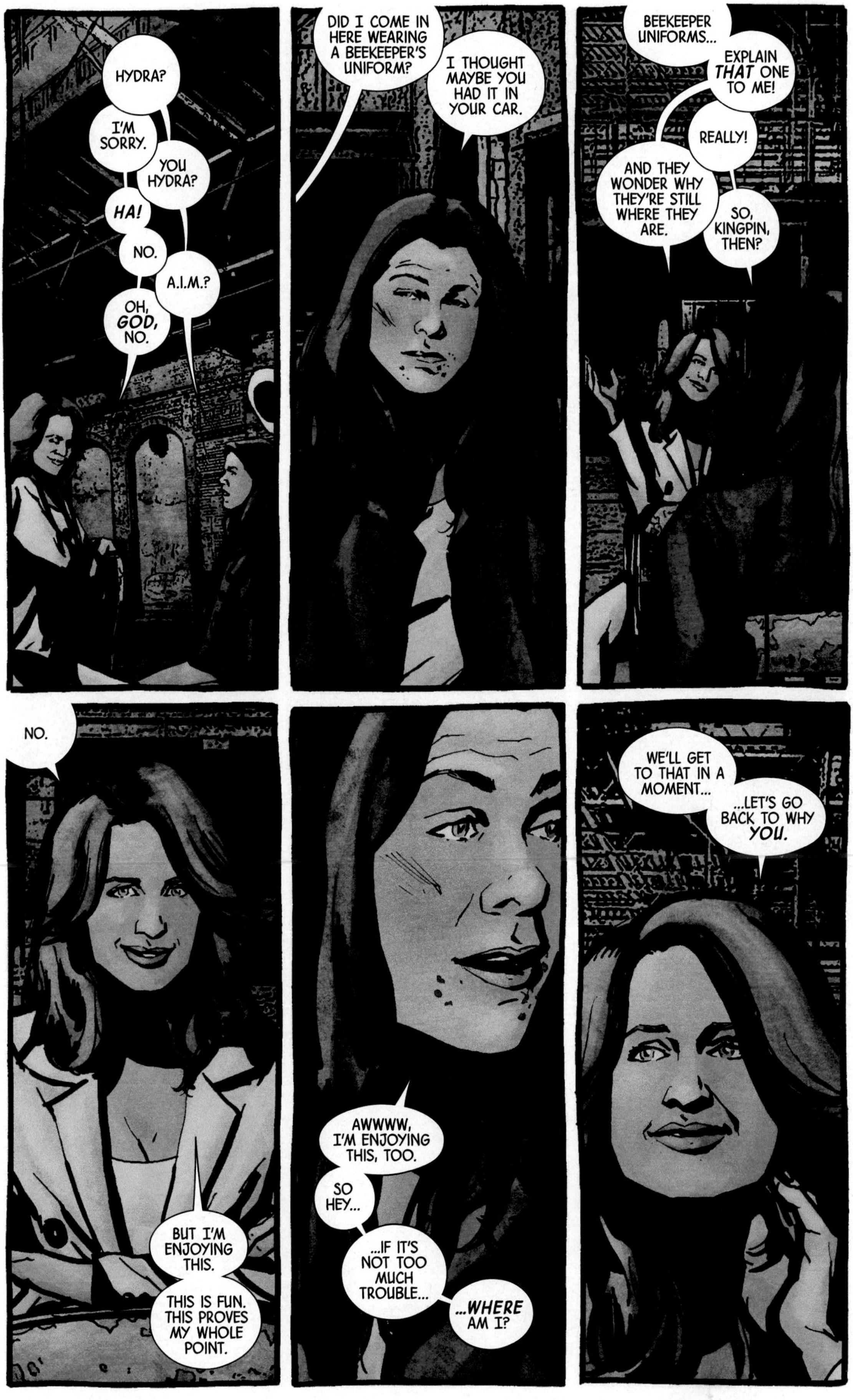
HYDRA?
I'M SORRY.
YOU HYDRA?
HA!
NO.
A.I.M.?
OH, GOD, NO.
DID I COME IN HERE WEARING A BEEKEEPER'S UNIFORM?
I THOUGHT MAYBE YOU HAD IT IN YOUR CAR.
BEEKEEPER UNIFORMS...
EXPLAIN THAT ONE TO ME!
REALLY!
AND THEY WONDER WHY THEY'RE STILL WHERE THEY ARE.
SO, KINGPIN, THEN?
NO.
BUT I'M ENJOYING THIS.
THIS IS FUN. THIS PROVES MY WHOLE POINT.
AWWWW, I'M ENJOYING THIS, TOO.
SO HEY...
...IF IT'S NOT TOO MUCH TROUBLE...
...WHERE AM I?
WE'LL GET TO THAT IN A MOMENT...
...LET'S GO BACK TO WHY YOU.

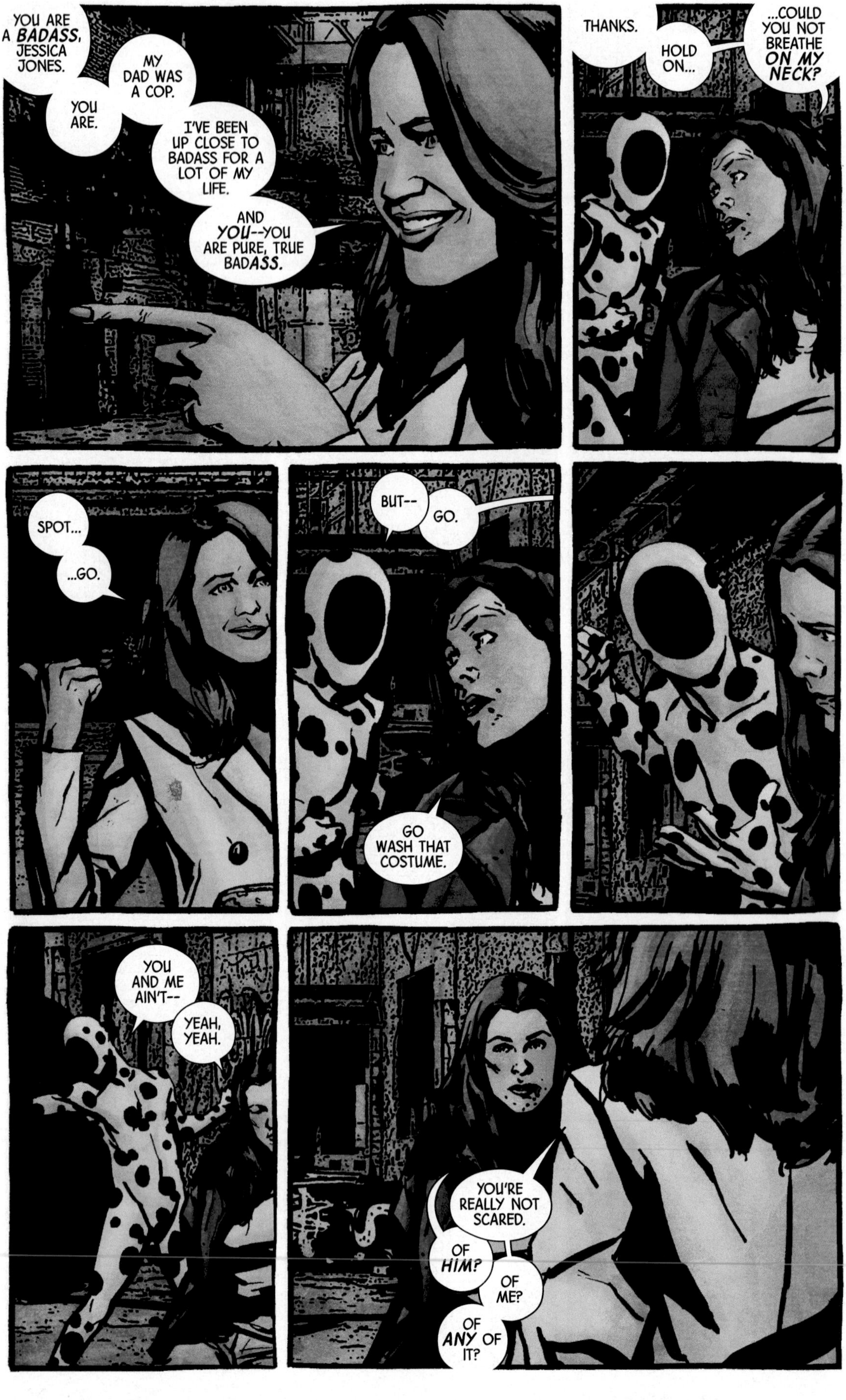
YOU ARE A BADASS, JESSICA JONES.
YOU ARE.
MY DAD WAS A COP.
I'VE BEEN UP CLOSE TO BADASS FOR A LOT OF MY LIFE.
AND YOU--YOU ARE PURE, TRUE BADASS.
THANKS.
HOLD ON...
...COULD YOU NOT BREATHE ON MY NECK?
SPOT...
...GO.
BUT--
GO.
GO WASH THAT COSTUME.
YOU AND ME AIN'T--
YEAH, YEAH.
YOU'RE REALLY NOT SCARED.
OF HIM?
OF ME?
OF ANY OF IT?

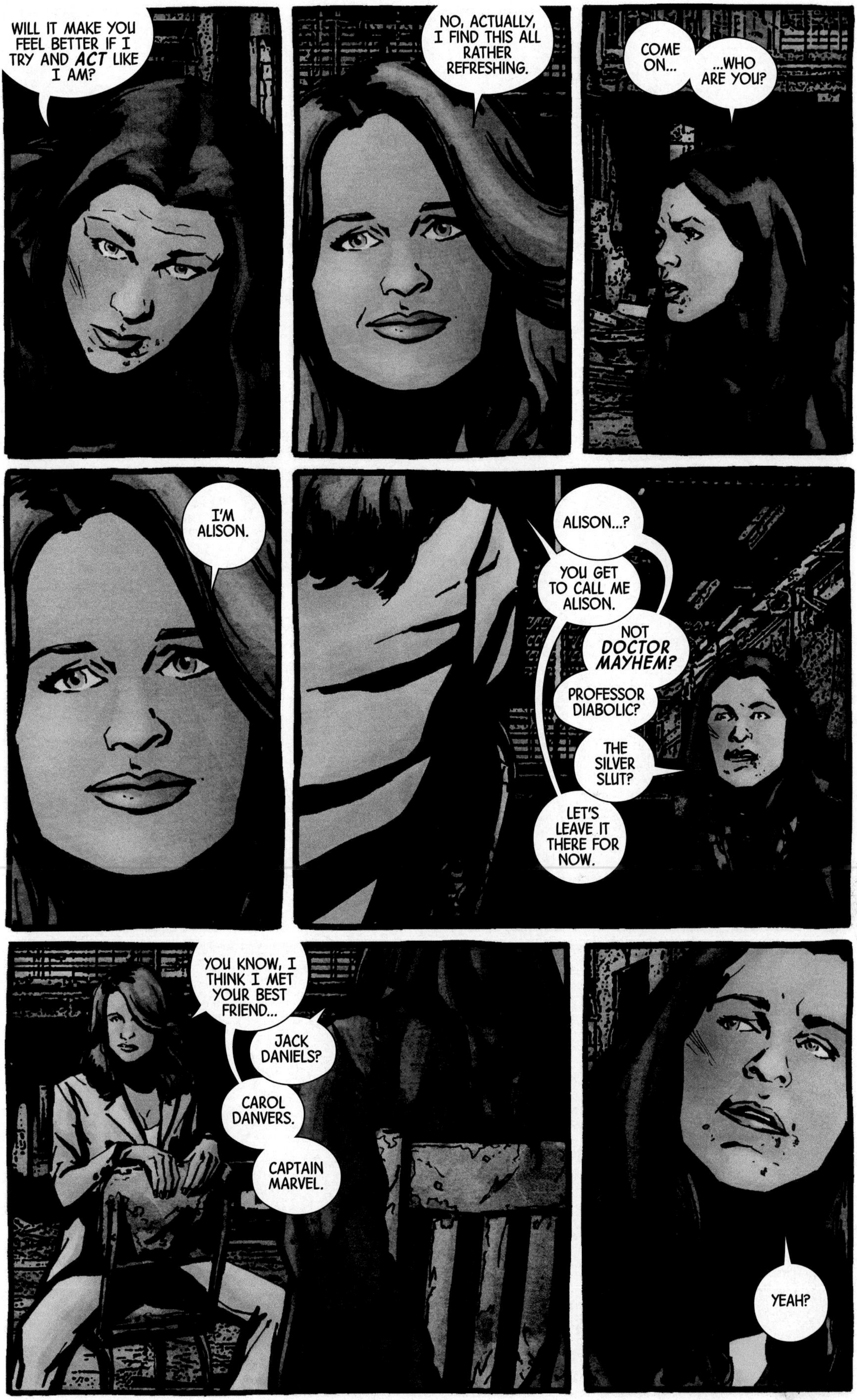
WILL IT MAKE YOU FEEL BETTER IF I TRY AND ACT LIKE I AM?
NO, ACTUALLY, I FIND THIS ALL RATHER REFRESHING.
COME ON...
...WHO ARE YOU?
I'M ALISON.
ALISON...?
YOU GET TO CALL ME ALISON.
NOT DOCTOR MAYHEM?
PROFESSOR DIABOLIC?
THE SILVER SLUT?
LET'S LEAVE IT THERE FOR NOW.
YOU KNOW, I THINK I MET YOUR BEST FRIEND...
JACK DANIELS?
CAROL DANVERS.
CAPTAIN MARVEL.
YEAH?

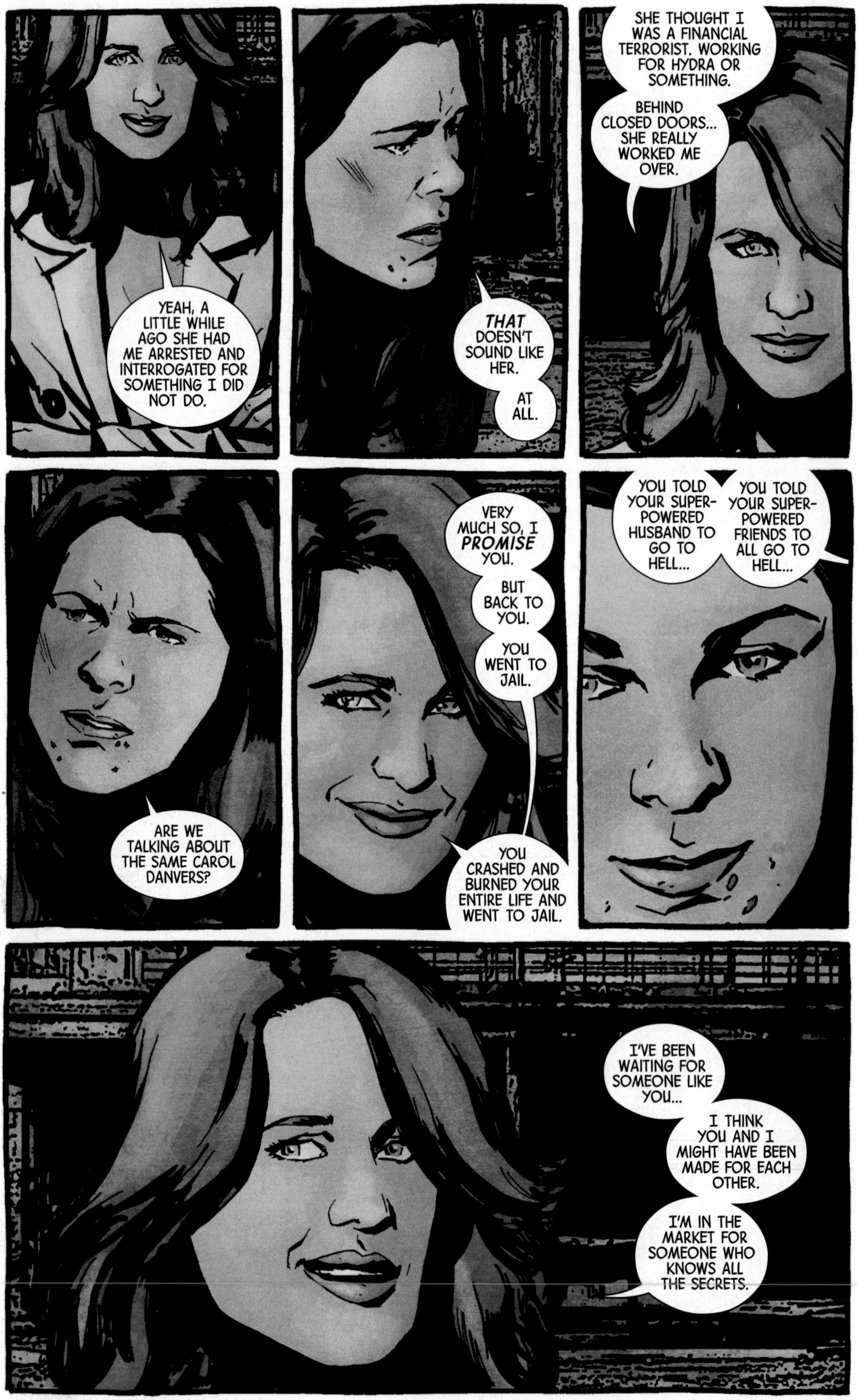

YEAH, A LITTLE WHILE AGO SHE HAD ME ARRESTED AND INTERROGATED FOR SOMETHING I DID NOT DO.
THAT DOESN'T SOUND LIKE HER.
AT ALL.
SHE THOUGHT I WAS A FINANCIAL TERRORIST. WORKING FOR HYDRA OR SOMETHING.
BEHIND CLOSED DOORS... SHE REALLY WORKED ME OVER.
ARE WE TALKING ABOUT THE SAME CAROL DANVERS?
VERY MUCH SO, I PROMISE YOU.
BUT BACK TO YOU.
YOU WENT TO JAIL.
YOU CRASHED AND BURNED YOUR ENTIRE LIFE AND WENT TO JAIL.
YOU TOLD YOUR SUPER-POWERED HUSBAND TO GO TO HELL...
YOU TOLD YOUR SUPER-POWERED FRIENDS TO ALL GO TO HELL...
I'VE BEEN WAITING FOR SOMEONE LIKE YOU...
I THINK YOU AND I MIGHT HAVE BEEN MADE FOR EACH OTHER.
I'M IN THE MARKET FOR SOMEONE WHO KNOWS ALL THE SECRETS.

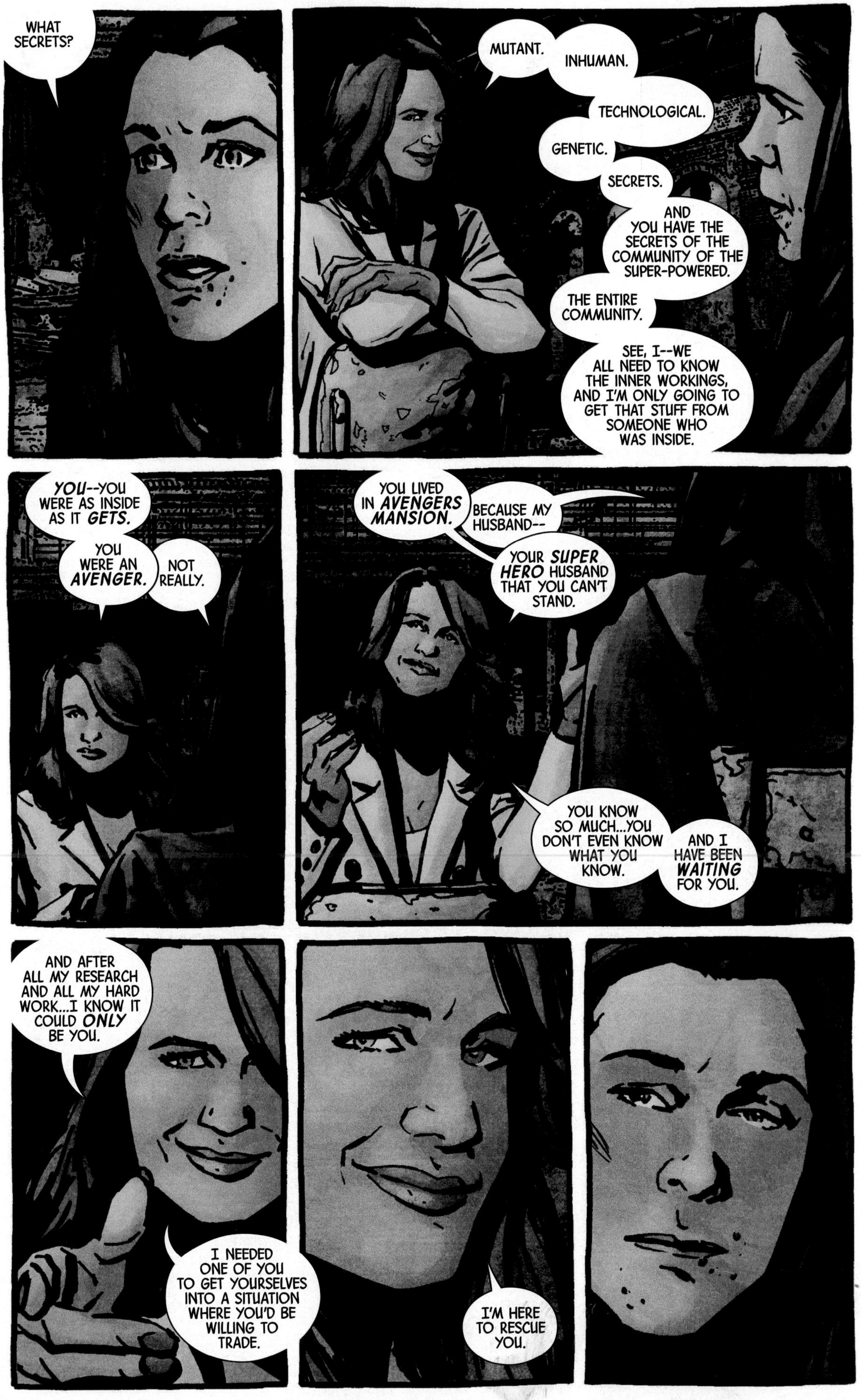
WHAT SECRETS?
MUTANT.
INHUMAN.
TECHNOLOGICAL.
GENETIC.
SECRETS.
AND YOU HAVE THE SECRETS OF THE COMMUNITY OF THE SUPER-POWERED.
THE ENTIRE COMMUNITY.
SEE, I--WE ALL NEED TO KNOW THE INNER WORKINGS, AND I'M ONLY GOING TO GET THAT STUFF FROM SOMEONE WHO WAS INSIDE.
YOU--YOU WERE AS INSIDE AS IT GETS.
YOU WERE AN AVENGER.
NOT REALLY.
YOU LIVED IN AVENGERS MANSION.
BECAUSE MY HUSBAND--
YOUR SUPER HERO HUSBAND THAT YOU CAN'T STAND.
YOU KNOW SO MUCH...YOU DON'T EVEN KNOW WHAT YOU KNOW.
AND I HAVE BEEN WAITING FOR YOU.
AND AFTER ALL MY RESEARCH AND ALL MY HARD WORK...I KNOW IT COULD ONLY BE YOU.
I NEEDED ONE OF YOU TO GET YOURSELVES INTO A SITUATION WHERE YOU'D BE WILLING TO TRADE.
I'M HERE TO RESCUE YOU.

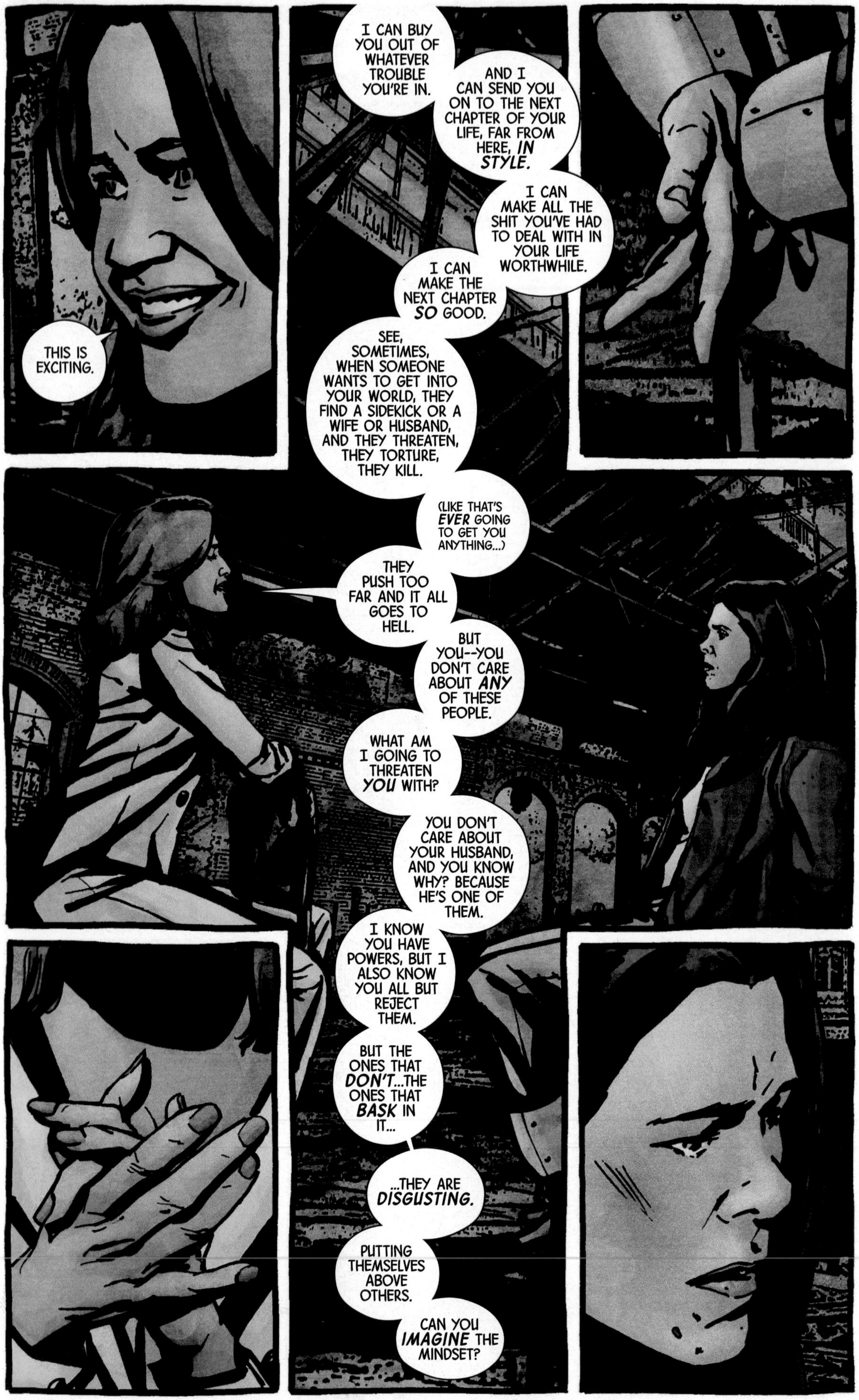

THIS IS EXCITING.
I CAN BUY YOU OUT OF WHATEVER TROUBLE YOU'RE IN.
AND I CAN SEND YOU ON TO THE NEXT CHAPTER OF YOUR LIFE, FAR FROM HERE, IN STYLE.
I CAN MAKE ALL THE SHIT YOU'VE HAD TO DEAL WITH IN YOUR LIFE WORTHWHILE.
I CAN MAKE THE NEXT CHAPTER SO GOOD.
SEE, SOMETIMES, WHEN SOMEONE WANTS TO GET INTO YOUR WORLD, THEY FIND A SIDEKICK OR A WIFE OR HUSBAND, AND THEY THREATEN, THEY TORTURE, THEY KILL.
(LIKE THAT'S EVER GOING TO GET YOU ANYTHING...)
THEY PUSH TOO FAR AND IT ALL GOES TO HELL.
BUT YOU--YOU DON'T CARE ABOUT ANY OF THESE PEOPLE.
WHAT AM I GOING TO THREATEN YOU WITH?
YOU DON'T CARE ABOUT YOUR HUSBAND, AND YOU KNOW WHY? BECAUSE HE'S ONE OF THEM.
I KNOW YOU HAVE POWERS, BUT I ALSO KNOW YOU ALL BUT REJECT THEM.
BUT THE ONES THAT DON'T...THE ONES THAT BASK IN IT...
...THEY ARE DISGUSTING.
PUTTING THEMSELVES ABOVE OTHERS.
CAN YOU IMAGINE THE MINDSET?

I MEAN, *YOU* CAN, YOU *LIVED* THERE.

YOU SAW IT FOR YOURSELF, DIDN'T YOU?

YOU HAD A FRONT ROW SEAT TO THAT PARADE OF NEVER-ENDING HUBRIS.

TO WEAR THE FLAG AND SAY YOU ARE AMERICA.

TO DECIDE YOU KNOW WHAT'S RIGHT AND WRONG FOR EVERYONE ELSE.

TO THINK YOU KNOW BETTER THAN EVERYONE ELSE.

AND NO ONE TO ANSWER TO.

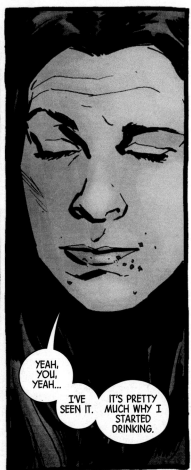

YEAH, YOU, YEAH...

I'VE SEEN IT.

IT'S PRETTY MUCH WHY I STARTED DRINKING.

YOU AND I ARE GOING TO BE--

--WE'RE GOING TO BE *VERY GOOD* TO EACH OTHER.

I KNOW I HAVE TO EARN MY WAY WITH YOU, BUT THIS IS GOING TO BE VERY BENEFICIAL.

I MEANT WHAT I SAID, JESSICA...

CLINK

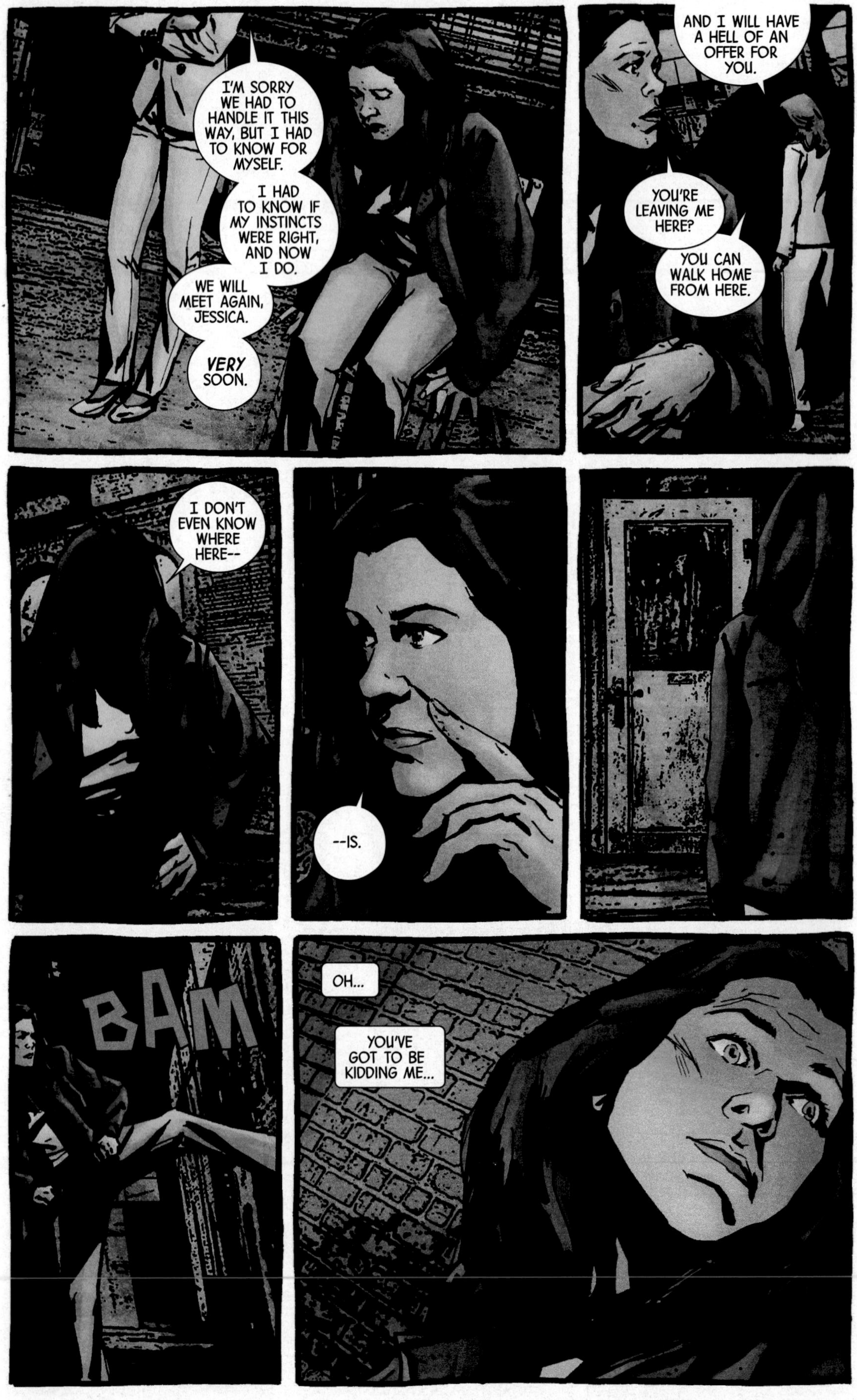
I'M SORRY WE HAD TO HANDLE IT THIS WAY, BUT I HAD TO KNOW FOR MYSELF.
I HAD TO KNOW IF MY INSTINCTS WERE RIGHT, AND NOW I DO.
WE WILL MEET AGAIN, JESSICA.
VERY SOON.
AND I WILL HAVE A HELL OF AN OFFER FOR YOU.
YOU'RE LEAVING ME HERE?
YOU CAN WALK HOME FROM HERE.
I DON'T EVEN KNOW WHERE HERE--
--IS.
BAM
OH...
YOU'VE GOT TO BE KIDDING ME...

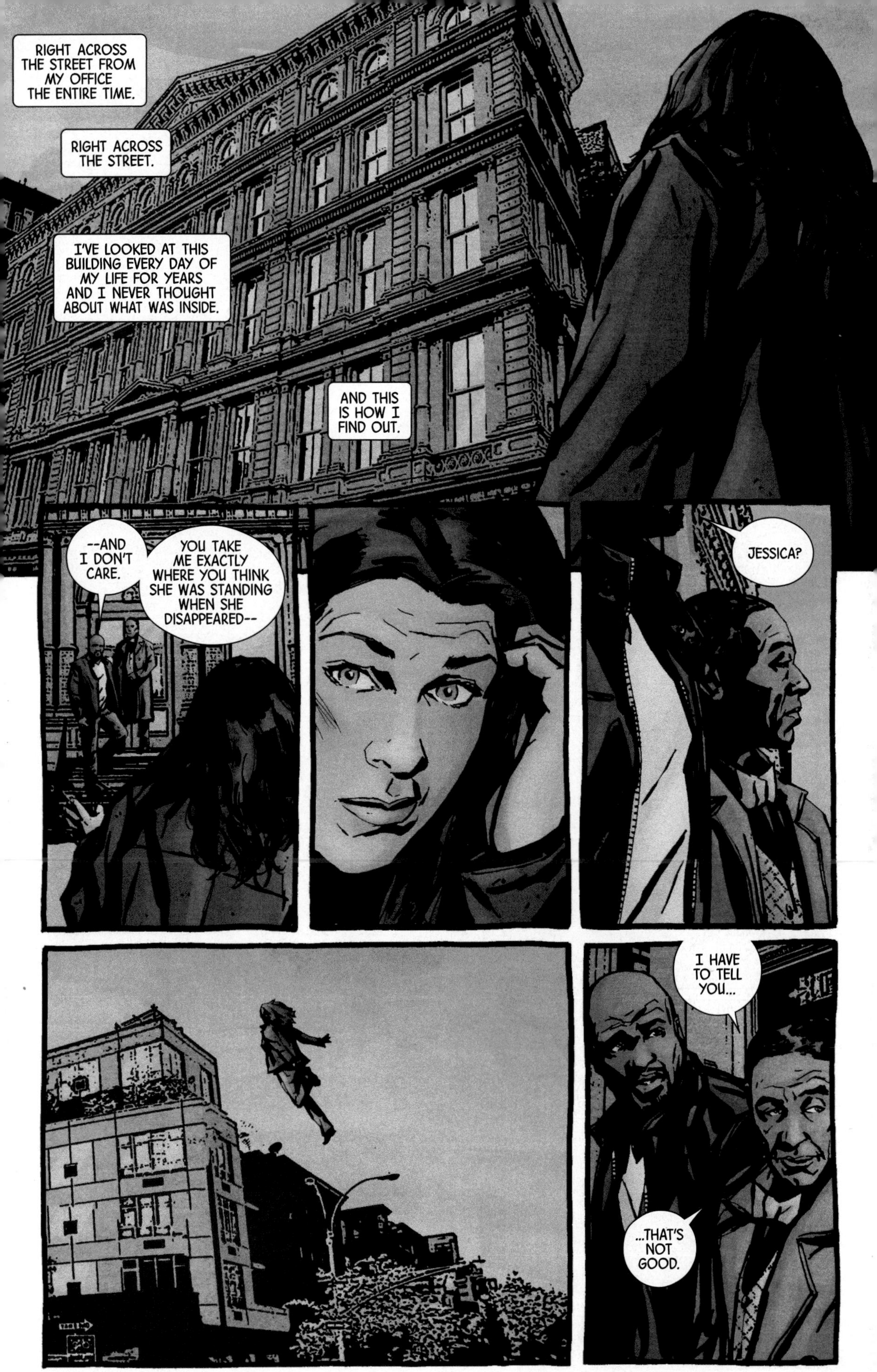
RIGHT ACROSS THE STREET FROM MY OFFICE THE ENTIRE TIME.
RIGHT ACROSS THE STREET.
I'VE LOOKED AT THIS BUILDING EVERY DAY OF MY LIFE FOR YEARS AND I NEVER THOUGHT ABOUT WHAT WAS INSIDE.
AND THIS IS HOW I FIND OUT.
--AND I DON'T CARE.
YOU TAKE ME EXACTLY WHERE YOU THINK SHE WAS STANDING WHEN SHE DISAPPEARED--
JESSICA?
I HAVE TO TELL YOU...
...THAT'S NOT GOOD.

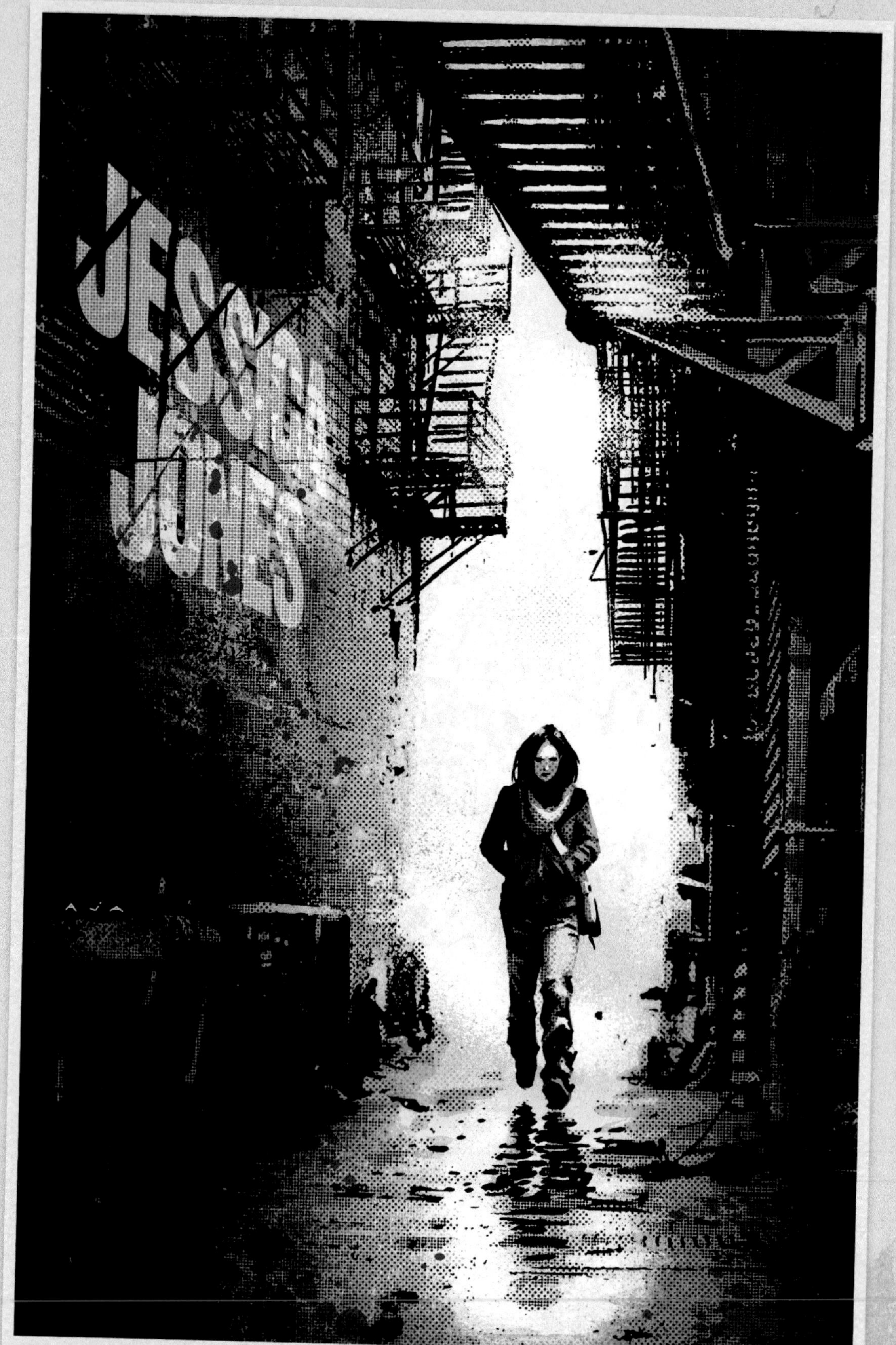
JESSICA
JONES

#1 variant by **David Aja**

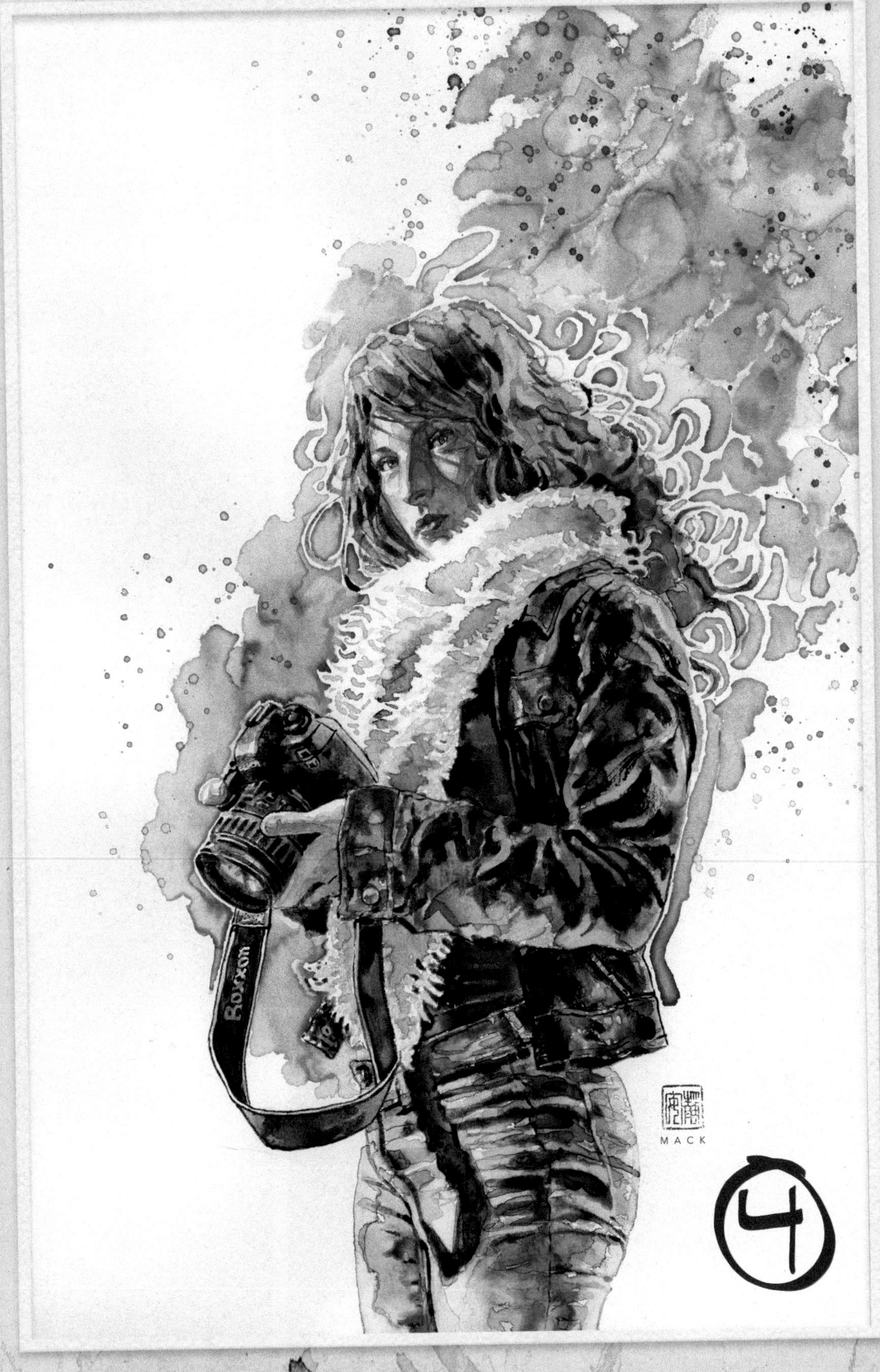
Roxxon
MACK
4

LUKE CAGE!

YOU *DID IT!*

YOU DID EXACTLY WHAT I TOLD YOU *NOT* TO DO!

YOU DID EXACTLY WHAT I *BEGGED* YOU NOT TO DO!

MISTY...

...YOU DON'T UNDERSTAND.

YOU ASKED FOR MY HELP, LUKE, AND I SAID I WOULD, BUT THAT YOU HAD TO SIT TIGHT!

DID YOU SIT TIGHT OR DID YOU CONFRONT HER?

SHE'S MY WIFE.

CAGE RAGE! STREET TANTRUM CAUGHT ON TAPE.

AND NOW YOU HAVE THIS!

WHAT THE HELL?

GE RAGE! EET TANTRUM GHT ON TAPE.

YOU LOOK *NUTS* HERE.

WHAT IS THIS FROM? WHAT--?

JAMESON'S "FACT" CHANNEL.

WHY WERE YOU LOOKING AT THAT CRAP?

WHY ARE YOU *ON HERE,* FOOL?

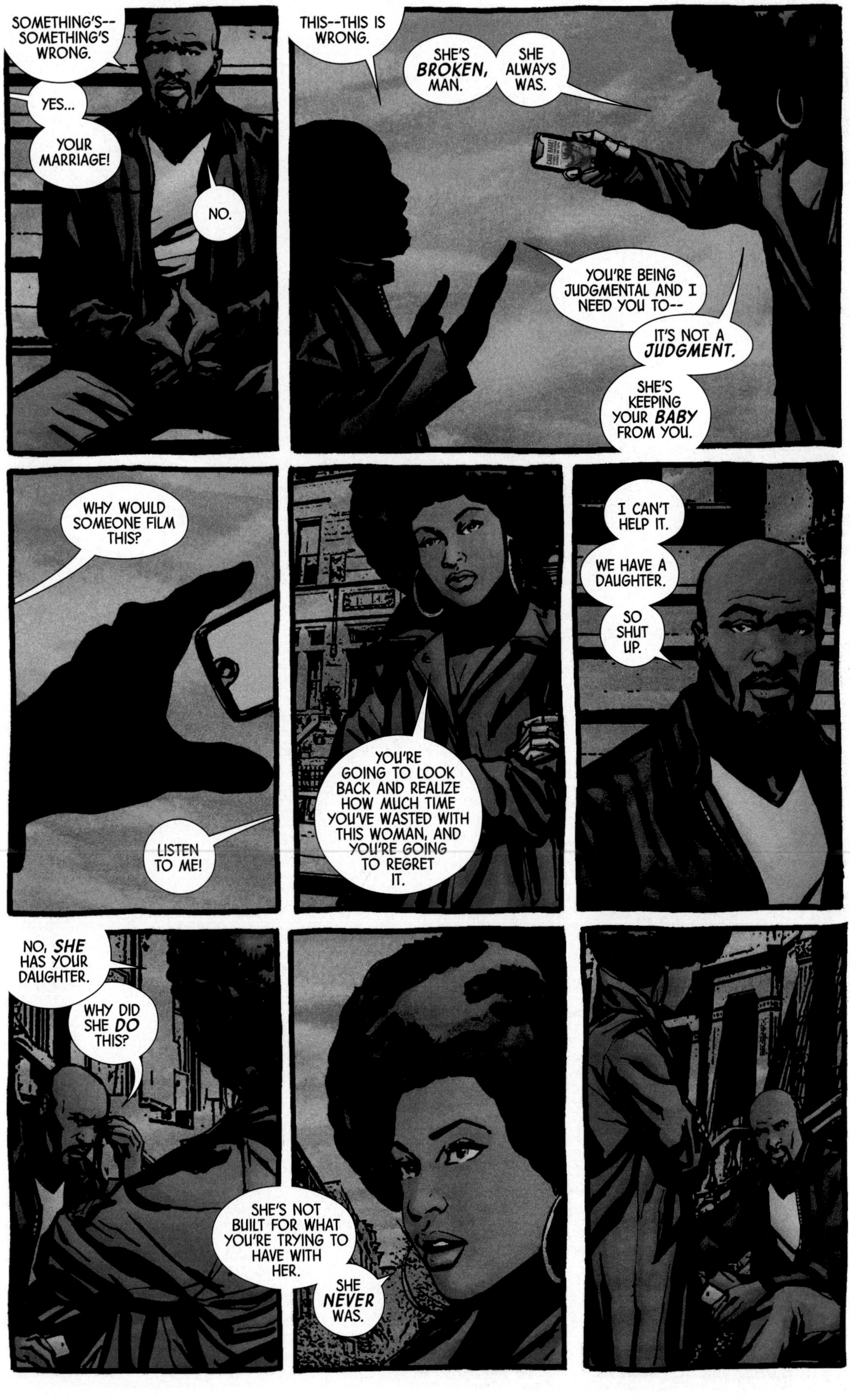
SOMETHING'S--
SOMETHING'S WRONG.
YES...
YOUR MARRIAGE!
NO.
THIS--THIS IS WRONG.
SHE'S *BROKEN,* MAN.
SHE ALWAYS WAS.
YOU'RE BEING JUDGMENTAL AND I NEED YOU TO--
IT'S NOT A *JUDGMENT.*
SHE'S KEEPING YOUR *BABY* FROM YOU.
WHY WOULD SOMEONE FILM THIS?
LISTEN TO ME!
YOU'RE GOING TO LOOK BACK AND REALIZE HOW MUCH TIME YOU'VE WASTED WITH THIS WOMAN, AND YOU'RE GOING TO REGRET IT.
I CAN'T HELP IT.
WE HAVE A DAUGHTER.
SO SHUT UP.
NO, *SHE* HAS YOUR DAUGHTER.
WHY DID SHE *DO* THIS?
SHE'S NOT BUILT FOR WHAT YOU'RE TRYING TO HAVE WITH HER.
SHE *NEVER* WAS.

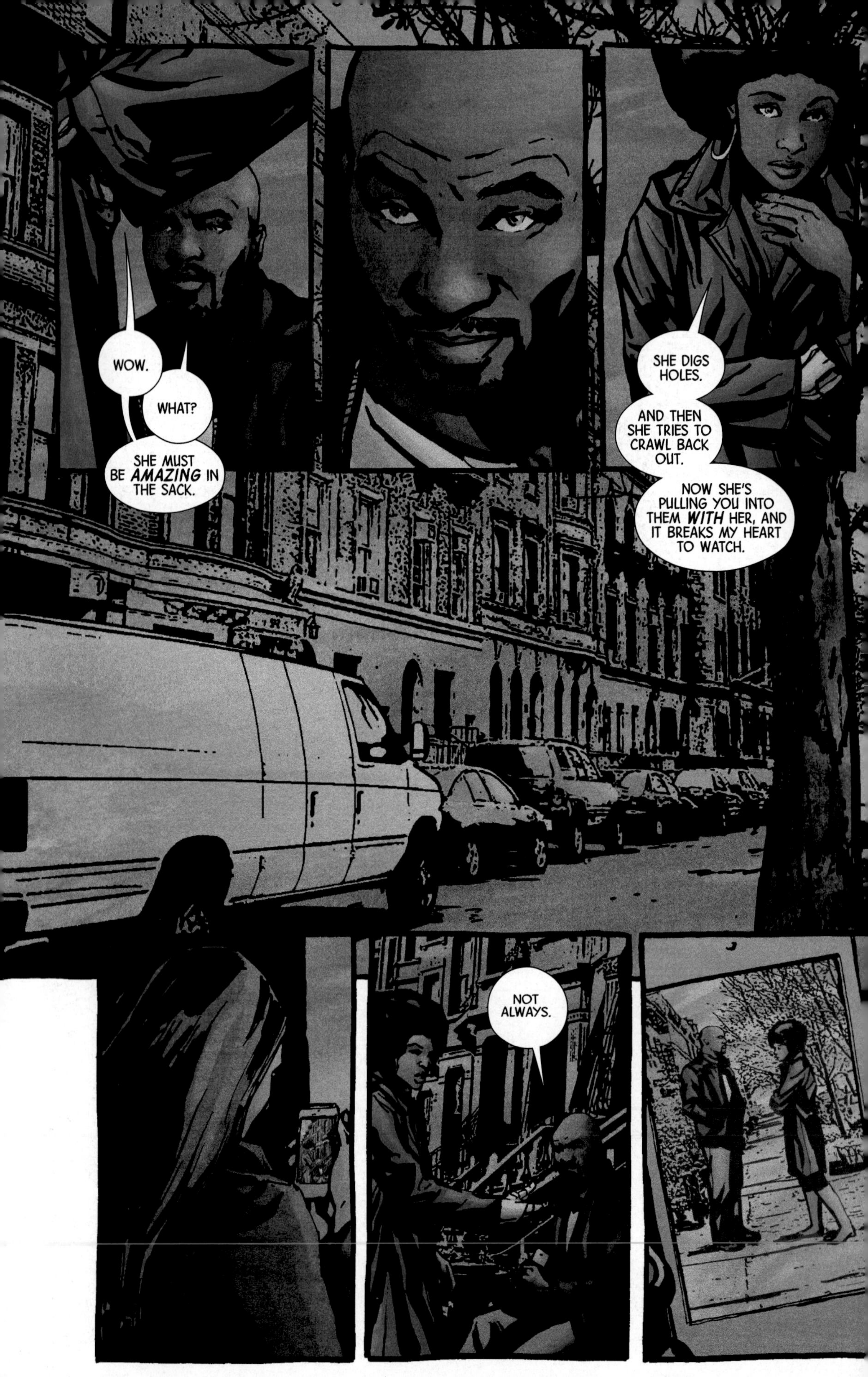

WOW.
WHAT?
SHE MUST BE AMAZING IN THE SACK.
SHE DIGS HOLES.
AND THEN SHE TRIES TO CRAWL BACK OUT.
NOW SHE'S PULLING YOU INTO THEM WITH HER, AND IT BREAKS MY HEART TO WATCH.
NOT ALWAYS.

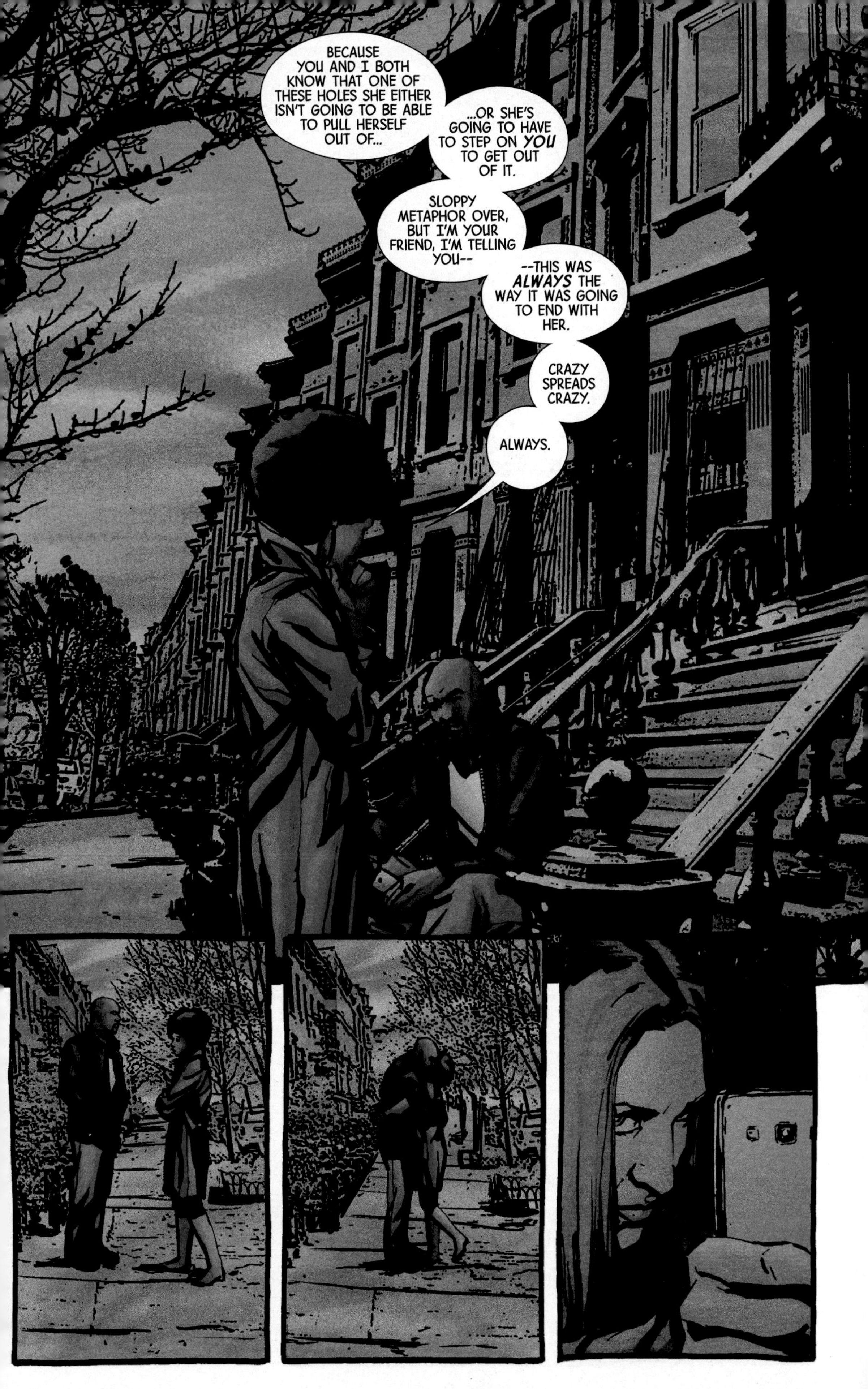
BECAUSE YOU AND I BOTH KNOW THAT ONE OF THESE HOLES SHE EITHER ISN'T GOING TO BE ABLE TO PULL HERSELF OUT OF...
...OR SHE'S GOING TO HAVE TO STEP ON *YOU* TO GET OUT OF IT.
SLOPPY METAPHOR OVER, BUT I'M YOUR FRIEND, I'M TELLING YOU--
--THIS WAS ***ALWAYS*** THE WAY IT WAS GOING TO END WITH HER.
CRAZY SPREADS CRAZY.
ALWAYS.

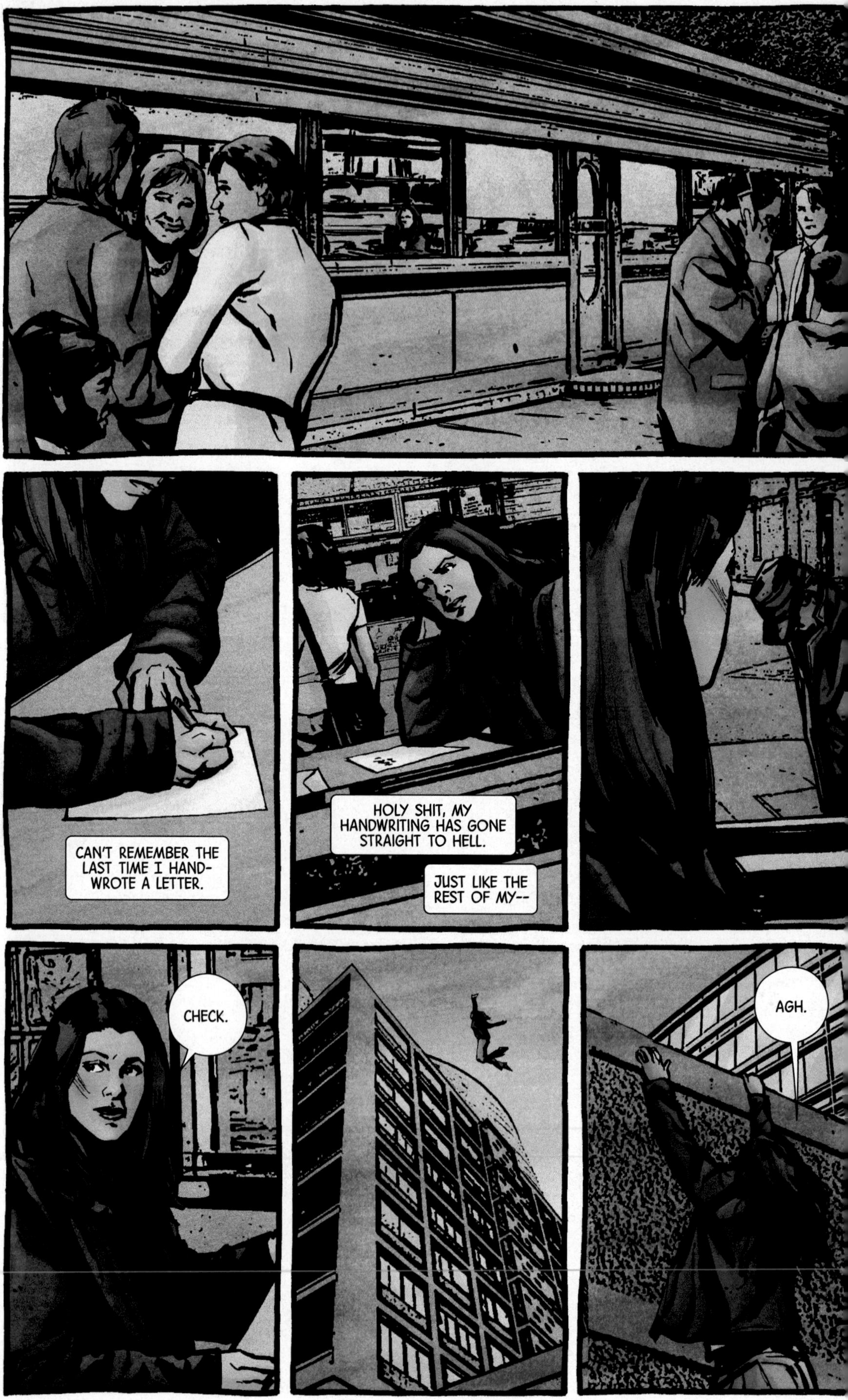
CAN'T REMEMBER THE LAST TIME I HAND-WROTE A LETTER.
HOLY SHIT, MY HANDWRITING HAS GONE STRAIGHT TO HELL.
JUST LIKE THE REST OF MY--
CHECK.
AGH.

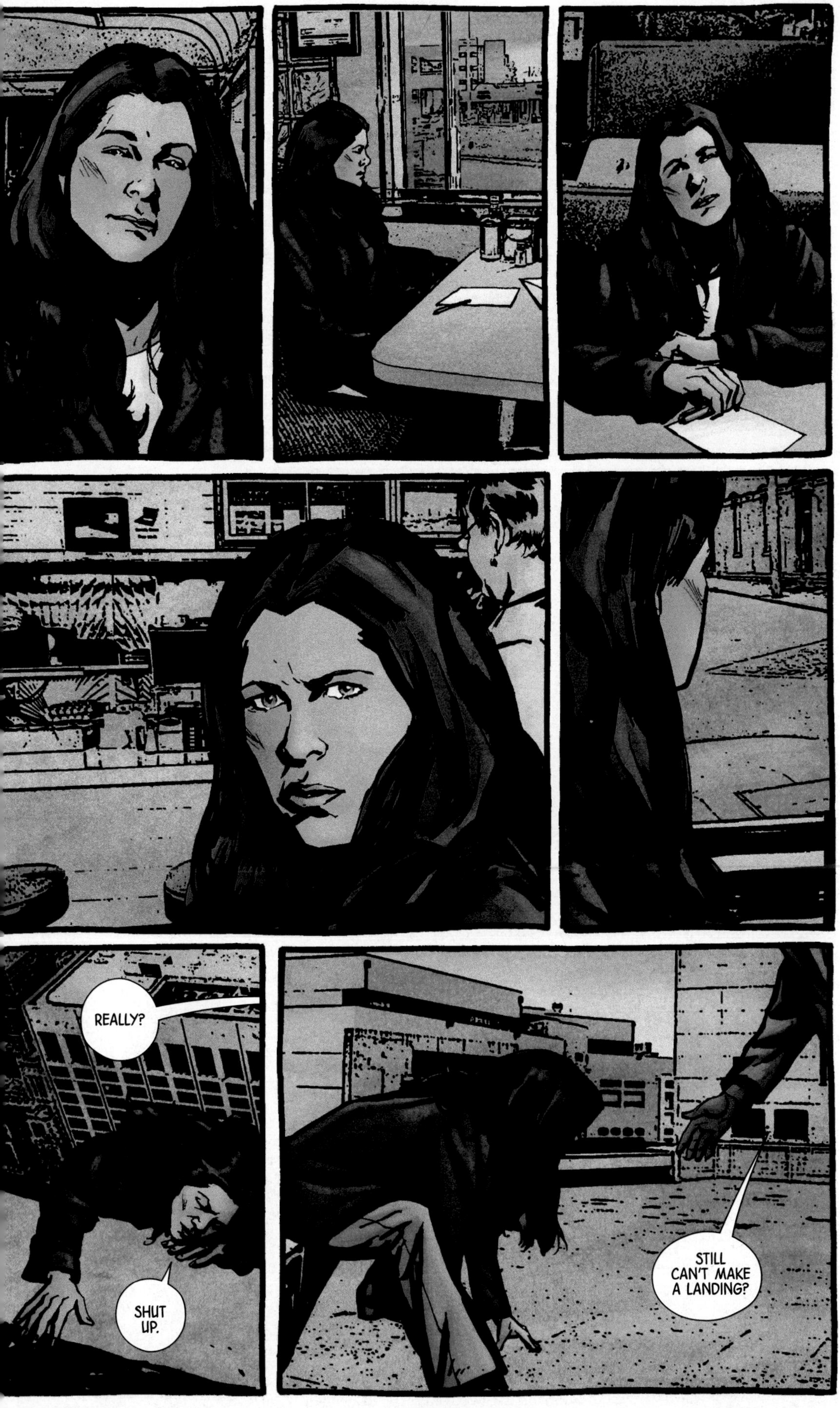
REALLY?
SHUT UP.
STILL CAN'T MAKE A LANDING?

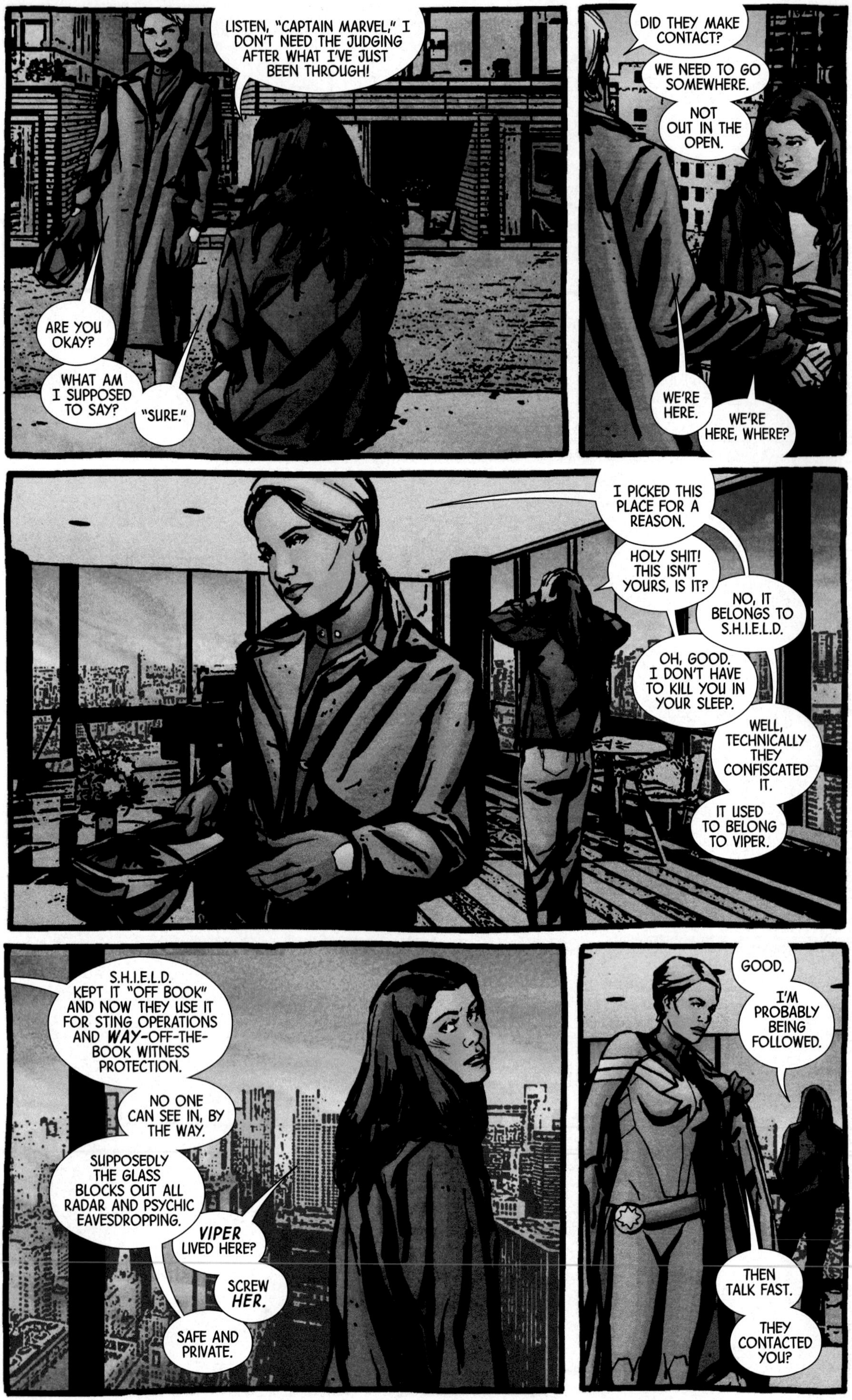
LISTEN, "CAPTAIN MARVEL," I DON'T NEED THE JUDGING AFTER WHAT I'VE JUST BEEN THROUGH!
ARE YOU OKAY?
WHAT AM I SUPPOSED TO SAY?
"SURE."
DID THEY MAKE CONTACT?
WE NEED TO GO SOMEWHERE.
NOT OUT IN THE OPEN.
WE'RE HERE.
WE'RE HERE, WHERE?
I PICKED THIS PLACE FOR A REASON.
HOLY SHIT! THIS ISN'T YOURS, IS IT?
NO, IT BELONGS TO S.H.I.E.L.D.
OH, GOOD. I DON'T HAVE TO KILL YOU IN YOUR SLEEP.
WELL, TECHNICALLY THEY CONFISCATED IT.
IT USED TO BELONG TO VIPER.
S.H.I.E.L.D. KEPT IT "OFF BOOK" AND NOW THEY USE IT FOR STING OPERATIONS AND WAY-OFF-THE-BOOK WITNESS PROTECTION.
NO ONE CAN SEE IN, BY THE WAY.
SUPPOSEDLY THE GLASS BLOCKS OUT ALL RADAR AND PSYCHIC EAVESDROPPING.
VIPER LIVED HERE?
SCREW HER.
SAFE AND PRIVATE.
GOOD.
I'M PROBABLY BEING FOLLOWED.
THEN TALK FAST.
THEY CONTACTED YOU?

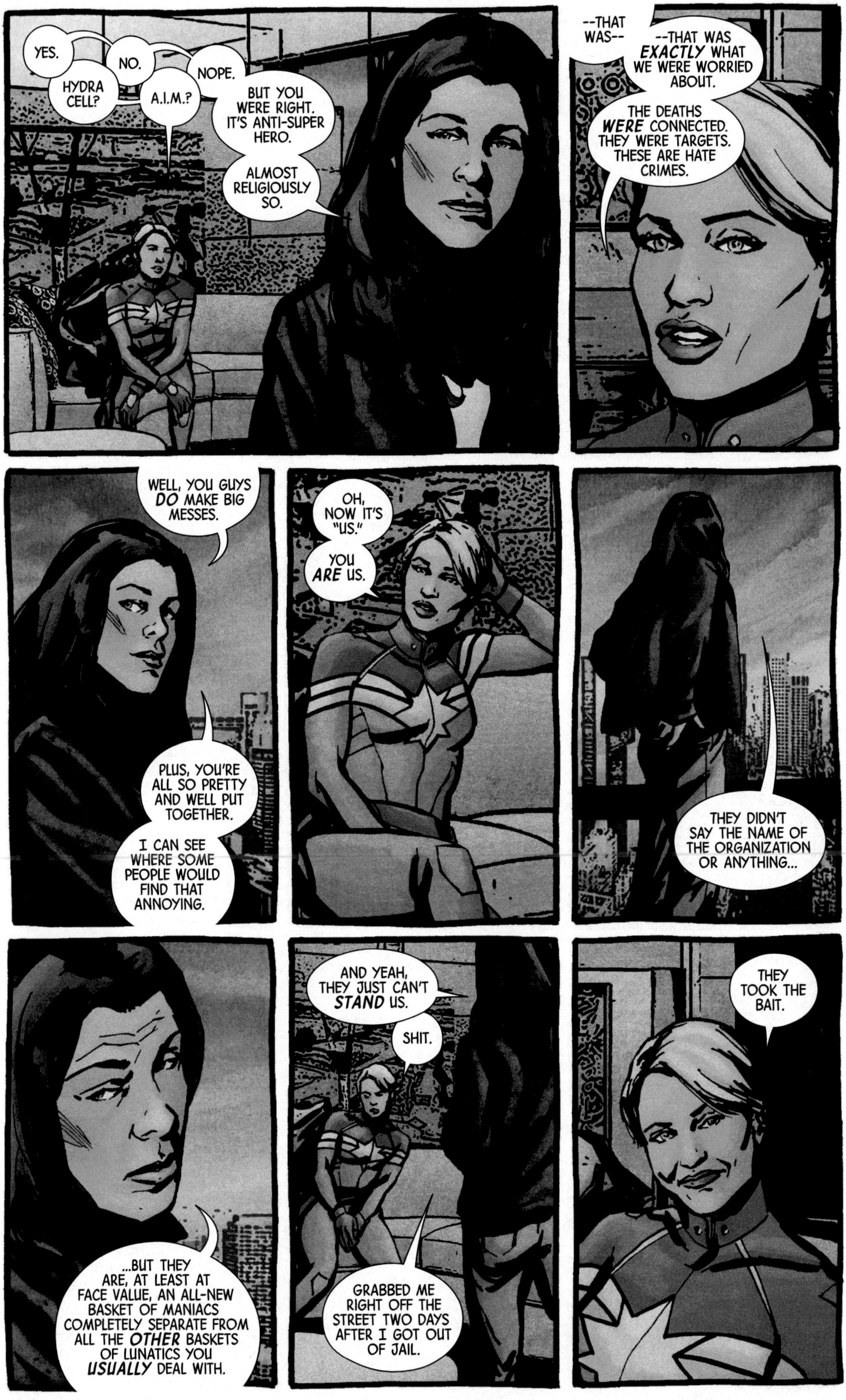
YES.
HYDRA CELL?
NO.
A.I.M.?
NOPE.
BUT YOU WERE RIGHT. IT'S ANTI-SUPER HERO.
ALMOST RELIGIOUSLY SO.
--THAT WAS--
--THAT WAS EXACTLY WHAT WE WERE WORRIED ABOUT.
THE DEATHS WERE CONNECTED. THEY WERE TARGETS. THESE ARE HATE CRIMES.
WELL, YOU GUYS DO MAKE BIG MESSES.
PLUS, YOU'RE ALL SO PRETTY AND WELL PUT TOGETHER.
I CAN SEE WHERE SOME PEOPLE WOULD FIND THAT ANNOYING.
OH, NOW IT'S "US."
YOU ARE US.
THEY DIDN'T SAY THE NAME OF THE ORGANIZATION OR ANYTHING...
...BUT THEY ARE, AT LEAST AT FACE VALUE, AN ALL-NEW BASKET OF MANIACS COMPLETELY SEPARATE FROM ALL THE OTHER BASKETS OF LUNATICS YOU USUALLY DEAL WITH.
AND YEAH, THEY JUST CAN'T STAND US.
SHIT.
GRABBED ME RIGHT OFF THE STREET TWO DAYS AFTER I GOT OUT OF JAIL.
THEY TOOK THE BAIT.

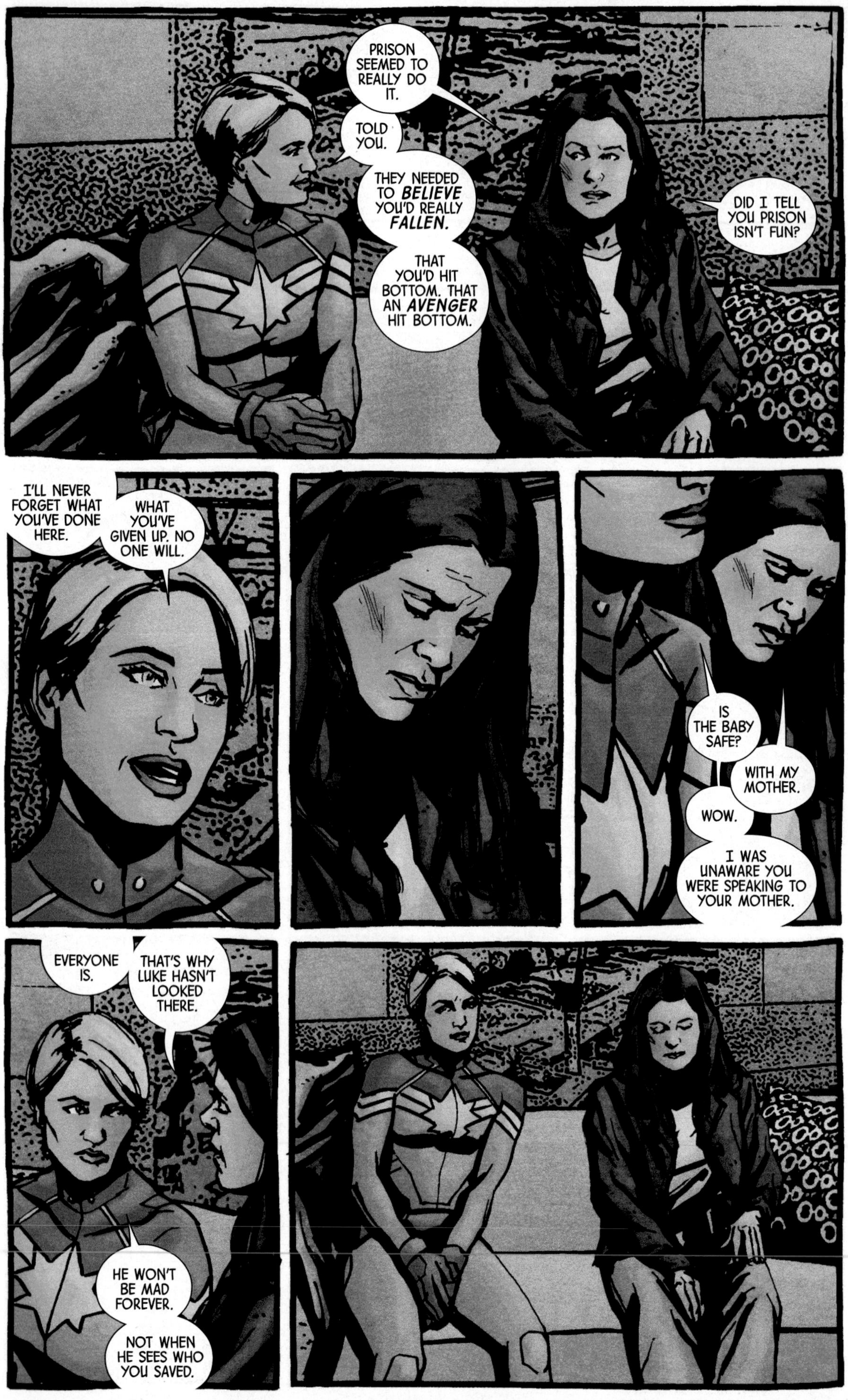
PRISON SEEMED TO REALLY DO IT.
TOLD YOU.
THEY NEEDED TO BELIEVE YOU'D REALLY FALLEN.
THAT YOU'D HIT BOTTOM. THAT AN AVENGER HIT BOTTOM.
DID I TELL YOU PRISON ISN'T FUN?
I'LL NEVER FORGET WHAT YOU'VE DONE HERE.
WHAT YOU'VE GIVEN UP. NO ONE WILL.
IS THE BABY SAFE?
WITH MY MOTHER.
WOW.
I WAS UNAWARE YOU WERE SPEAKING TO YOUR MOTHER.
EVERYONE IS.
THAT'S WHY LUKE HASN'T LOOKED THERE.
HE WON'T BE MAD FOREVER.
NOT WHEN HE SEES WHO YOU SAVED.

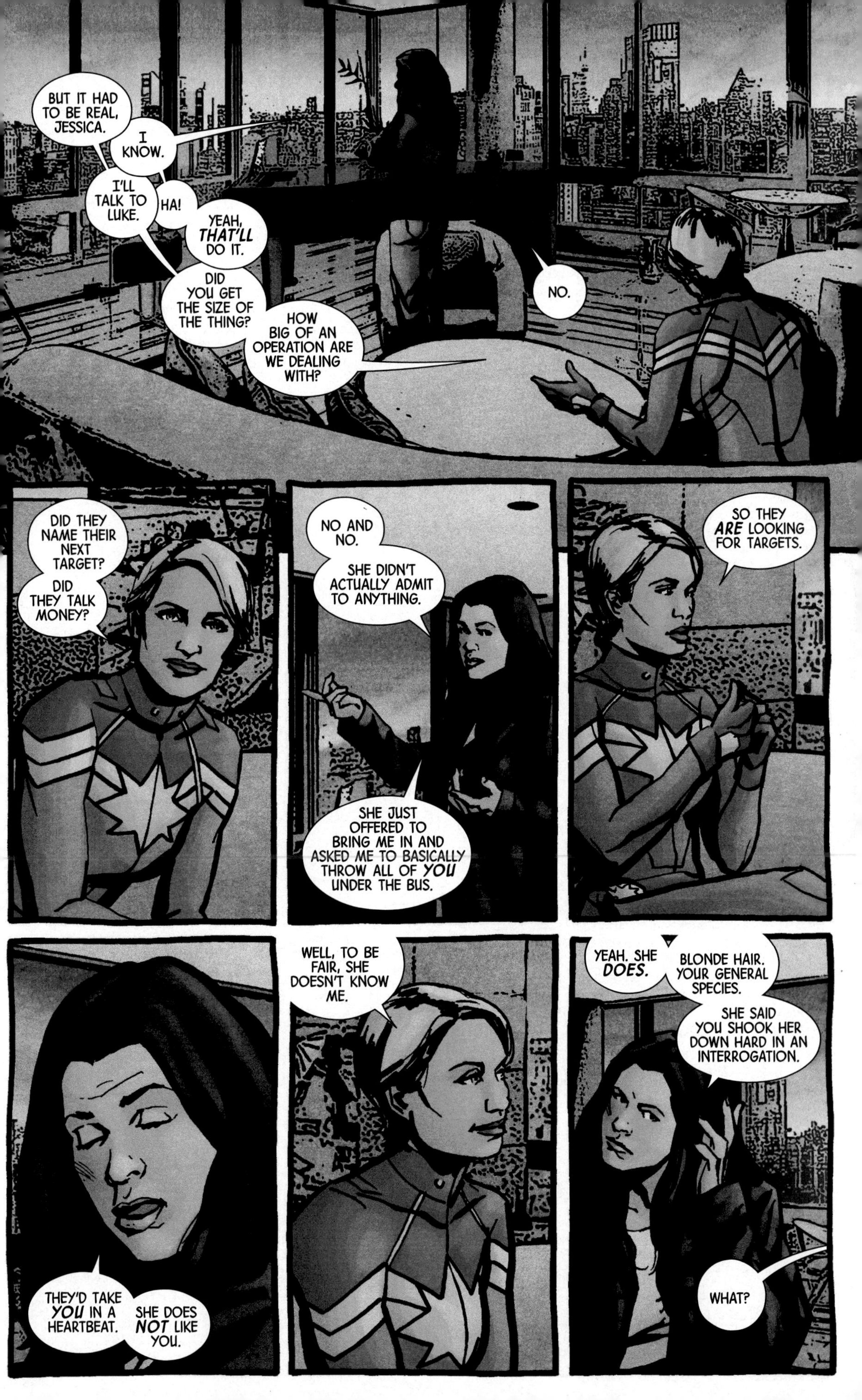
BUT IT HAD TO BE REAL, JESSICA.
I KNOW.
I'LL TALK TO LUKE.
HA!
YEAH, THAT'LL DO IT.
DID YOU GET THE SIZE OF THE THING?
NO.
HOW BIG OF AN OPERATION ARE WE DEALING WITH?
DID THEY NAME THEIR NEXT TARGET?
DID THEY TALK MONEY?
NO AND NO.
SHE DIDN'T ACTUALLY ADMIT TO ANYTHING.
SHE JUST OFFERED TO BRING ME IN AND ASKED ME TO BASICALLY THROW ALL OF YOU UNDER THE BUS.
SO THEY ARE LOOKING FOR TARGETS.
THEY'D TAKE YOU IN A HEARTBEAT.
SHE DOES NOT LIKE YOU.
WELL, TO BE FAIR, SHE DOESN'T KNOW ME.
YEAH. SHE DOES.
BLONDE HAIR. YOUR GENERAL SPECIES.
SHE SAID YOU SHOOK HER DOWN HARD IN AN INTERROGATION.
WHAT?

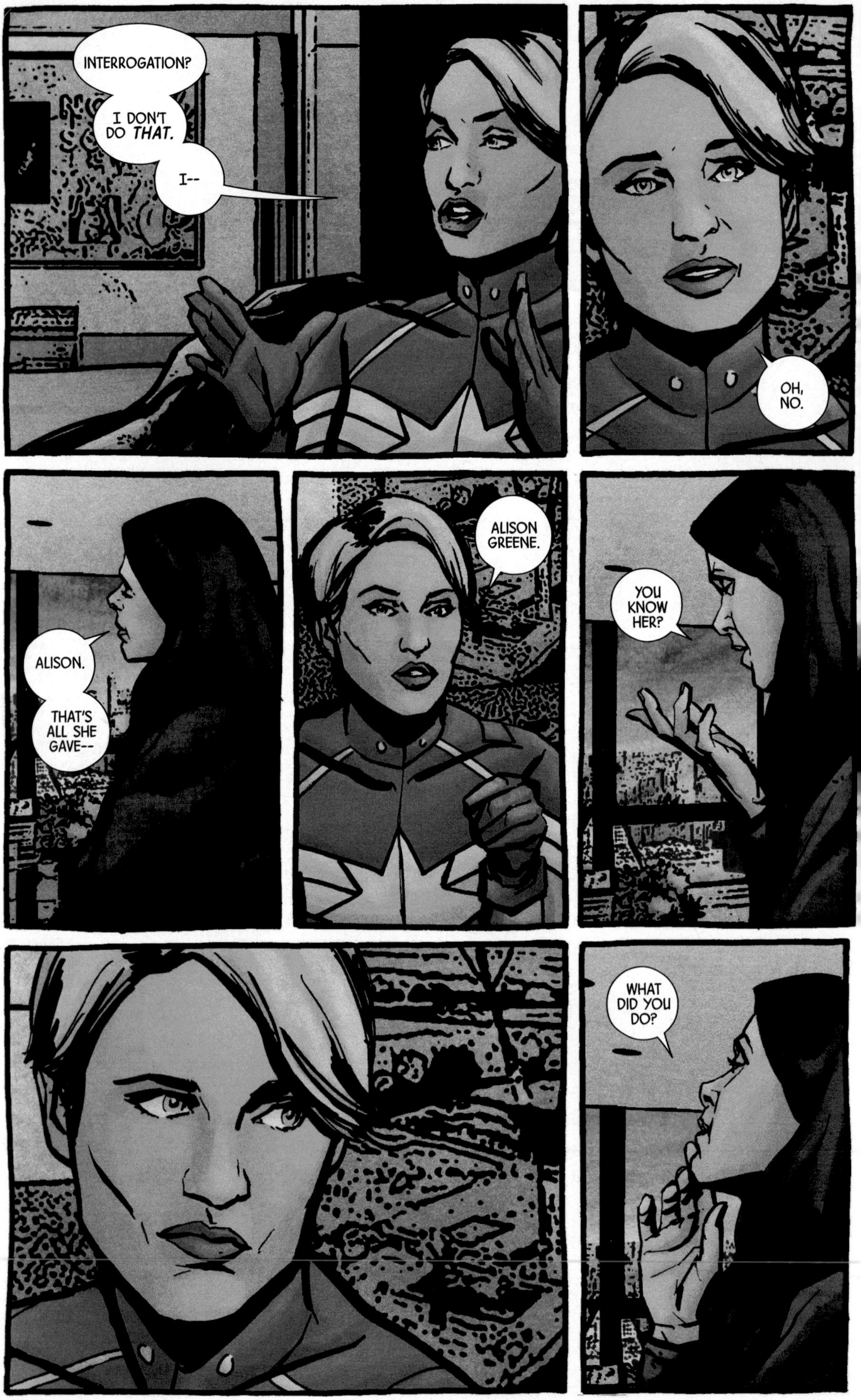
INTERROGATION?
I DON'T DO *THAT.*
I--
OH, NO.
ALISON.
THAT'S ALL SHE GAVE--
ALISON GREENE.
YOU KNOW HER?
WHAT DID YOU DO?

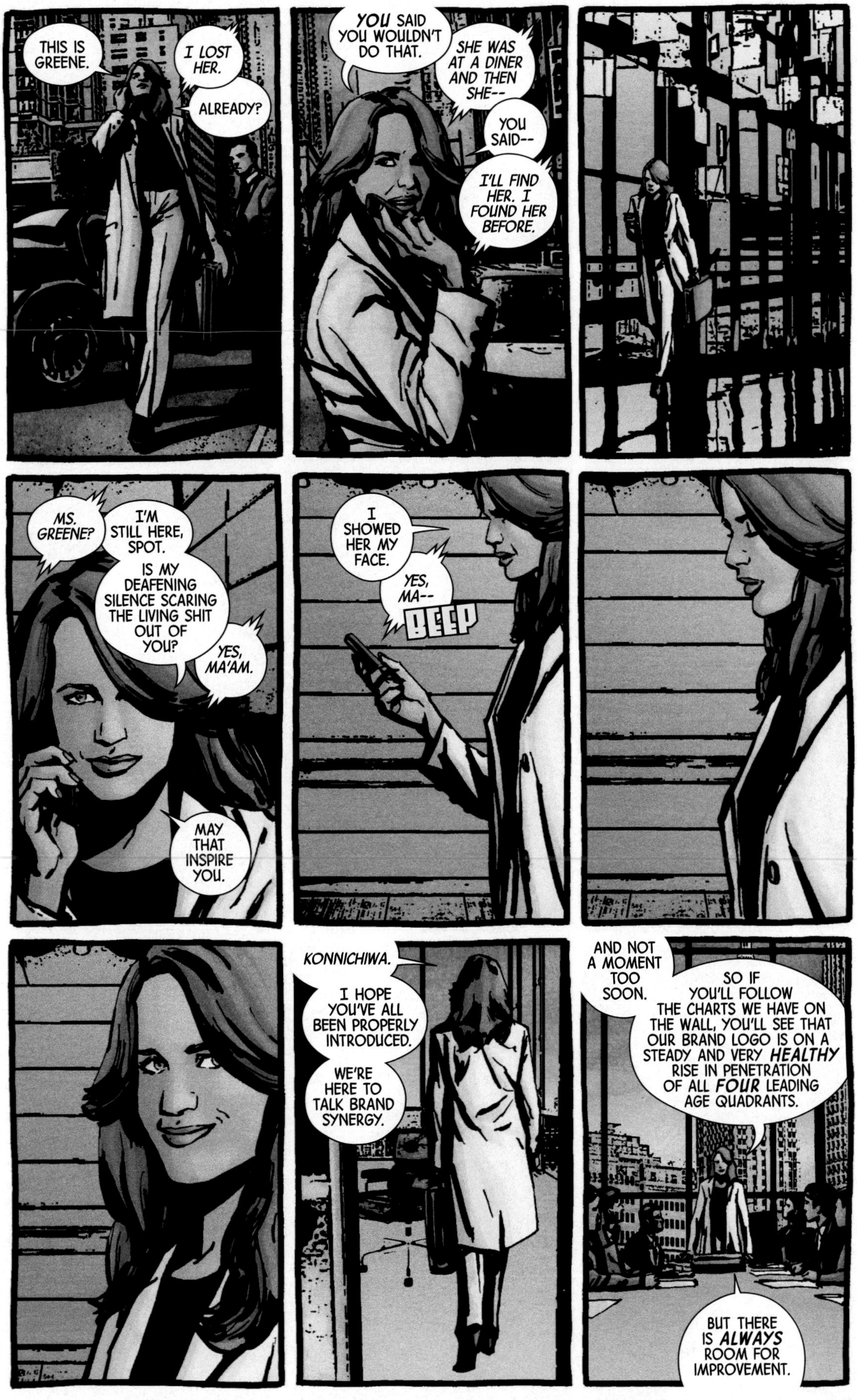
THIS IS GREENE.
I LOST HER.
ALREADY?
YOU SAID YOU WOULDN'T DO THAT.
SHE WAS AT A DINER AND THEN SHE--
YOU SAID--
I'LL FIND HER. I FOUND HER BEFORE.
MS. GREENE?
I'M STILL HERE, SPOT.
IS MY DEAFENING SILENCE SCARING THE LIVING SHIT OUT OF YOU?
YES, MA'AM.
MAY THAT INSPIRE YOU.
I SHOWED HER MY FACE.
YES, MA--
BEEP
KONNICHIWA.
I HOPE YOU'VE ALL BEEN PROPERLY INTRODUCED.
WE'RE HERE TO TALK BRAND SYNERGY.
AND NOT A MOMENT TOO SOON.
SO IF YOU'LL FOLLOW THE CHARTS WE HAVE ON THE WALL, YOU'LL SEE THAT OUR BRAND LOGO IS ON A STEADY AND VERY HEALTHY RISE IN PENETRATION OF ALL FOUR LEADING AGE QUADRANTS.
BUT THERE IS ALWAYS ROOM FOR IMPROVEMENT.

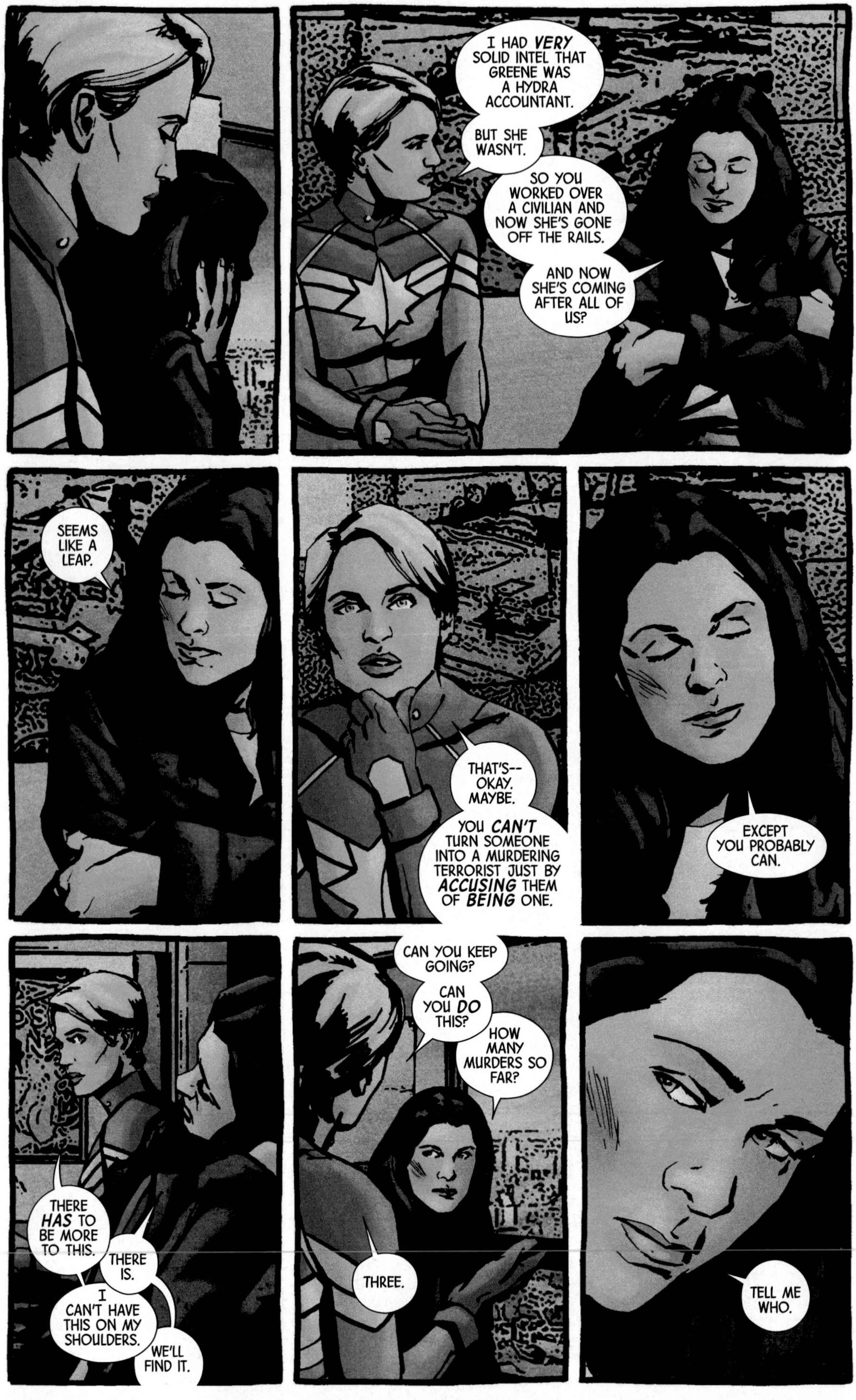
I HAD VERY SOLID INTEL THAT GREENE WAS A HYDRA ACCOUNTANT.
BUT SHE WASN'T.
SO YOU WORKED OVER A CIVILIAN AND NOW SHE'S GONE OFF THE RAILS.
AND NOW SHE'S COMING AFTER ALL OF US?
SEEMS LIKE A LEAP.
THAT'S-- OKAY. MAYBE.
YOU CAN'T TURN SOMEONE INTO A MURDERING TERRORIST JUST BY ACCUSING THEM OF BEING ONE.
EXCEPT YOU PROBABLY CAN.
THERE HAS TO BE MORE TO THIS.
THERE IS.
I CAN'T HAVE THIS ON MY SHOULDERS.
WE'LL FIND IT.
CAN YOU KEEP GOING?
CAN YOU DO THIS?
HOW MANY MURDERS SO FAR?
THREE.
TELL ME WHO.

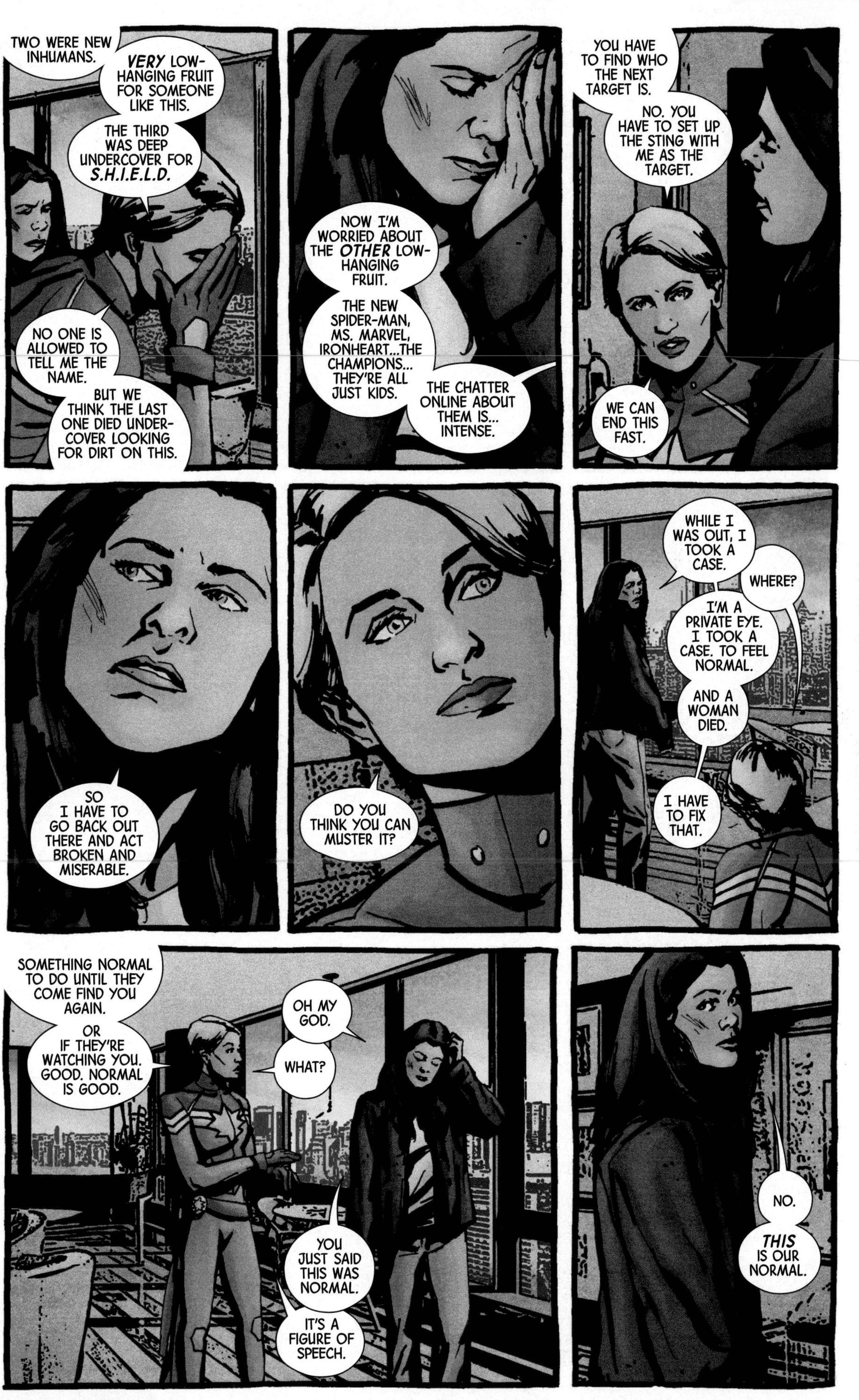
TWO WERE NEW INHUMANS.
VERY LOW-HANGING FRUIT FOR SOMEONE LIKE THIS.
THE THIRD WAS DEEP UNDERCOVER FOR S.H.I.E.L.D.
NO ONE IS ALLOWED TO TELL ME THE NAME.
BUT WE THINK THE LAST ONE DIED UNDER-COVER LOOKING FOR DIRT ON THIS.
NOW I'M WORRIED ABOUT THE OTHER LOW-HANGING FRUIT.
THE NEW SPIDER-MAN, MS. MARVEL, IRONHEART...THE CHAMPIONS... THEY'RE ALL JUST KIDS.
THE CHATTER ONLINE ABOUT THEM IS... INTENSE.
YOU HAVE TO FIND WHO THE NEXT TARGET IS.
NO. YOU HAVE TO SET UP THE STING WITH ME AS THE TARGET.
WE CAN END THIS FAST.
SO I HAVE TO GO BACK OUT THERE AND ACT BROKEN AND MISERABLE.
DO YOU THINK YOU CAN MUSTER IT?
WHILE I WAS OUT, I TOOK A CASE.
WHERE?
I'M A PRIVATE EYE. I TOOK A CASE. TO FEEL NORMAL.
AND A WOMAN DIED.
I HAVE TO FIX THAT.
SOMETHING NORMAL TO DO UNTIL THEY COME FIND YOU AGAIN.
OR IF THEY'RE WATCHING YOU. GOOD. NORMAL IS GOOD.
OH MY GOD.
WHAT?
YOU JUST SAID THIS WAS NORMAL.
IT'S A FIGURE OF SPEECH.
NO.
THIS IS OUR NORMAL.

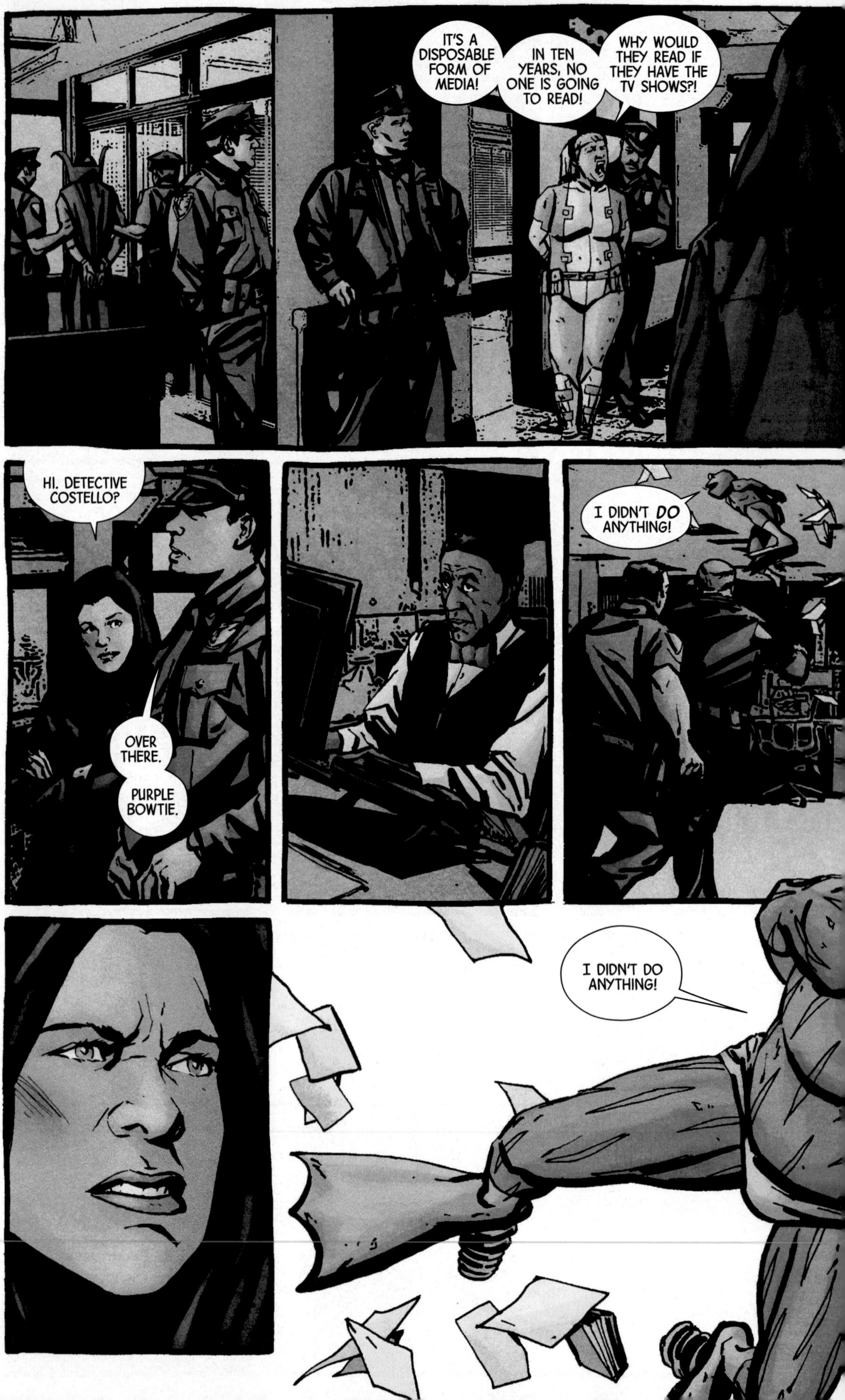
IT'S A DISPOSABLE FORM OF MEDIA!
IN TEN YEARS, NO ONE IS GOING TO READ!
WHY WOULD THEY READ IF THEY HAVE THE TV SHOWS?!
HI. DETECTIVE COSTELLO?
OVER THERE.
PURPLE BOWTIE.
I DIDN'T *DO* ANYTHING!
I DIDN'T DO ANYTHING!

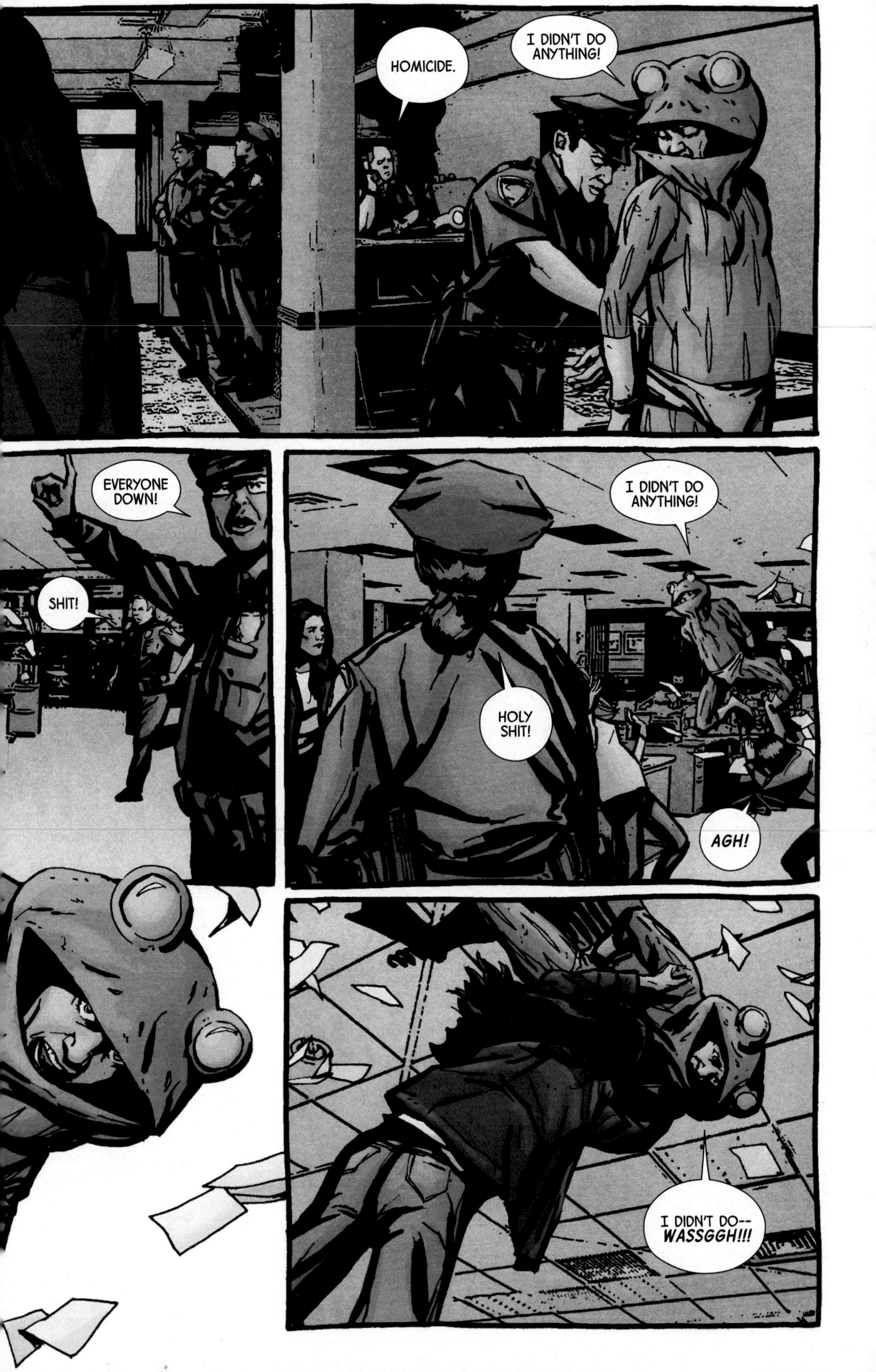
HOMICIDE.
I DIDN'T DO ANYTHING!
EVERYONE DOWN!
SHIT!
I DIDN'T DO ANYTHING!
HOLY SHIT!
AGH!
I DIDN'T DO-- WASSGGH!!!

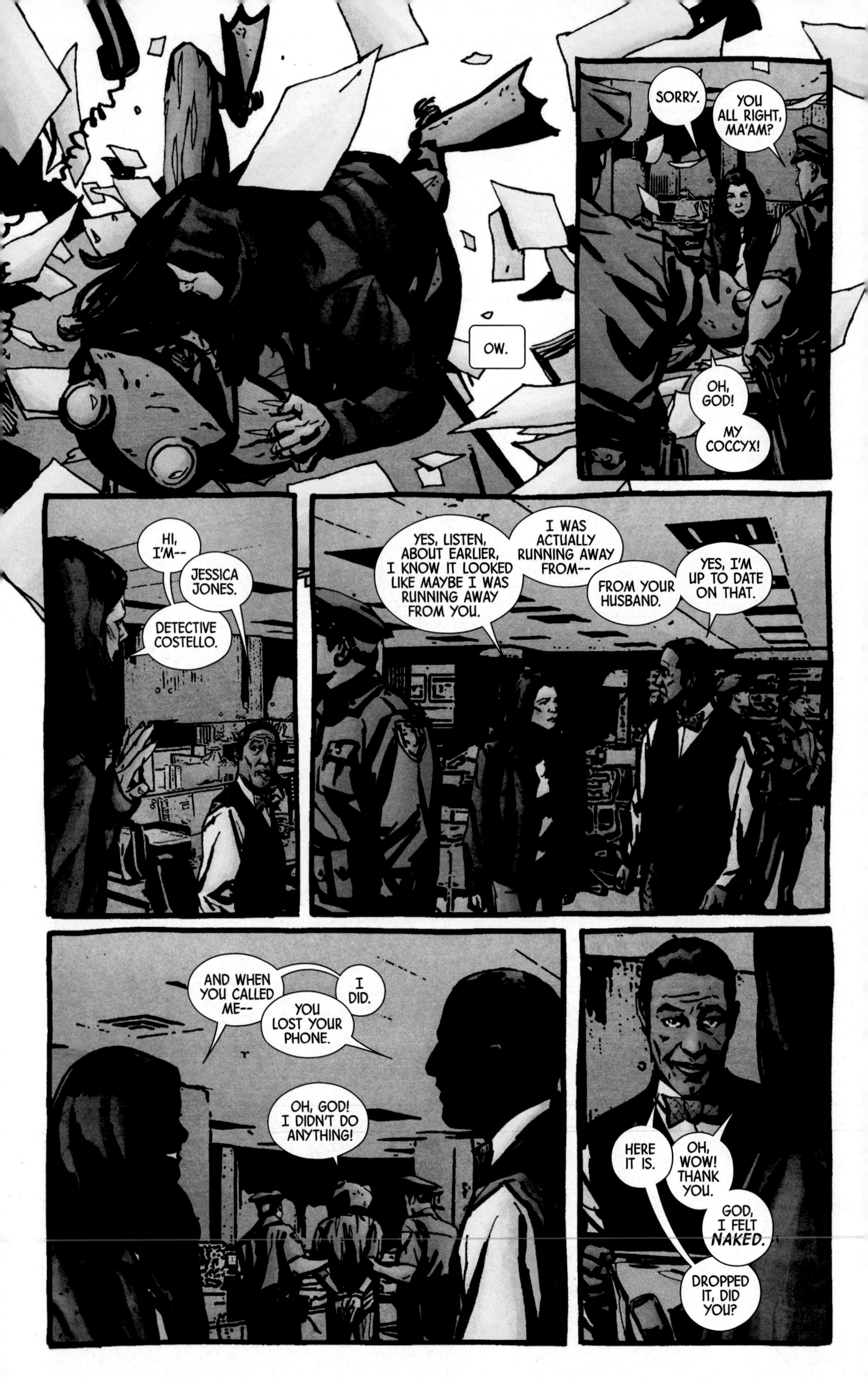
OW.
SORRY.
YOU ALL RIGHT, MA'AM?
OH, GOD!
MY COCCYX!
HI, I'M--
JESSICA JONES.
DETECTIVE COSTELLO.
YES, LISTEN, ABOUT EARLIER, I KNOW IT LOOKED LIKE MAYBE I WAS RUNNING AWAY FROM YOU.
I WAS ACTUALLY RUNNING AWAY FROM--
FROM YOUR HUSBAND.
YES, I'M UP TO DATE ON THAT.
AND WHEN YOU CALLED ME--
I DID.
YOU LOST YOUR PHONE.
OH, GOD! I DIDN'T DO ANYTHING!
HERE IT IS.
OH, WOW! THANK YOU.
GOD, I FELT *NAKED.*
DROPPED IT, DID YOU?

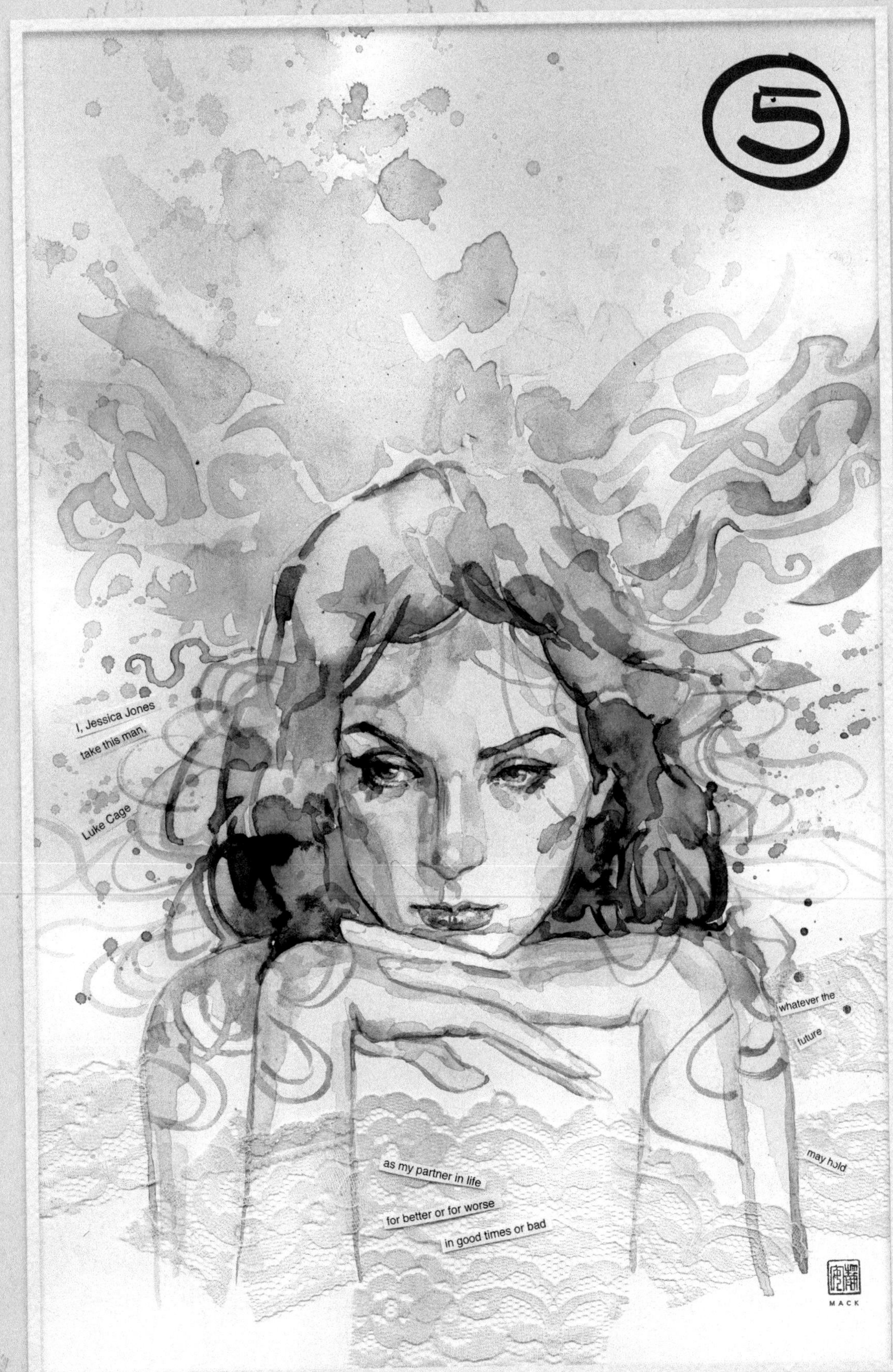
5
I, Jessica Jones
take this man,
Luke Cage
as my partner in life
for better or for worse
in good times or bad
whatever the
future
may hold
MACK

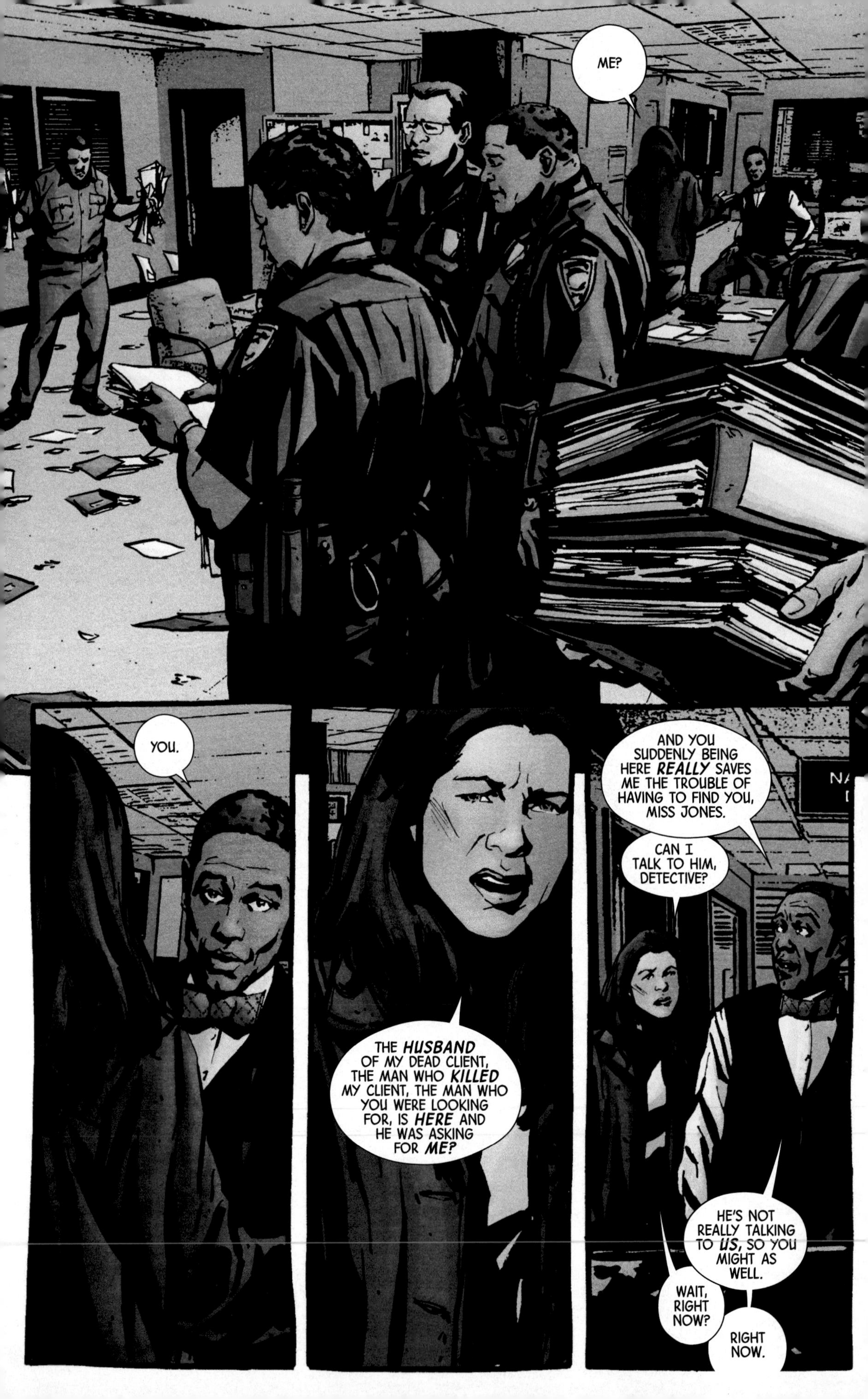
ME?
YOU.
THE HUSBAND OF MY DEAD CLIENT, THE MAN WHO KILLED MY CLIENT, THE MAN WHO YOU WERE LOOKING FOR, IS HERE AND HE WAS ASKING FOR ME?
AND YOU SUDDENLY BEING HERE REALLY SAVES ME THE TROUBLE OF HAVING TO FIND YOU, MISS JONES.
CAN I TALK TO HIM, DETECTIVE?
HE'S NOT REALLY TALKING TO US, SO YOU MIGHT AS WELL.
WAIT, RIGHT NOW?
RIGHT NOW.

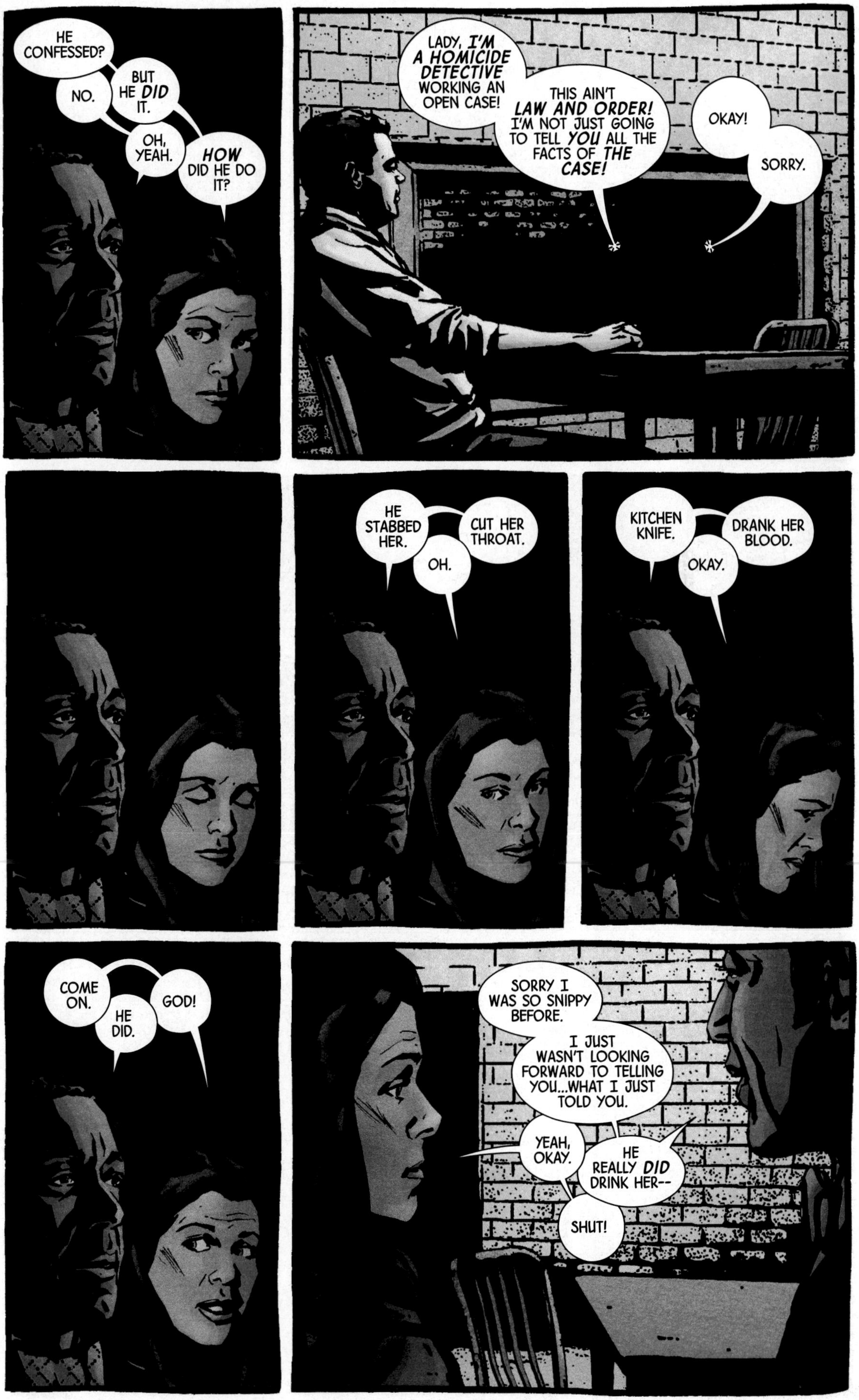
HE CONFESSED?
NO.
BUT HE DID IT.
OH, YEAH.
HOW DID HE DO IT?
LADY, I'M A HOMICIDE DETECTIVE WORKING AN OPEN CASE!
THIS AIN'T LAW AND ORDER! I'M NOT JUST GOING TO TELL YOU ALL THE FACTS OF THE CASE!
OKAY!
SORRY.
HE STABBED HER.
CUT HER THROAT.
OH.
KITCHEN KNIFE.
DRANK HER BLOOD.
OKAY.
COME ON.
HE DID.
GOD!
SORRY I WAS SO SNIPPY BEFORE.
I JUST WASN'T LOOKING FORWARD TO TELLING YOU...WHAT I JUST TOLD YOU.
YEAH, OKAY.
HE REALLY DID DRINK HER--
SHUT!

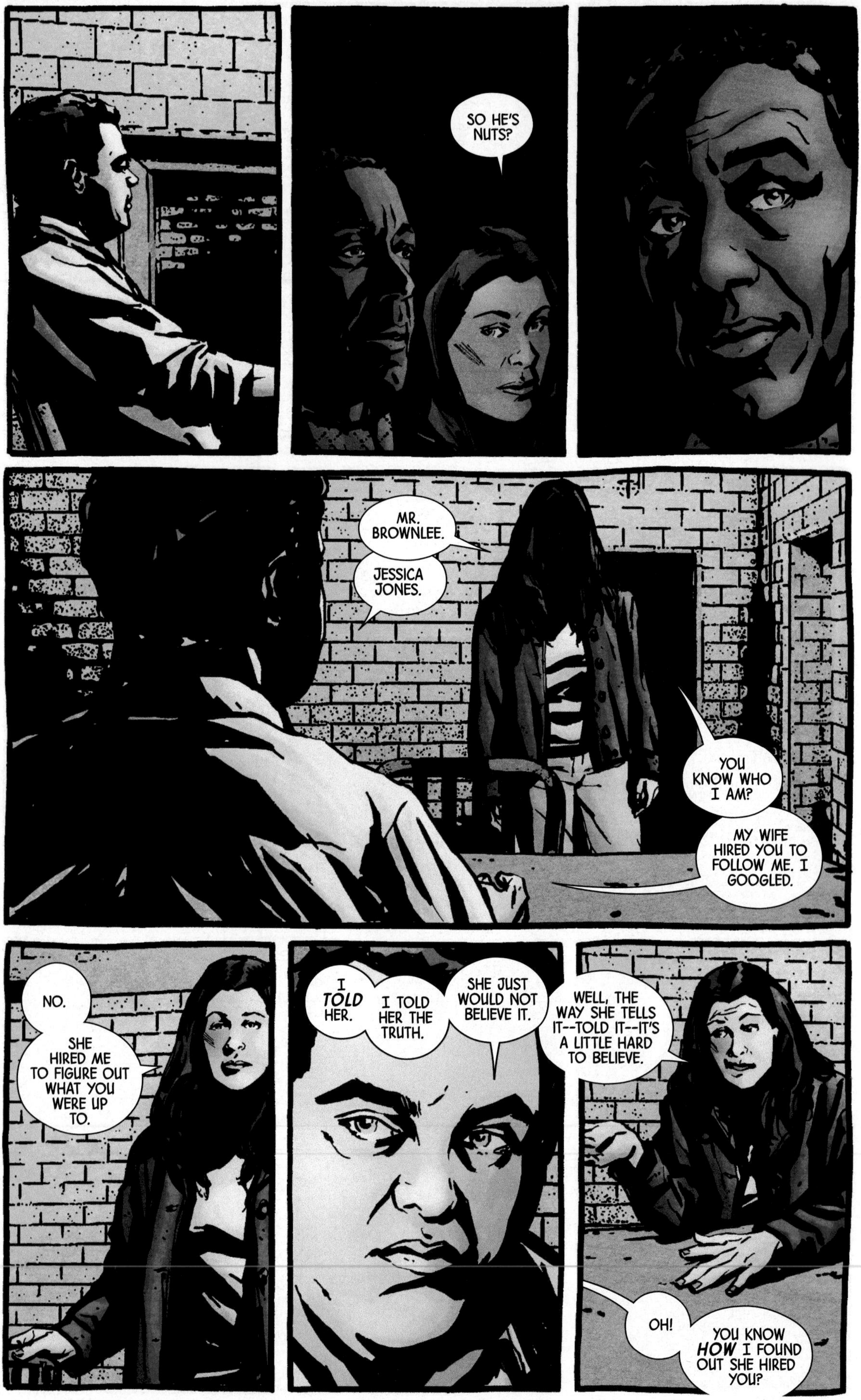
SO HE'S NUTS?
MR. BROWNLEE.
JESSICA JONES.
YOU KNOW WHO I AM?
MY WIFE HIRED YOU TO FOLLOW ME. I GOOGLED.
NO.
SHE HIRED ME TO FIGURE OUT WHAT YOU WERE UP TO.
I TOLD HER.
I TOLD HER THE TRUTH.
SHE JUST WOULD NOT BELIEVE IT.
WELL, THE WAY SHE TELLS IT--TOLD IT--IT'S A LITTLE HARD TO BELIEVE.
OH!
YOU KNOW HOW I FOUND OUT SHE HIRED YOU?

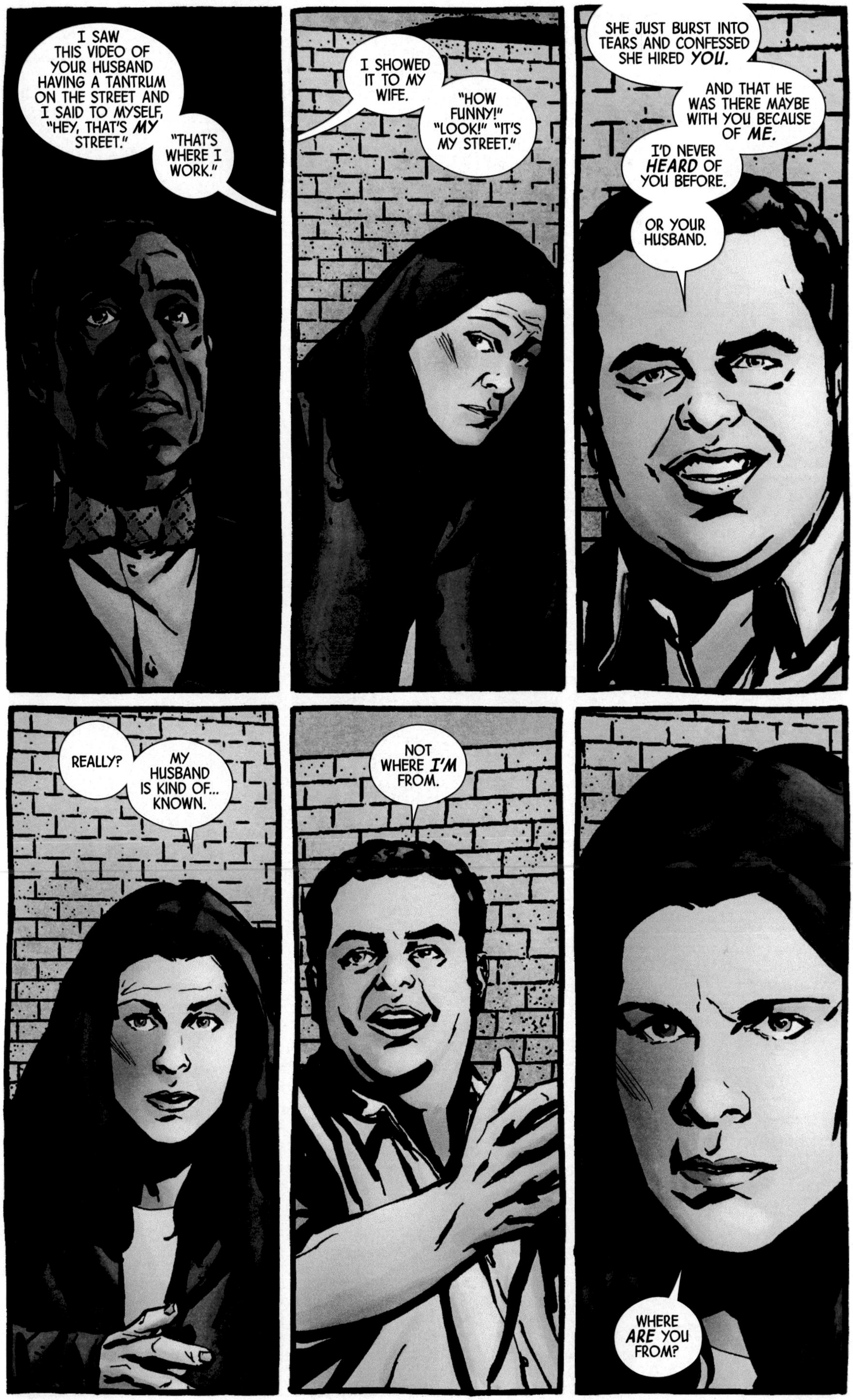
I SAW THIS VIDEO OF YOUR HUSBAND HAVING A TANTRUM ON THE STREET AND I SAID TO MYSELF, "HEY, THAT'S MY STREET."
"THAT'S WHERE I WORK."
I SHOWED IT TO MY WIFE.
"HOW FUNNY!" "LOOK!" "IT'S MY STREET."
SHE JUST BURST INTO TEARS AND CONFESSED SHE HIRED YOU.
AND THAT HE WAS THERE MAYBE WITH YOU BECAUSE OF ME.
I'D NEVER HEARD OF YOU BEFORE.
OR YOUR HUSBAND.
REALLY?
MY HUSBAND IS KIND OF... KNOWN.
NOT WHERE I'M FROM.
WHERE ARE YOU FROM?

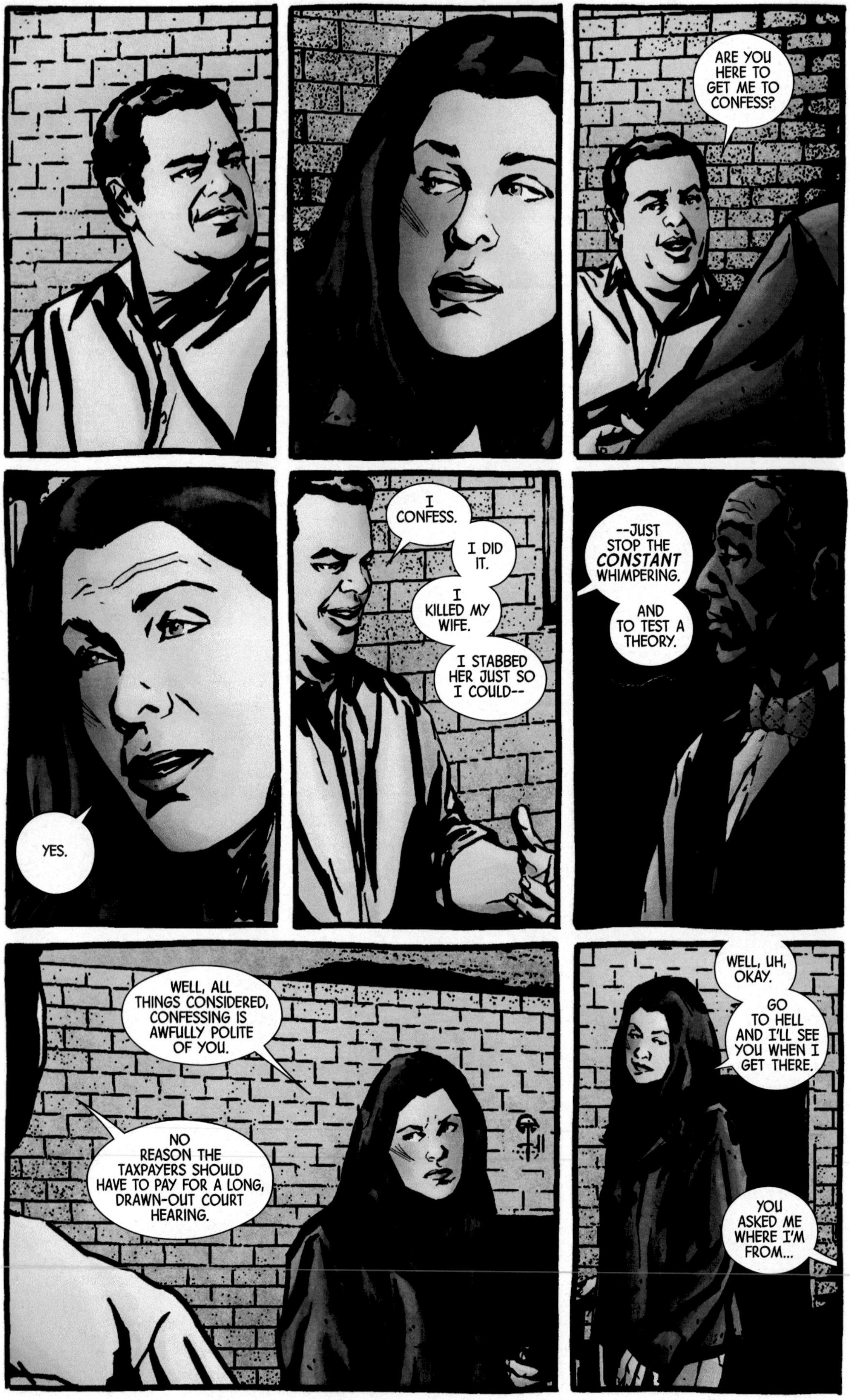
ARE YOU HERE TO GET ME TO CONFESS?
YES.
I CONFESS.
I DID IT.
I KILLED MY WIFE.
I STABBED HER JUST SO I COULD--
--JUST STOP THE *CONSTANT* WHIMPERING.
AND TO TEST A THEORY.
WELL, ALL THINGS CONSIDERED, CONFESSING IS AWFULLY POLITE OF YOU.
NO REASON THE TAXPAYERS SHOULD HAVE TO PAY FOR A LONG, DRAWN-OUT COURT HEARING.
WELL, UH, OKAY.
GO TO HELL AND I'LL SEE YOU WHEN I GET THERE.
YOU ASKED ME WHERE I'M FROM...

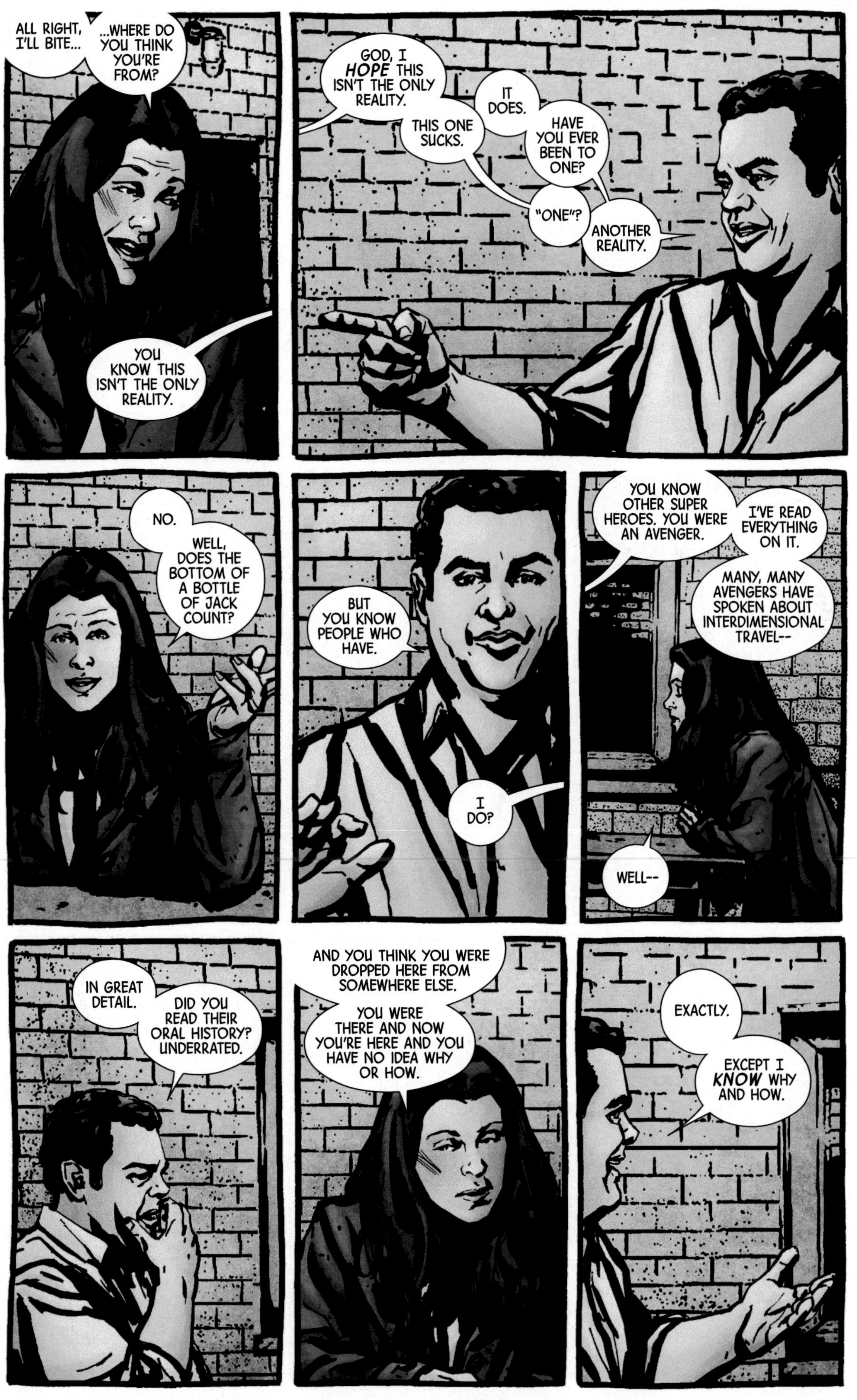
ALL RIGHT, I'LL BITE...
...WHERE DO YOU THINK YOU'RE FROM?
YOU KNOW THIS ISN'T THE ONLY REALITY.
GOD, I HOPE THIS ISN'T THE ONLY REALITY.
THIS ONE SUCKS.
IT DOES.
HAVE YOU EVER BEEN TO ONE?
"ONE"?
ANOTHER REALITY.
NO.
WELL, DOES THE BOTTOM OF A BOTTLE OF JACK COUNT?
BUT YOU KNOW PEOPLE WHO HAVE.
I DO?
YOU KNOW OTHER SUPER HEROES. YOU WERE AN AVENGER.
WELL--
I'VE READ EVERYTHING ON IT.
MANY, MANY AVENGERS HAVE SPOKEN ABOUT INTERDIMENSIONAL TRAVEL--
IN GREAT DETAIL.
DID YOU READ THEIR ORAL HISTORY? UNDERRATED.
AND YOU THINK YOU WERE DROPPED HERE FROM SOMEWHERE ELSE.
YOU WERE THERE AND NOW YOU'RE HERE AND YOU HAVE NO IDEA WHY OR HOW.
EXACTLY.
EXCEPT I KNOW WHY AND HOW.

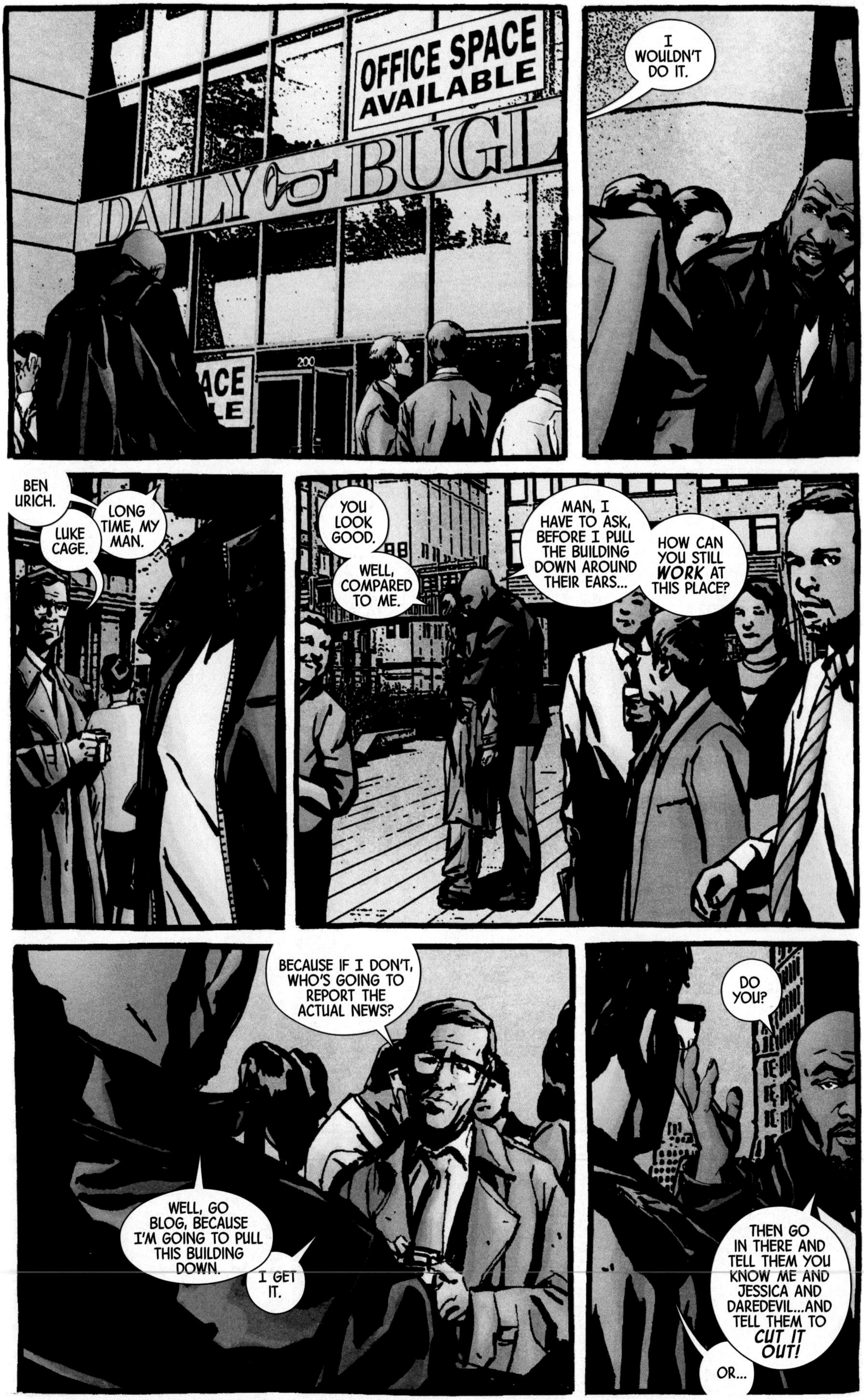
OFFICE SPACE AVAILABLE
DAILY BUGL
I WOULDN'T DO IT.
BEN URICH.
LUKE CAGE.
LONG TIME, MY MAN.
YOU LOOK GOOD.
WELL, COMPARED TO ME.
MAN, I HAVE TO ASK, BEFORE I PULL THE BUILDING DOWN AROUND THEIR EARS...
HOW CAN YOU STILL WORK AT THIS PLACE?
BECAUSE IF I DON'T, WHO'S GOING TO REPORT THE ACTUAL NEWS?
WELL, GO BLOG, BECAUSE I'M GOING TO PULL THIS BUILDING DOWN.
I GET IT.
DO YOU?
THEN GO IN THERE AND TELL THEM YOU KNOW ME AND JESSICA AND DAREDEVIL...AND TELL THEM TO CUT IT OUT!
OR...

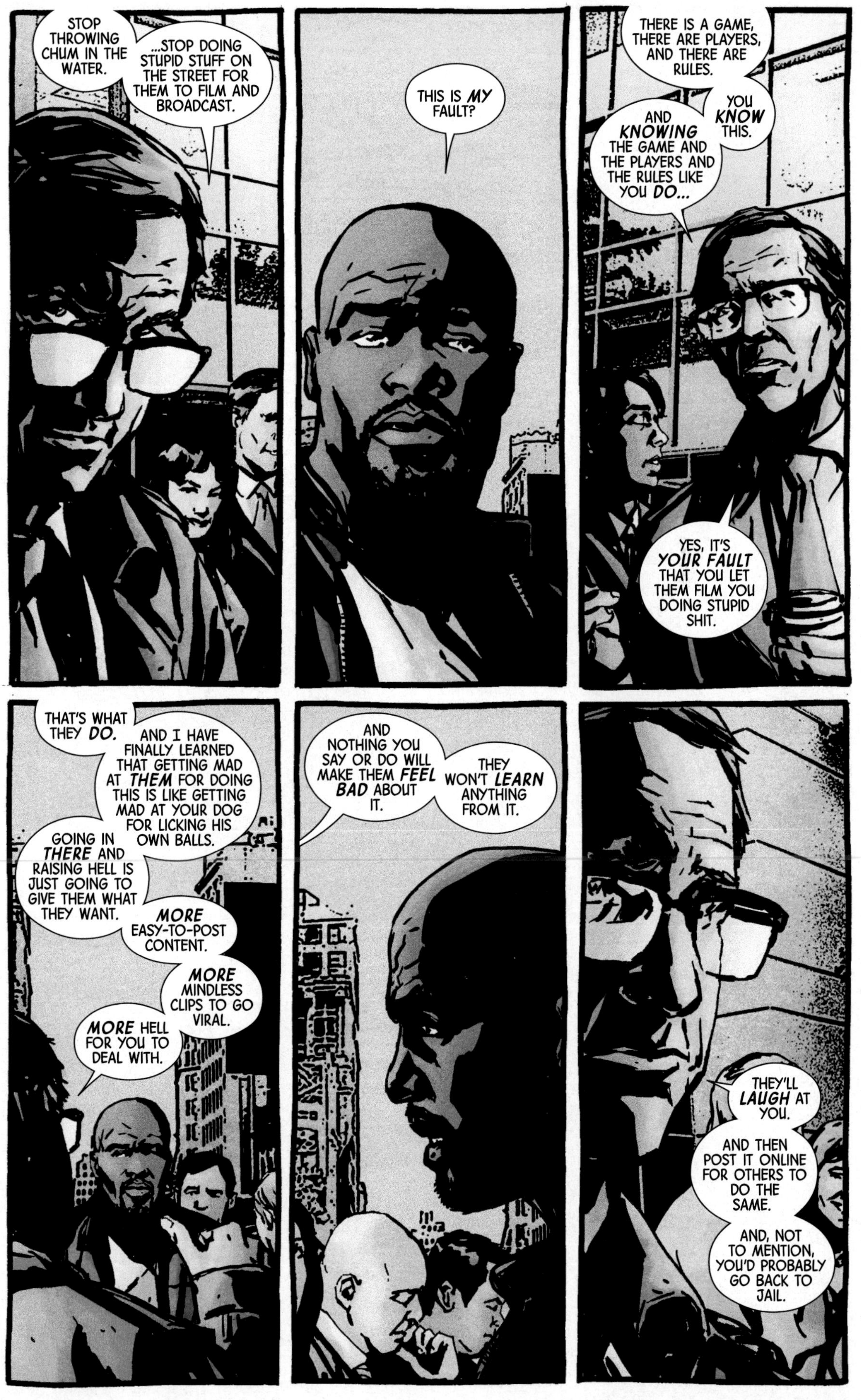
STOP THROWING CHUM IN THE WATER.
...STOP DOING STUPID STUFF ON THE STREET FOR THEM TO FILM AND BROADCAST.
THIS IS MY FAULT?
THERE IS A GAME, THERE ARE PLAYERS, AND THERE ARE RULES.
YOU KNOW THIS.
AND KNOWING THE GAME AND THE PLAYERS AND THE RULES LIKE YOU DO...
YES, IT'S YOUR FAULT THAT YOU LET THEM FILM YOU DOING STUPID SHIT.
THAT'S WHAT THEY DO.
AND I HAVE FINALLY LEARNED THAT GETTING MAD AT THEM FOR DOING THIS IS LIKE GETTING MAD AT YOUR DOG FOR LICKING HIS OWN BALLS.
GOING IN THERE AND RAISING HELL IS JUST GOING TO GIVE THEM WHAT THEY WANT.
MORE EASY-TO-POST CONTENT.
MORE MINDLESS CLIPS TO GO VIRAL.
MORE HELL FOR YOU TO DEAL WITH.
AND NOTHING YOU SAY OR DO WILL MAKE THEM FEEL BAD ABOUT IT.
THEY WON'T LEARN ANYTHING FROM IT.
THEY'LL LAUGH AT YOU.
AND THEN POST IT ONLINE FOR OTHERS TO DO THE SAME.
AND, NOT TO MENTION, YOU'D PROBABLY GO BACK TO JAIL.

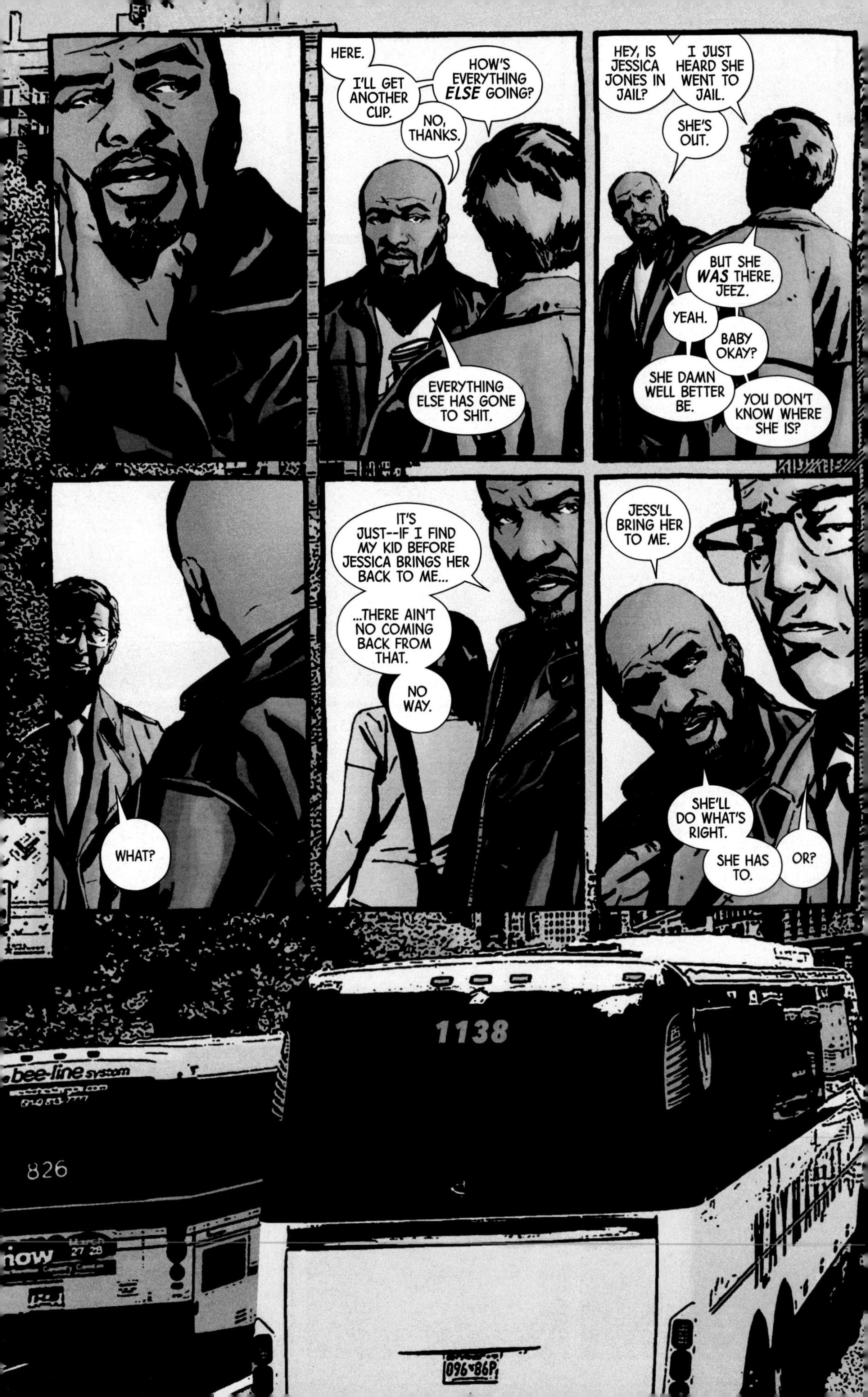
HERE.
I'LL GET ANOTHER CUP.
HOW'S EVERYTHING *ELSE* GOING?
NO, THANKS.
EVERYTHING ELSE HAS GONE TO SHIT.
HEY, IS JESSICA JONES IN JAIL?
I JUST HEARD SHE WENT TO JAIL.
SHE'S OUT.
BUT SHE *WAS* THERE. JEEZ.
YEAH.
BABY OKAY?
SHE DAMN WELL BETTER BE.
YOU DON'T KNOW WHERE SHE IS?
WHAT?
IT'S JUST--IF I FIND MY KID BEFORE JESSICA BRINGS HER BACK TO ME...
...THERE AIN'T NO COMING BACK FROM THAT.
NO WAY.
JESS'LL BRING HER TO ME.
SHE'LL DO WHAT'S RIGHT.
SHE HAS TO.
OR?
1138
bee-line system
826

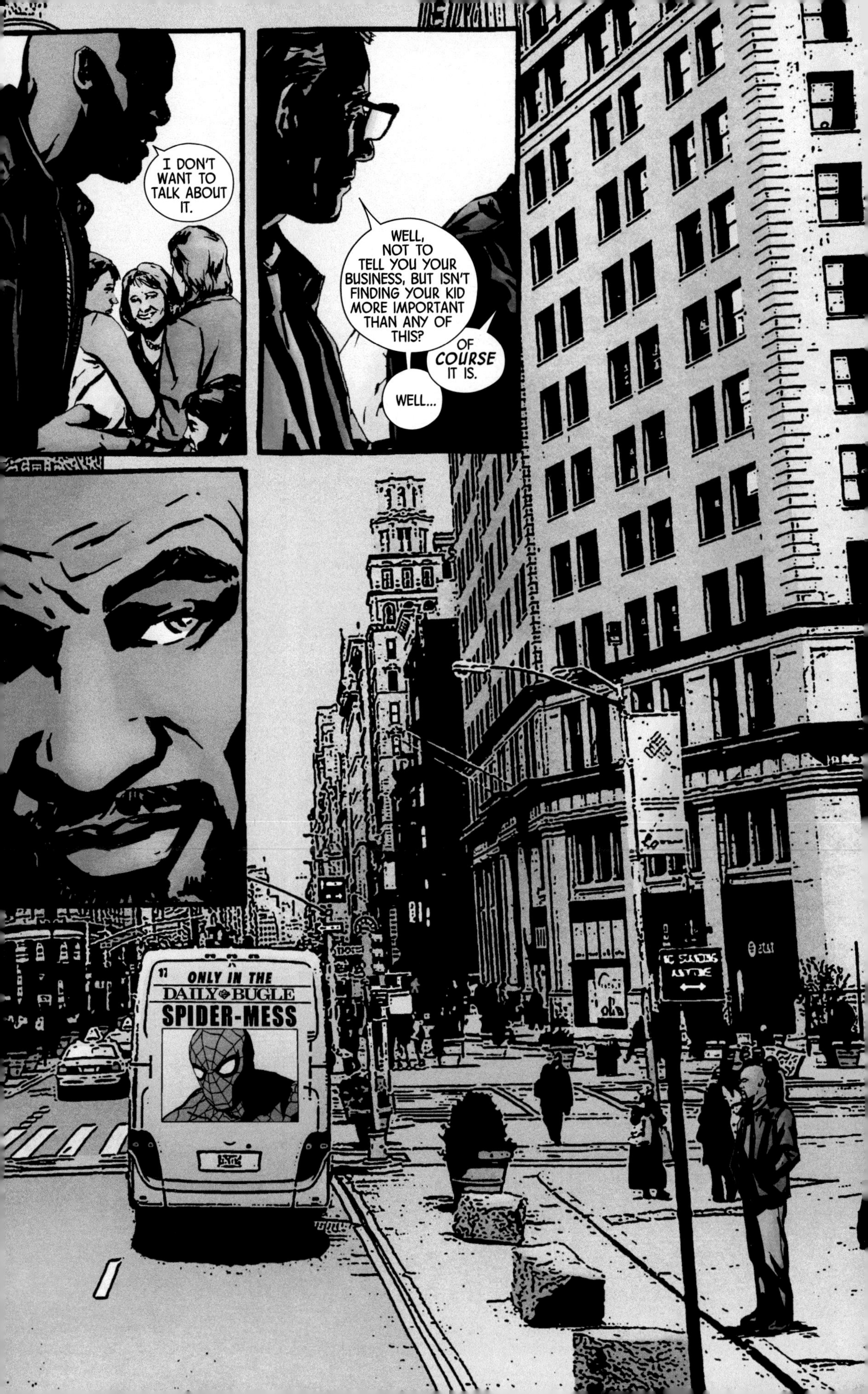
I DON'T WANT TO TALK ABOUT IT.
WELL, NOT TO TELL YOU YOUR BUSINESS, BUT ISN'T FINDING YOUR KID MORE IMPORTANT THAN ANY OF THIS?
OF COURSE IT IS.
WELL...
ONLY IN THE
DAILY BUGLE
SPIDER-MESS

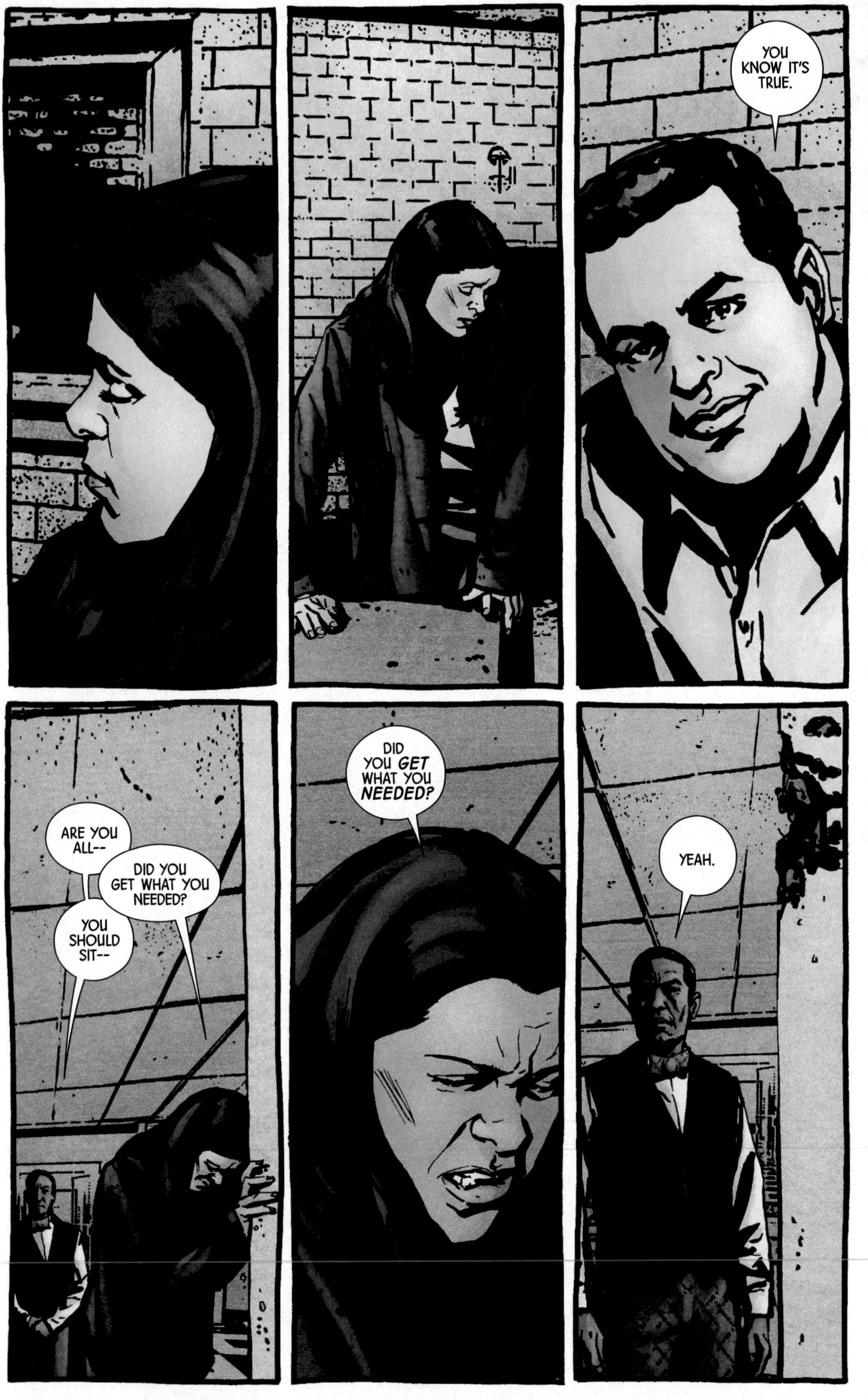
YOU KNOW IT'S TRUE.
ARE YOU ALL--
DID YOU GET WHAT YOU NEEDED?
YOU SHOULD SIT--
DID YOU *GET* WHAT YOU *NEEDED?*
YEAH.

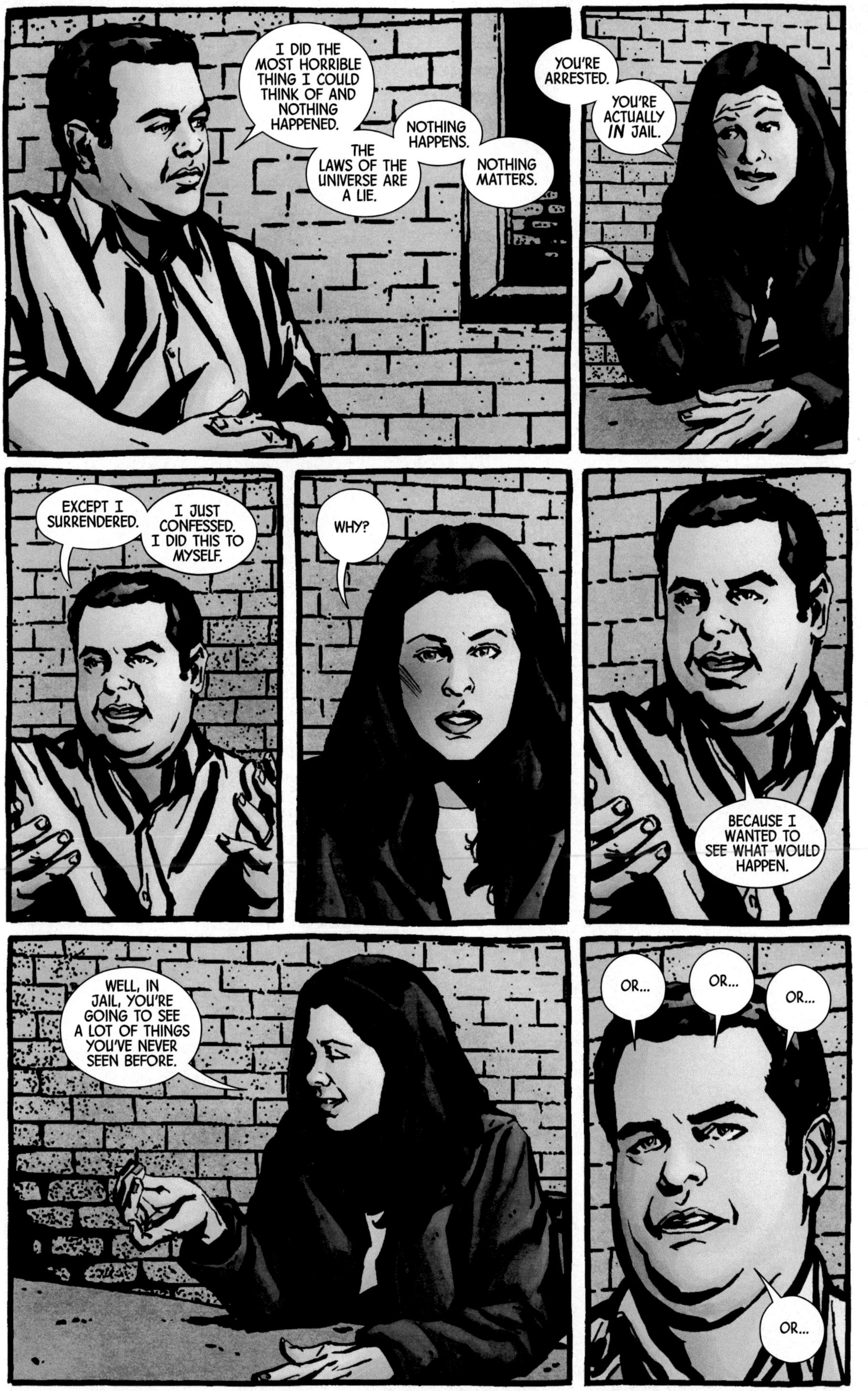
I DID THE MOST HORRIBLE THING I COULD THINK OF AND NOTHING HAPPENED.
THE LAWS OF THE UNIVERSE ARE A LIE.
NOTHING HAPPENS.
NOTHING MATTERS.
YOU'RE ARRESTED.
YOU'RE ACTUALLY *IN* JAIL.
EXCEPT I SURRENDERED.
I JUST CONFESSED. I DID THIS TO MYSELF.
WHY?
BECAUSE I WANTED TO SEE WHAT WOULD HAPPEN.
WELL, IN JAIL, YOU'RE GOING TO SEE A LOT OF THINGS YOU'VE NEVER SEEN BEFORE.
OR...
OR...
OR...
OR...

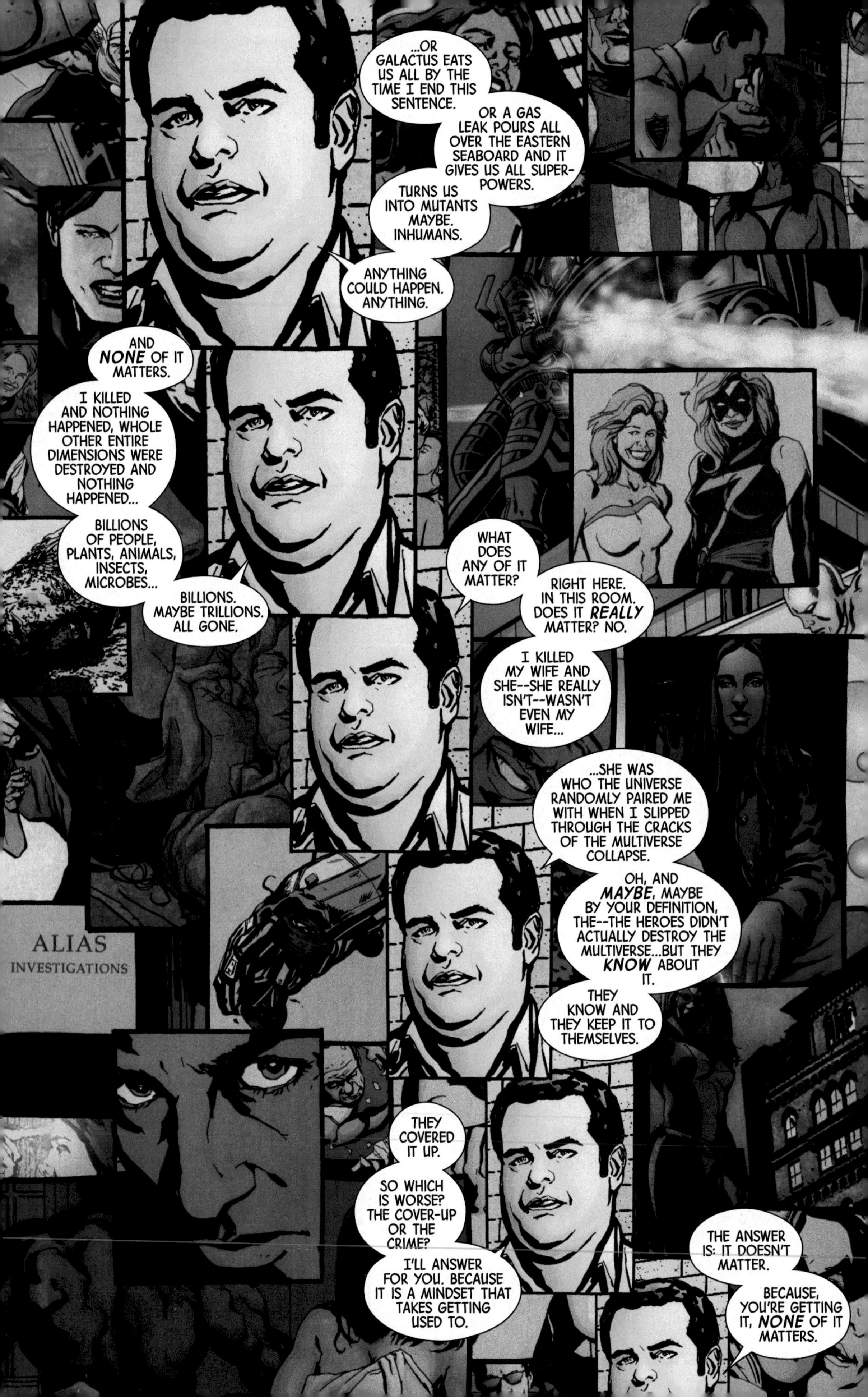
...OR GALACTUS EATS US ALL BY THE TIME I END THIS SENTENCE.
OR A GAS LEAK POURS ALL OVER THE EASTERN SEABOARD AND IT GIVES US ALL SUPER-POWERS.
TURNS US INTO MUTANTS MAYBE. INHUMANS.
ANYTHING COULD HAPPEN. ANYTHING.
AND *NONE* OF IT MATTERS.
I KILLED AND NOTHING HAPPENED, WHOLE OTHER ENTIRE DIMENSIONS WERE DESTROYED AND NOTHING HAPPENED...
BILLIONS OF PEOPLE, PLANTS, ANIMALS, INSECTS, MICROBES...
BILLIONS. MAYBE TRILLIONS. ALL GONE.
WHAT DOES ANY OF IT MATTER?
RIGHT HERE. IN THIS ROOM. DOES IT *REALLY* MATTER? NO.
I KILLED MY WIFE AND SHE--SHE REALLY ISN'T--WASN'T EVEN MY WIFE...
...SHE WAS WHO THE UNIVERSE RANDOMLY PAIRED ME WITH WHEN I SLIPPED THROUGH THE CRACKS OF THE MULTIVERSE COLLAPSE.
OH, AND *MAYBE*, MAYBE BY YOUR DEFINITION, THE--THE HEROES DIDN'T ACTUALLY DESTROY THE MULTIVERSE...BUT THEY *KNOW* ABOUT IT.
THEY KNOW AND THEY KEEP IT TO THEMSELVES.
ALIAS INVESTIGATIONS
THEY COVERED IT UP.
SO WHICH IS WORSE? THE COVER-UP OR THE CRIME?
I'LL ANSWER FOR YOU. BECAUSE IT IS A MINDSET THAT TAKES GETTING USED TO.
THE ANSWER IS: IT DOESN'T MATTER.
BECAUSE, YOU'RE GETTING IT, *NONE* OF IT MATTERS.

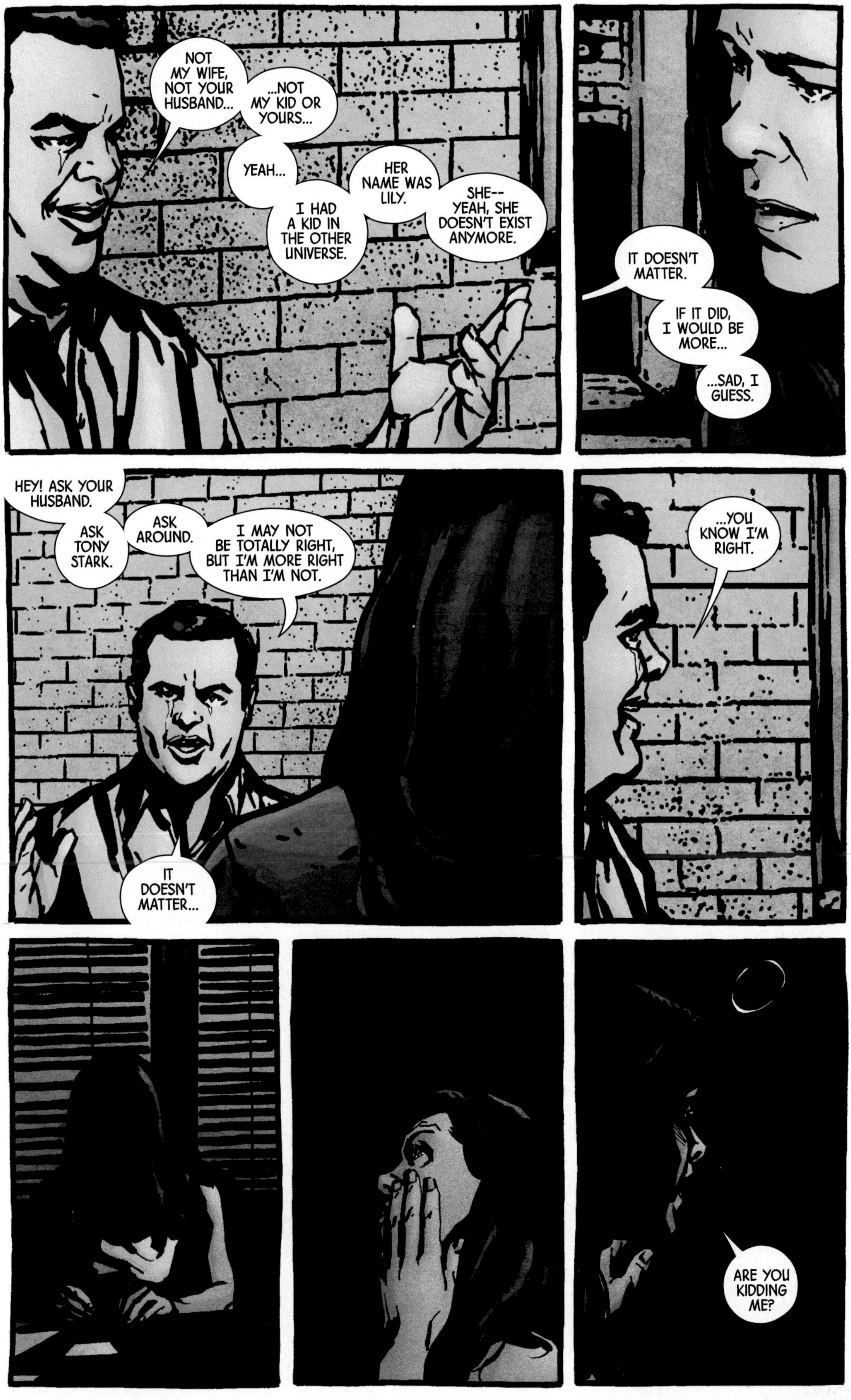
NOT MY WIFE, NOT YOUR HUSBAND...
...NOT MY KID OR YOURS...
YEAH...
I HAD A KID IN THE OTHER UNIVERSE.
HER NAME WAS LILY.
SHE-- YEAH, SHE DOESN'T EXIST ANYMORE.
IT DOESN'T MATTER.
IF IT DID, I WOULD BE MORE...
...SAD, I GUESS.
HEY! ASK YOUR HUSBAND.
ASK TONY STARK.
ASK AROUND.
I MAY NOT BE TOTALLY RIGHT, BUT I'M MORE RIGHT THAN I'M NOT.
IT DOESN'T MATTER...
...YOU KNOW I'M RIGHT.
ARE YOU KIDDING ME?

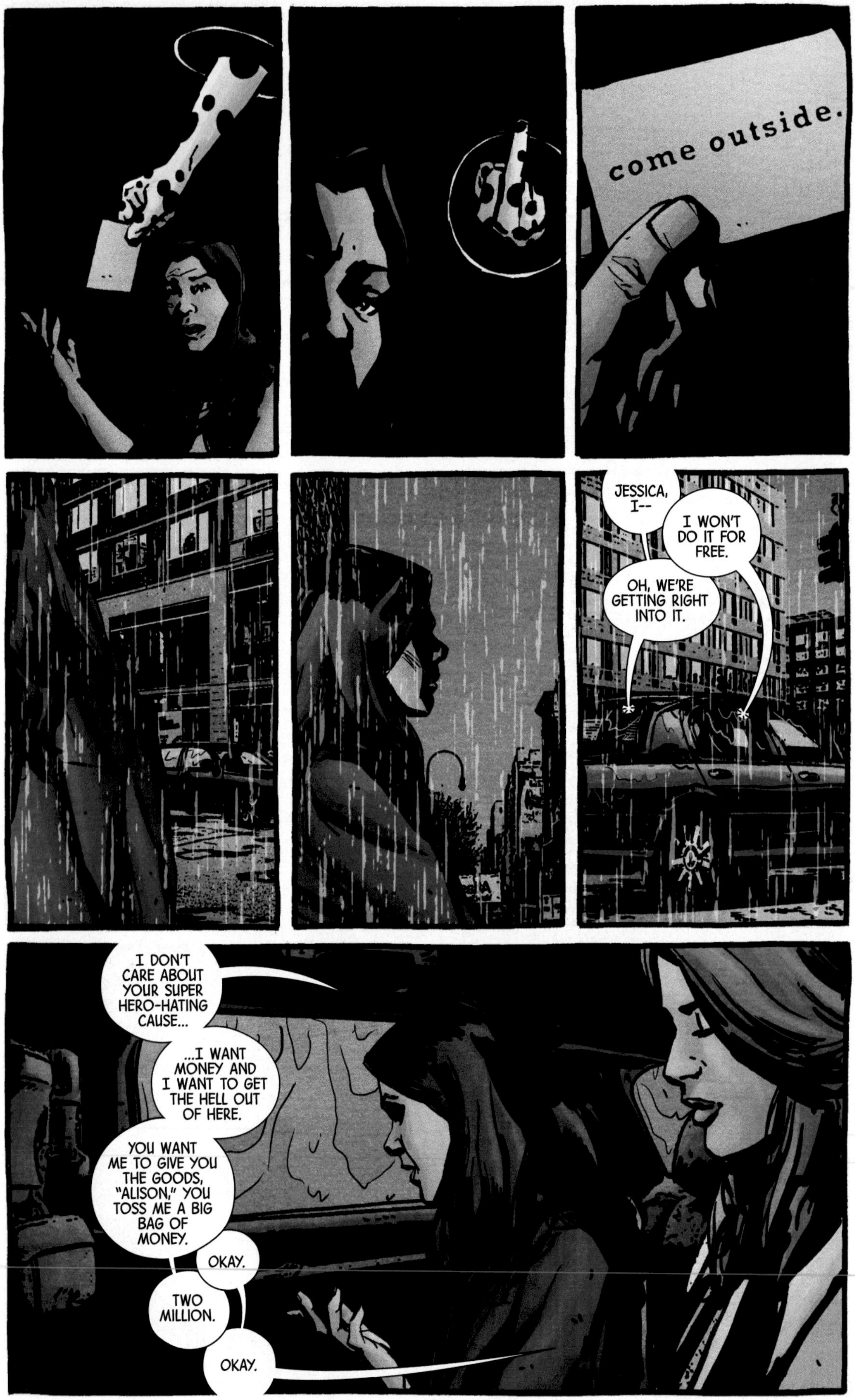
come outside.
JESSICA, I--
I WON'T DO IT FOR FREE.
OH, WE'RE GETTING RIGHT INTO IT.
I DON'T CARE ABOUT YOUR SUPER HERO-HATING CAUSE...
...I WANT MONEY AND I WANT TO GET THE HELL OUT OF HERE.
YOU WANT ME TO GIVE YOU THE GOODS, "ALISON," YOU TOSS ME A BIG BAG OF MONEY.
OKAY.
TWO MILLION.
OKAY.

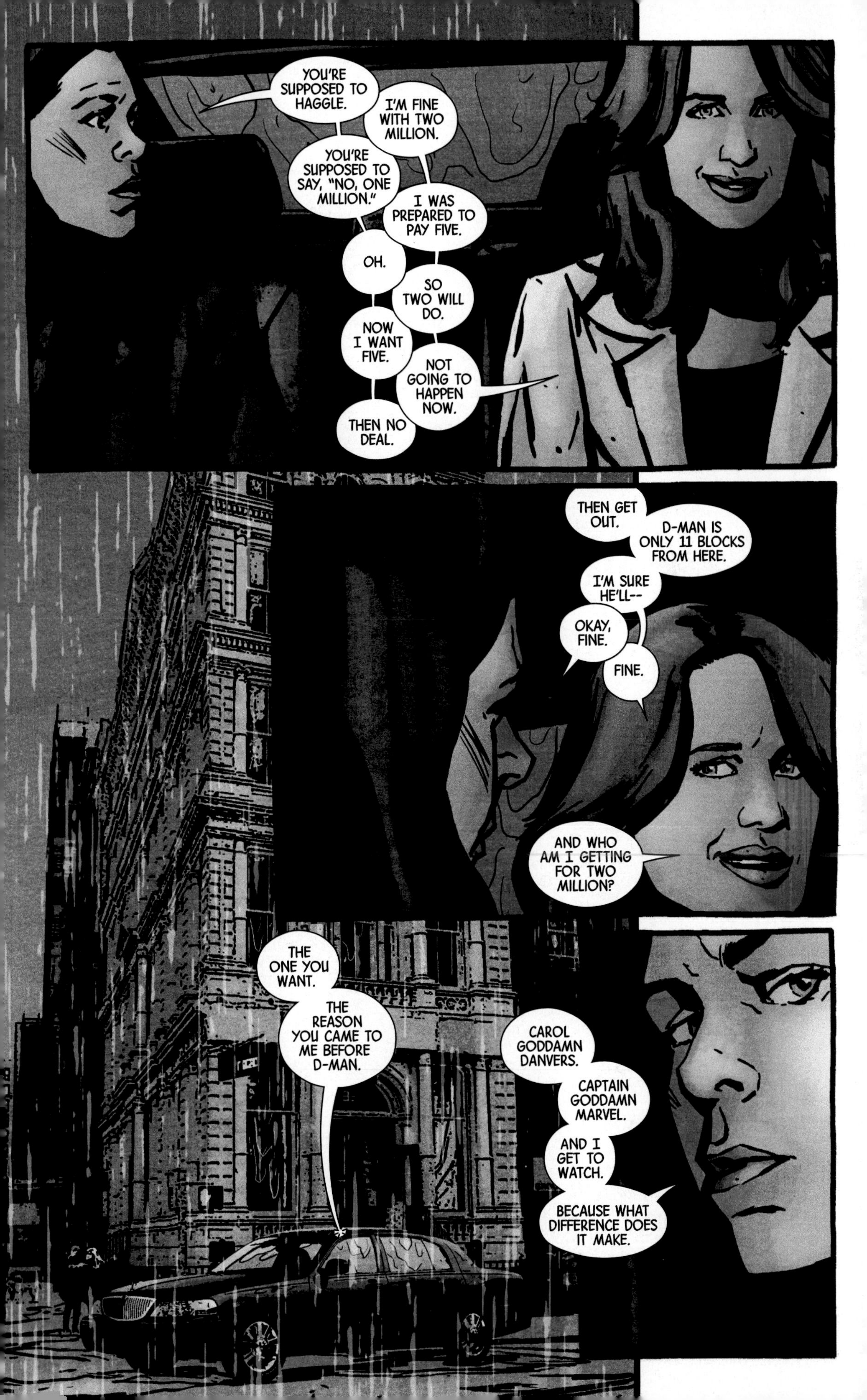
YOU'RE SUPPOSED TO HAGGLE.
I'M FINE WITH TWO MILLION.
YOU'RE SUPPOSED TO SAY, "NO, ONE MILLION."
I WAS PREPARED TO PAY FIVE.
OH.
SO TWO WILL DO.
NOW I WANT FIVE.
NOT GOING TO HAPPEN NOW.
THEN NO DEAL.
THEN GET OUT.
D-MAN IS ONLY 11 BLOCKS FROM HERE.
I'M SURE HE'LL--
OKAY, FINE.
FINE.
AND WHO AM I GETTING FOR TWO MILLION?
THE ONE YOU WANT.
THE REASON YOU CAME TO ME BEFORE D-MAN.
CAROL GODDAMN DANVERS.
CAPTAIN GODDAMN MARVEL.
AND I GET TO WATCH.
BECAUSE WHAT DIFFERENCE DOES IT MAKE.

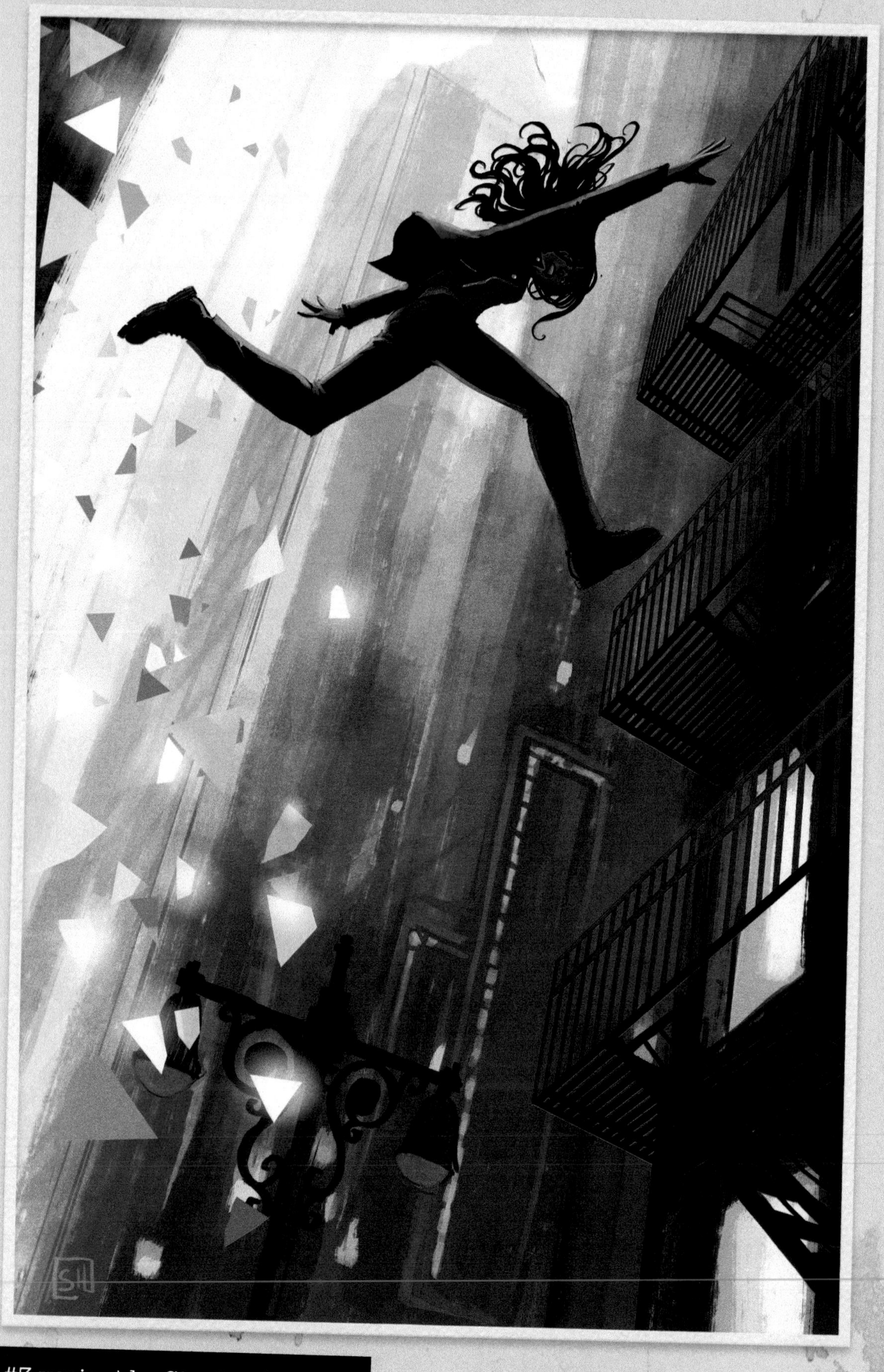

#3 variant by **Stephanie Hans**

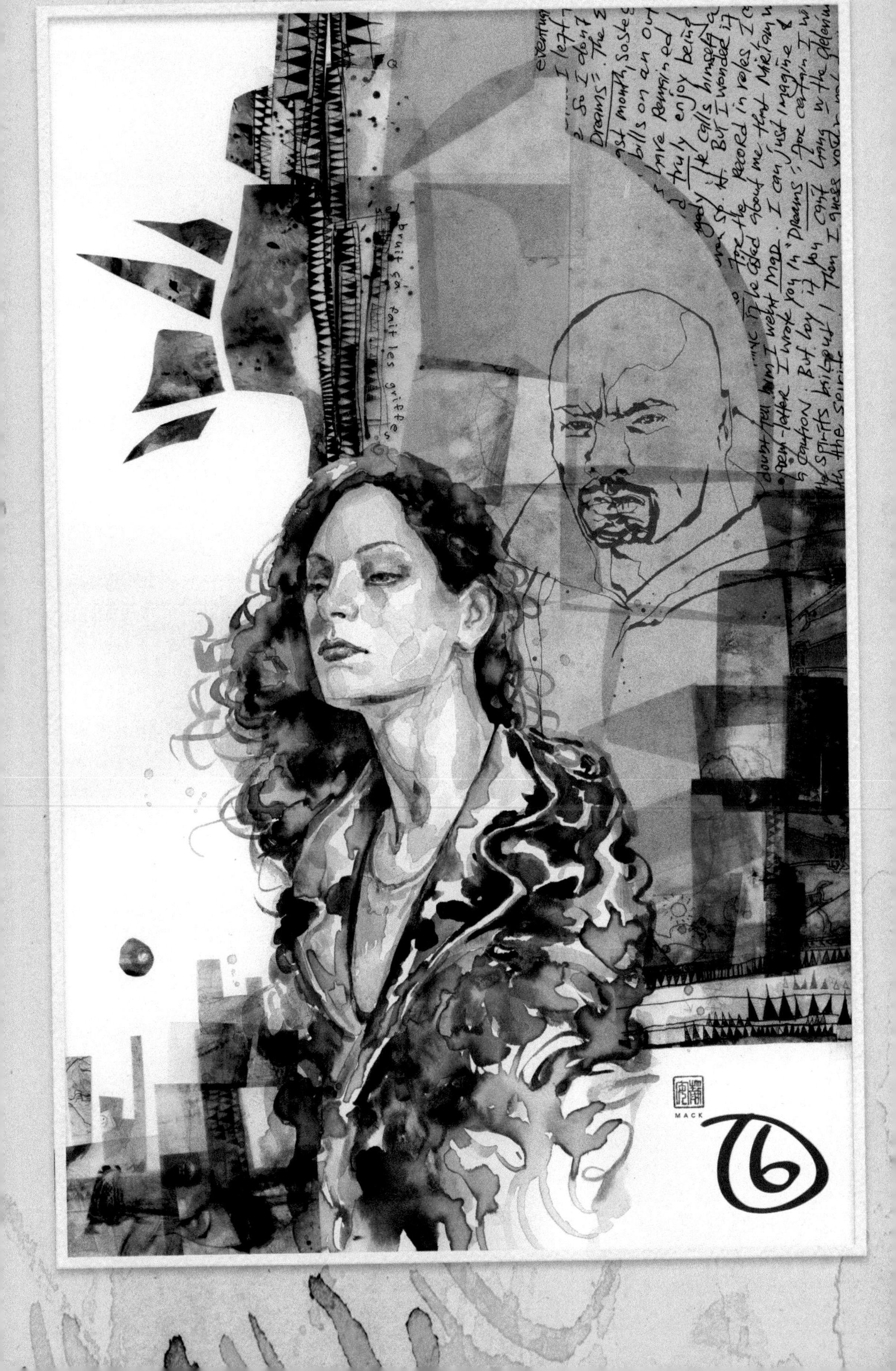
MACK

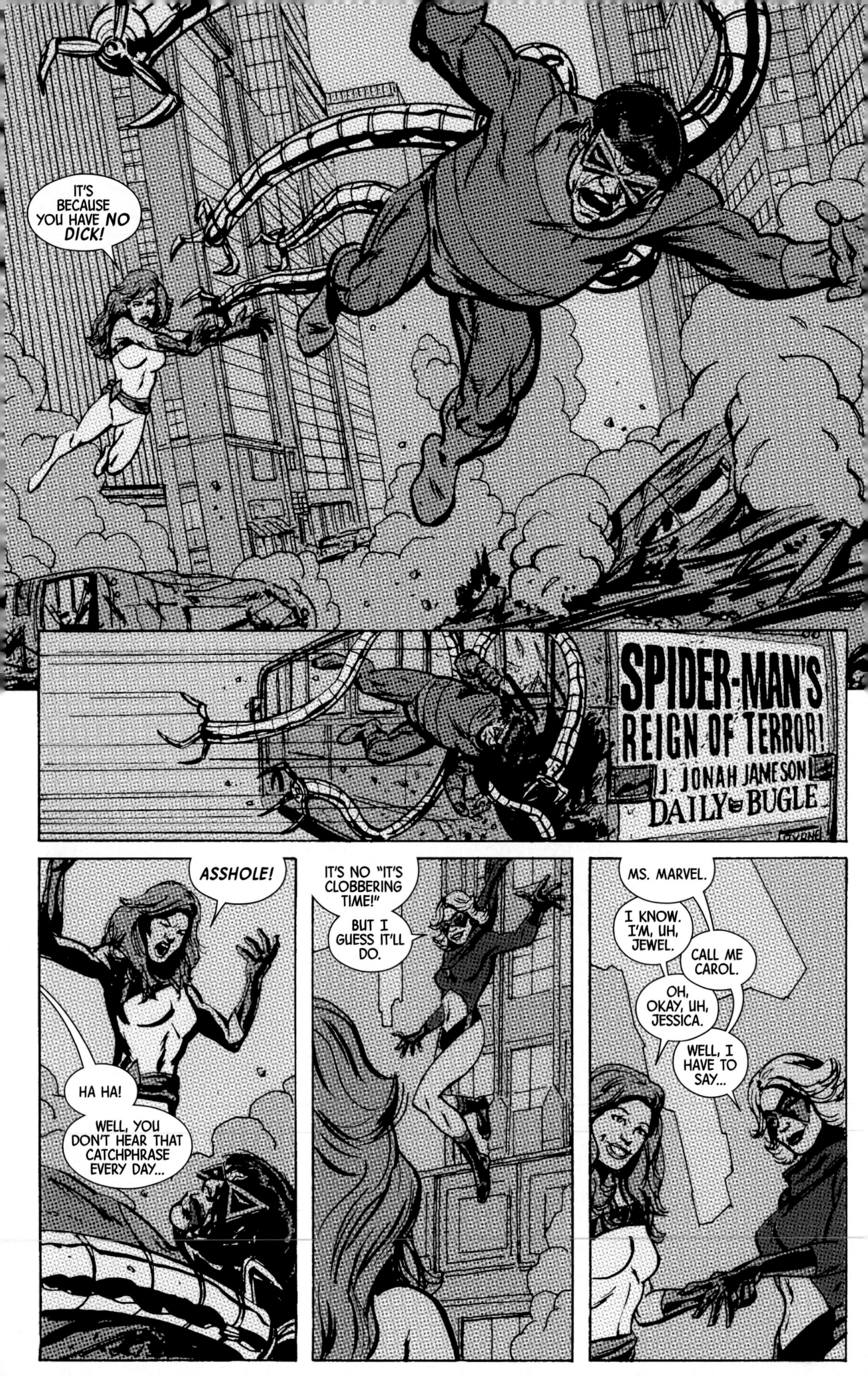
IT'S BECAUSE YOU HAVE NO DICK!
SPIDER-MAN'S REIGN OF TERROR!
J. JONAH JAMESON
DAILY BUGLE
ASSHOLE!
HA HA!
WELL, YOU DON'T HEAR THAT CATCHPHRASE EVERY DAY...
IT'S NO "IT'S CLOBBERING TIME!"
BUT I GUESS IT'LL DO.
MS. MARVEL.
I KNOW. I'M, UH, JEWEL.
CALL ME CAROL.
OH, OKAY, UH, JESSICA.
WELL, I HAVE TO SAY...

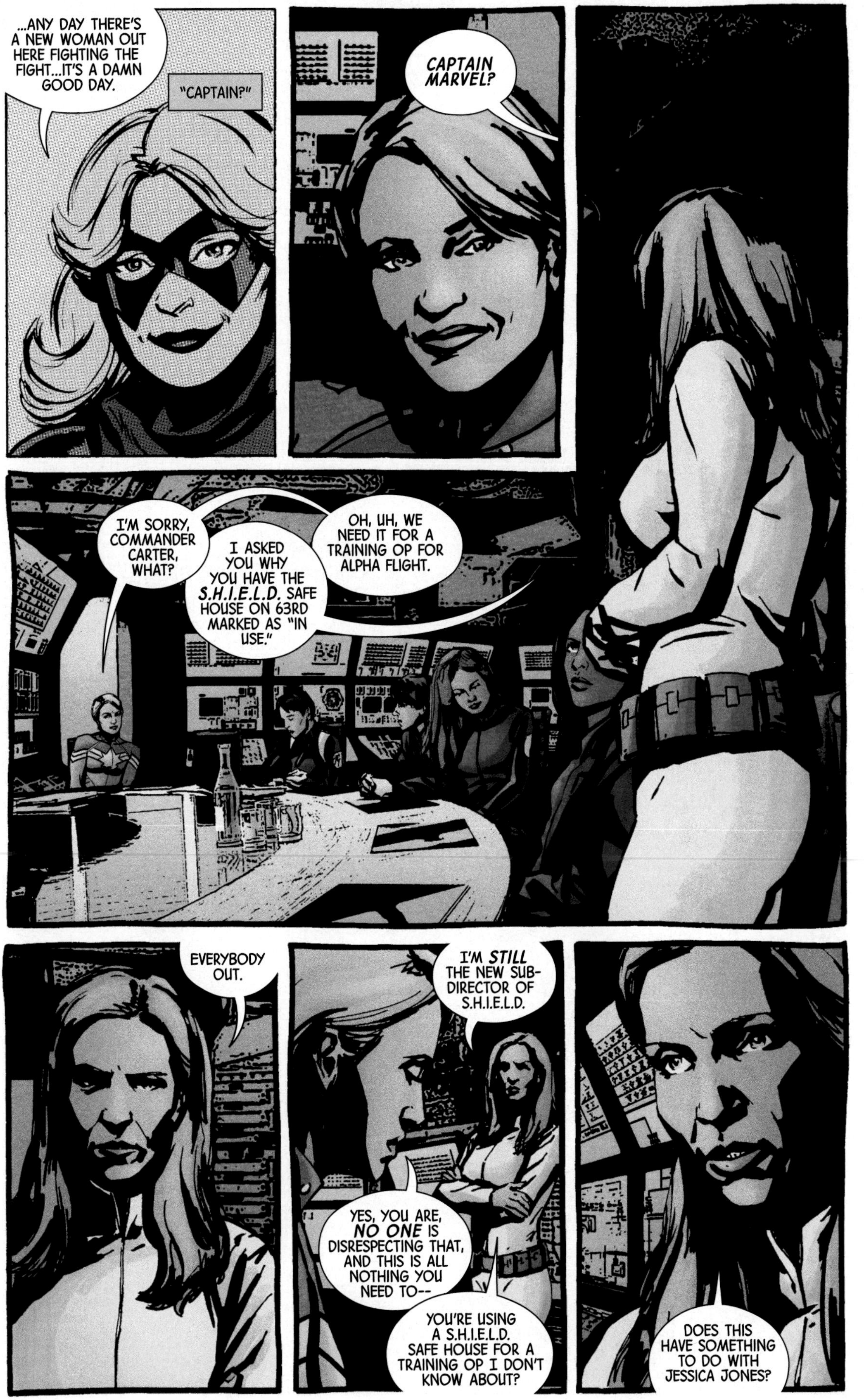
...ANY DAY THERE'S A NEW WOMAN OUT HERE FIGHTING THE FIGHT...IT'S A DAMN GOOD DAY.
"CAPTAIN?"
CAPTAIN MARVEL?
I'M SORRY, COMMANDER CARTER, WHAT?
I ASKED YOU WHY YOU HAVE THE S.H.I.E.L.D. SAFE HOUSE ON 63RD MARKED AS "IN USE."
OH, UH, WE NEED IT FOR A TRAINING OP FOR ALPHA FLIGHT.
EVERYBODY OUT.
I'M STILL THE NEW SUB-DIRECTOR OF S.H.I.E.L.D.
YES, YOU ARE, NO ONE IS DISRESPECTING THAT, AND THIS IS ALL NOTHING YOU NEED TO--
YOU'RE USING A S.H.I.E.L.D. SAFE HOUSE FOR A TRAINING OP I DON'T KNOW ABOUT?
DOES THIS HAVE SOMETHING TO DO WITH JESSICA JONES?

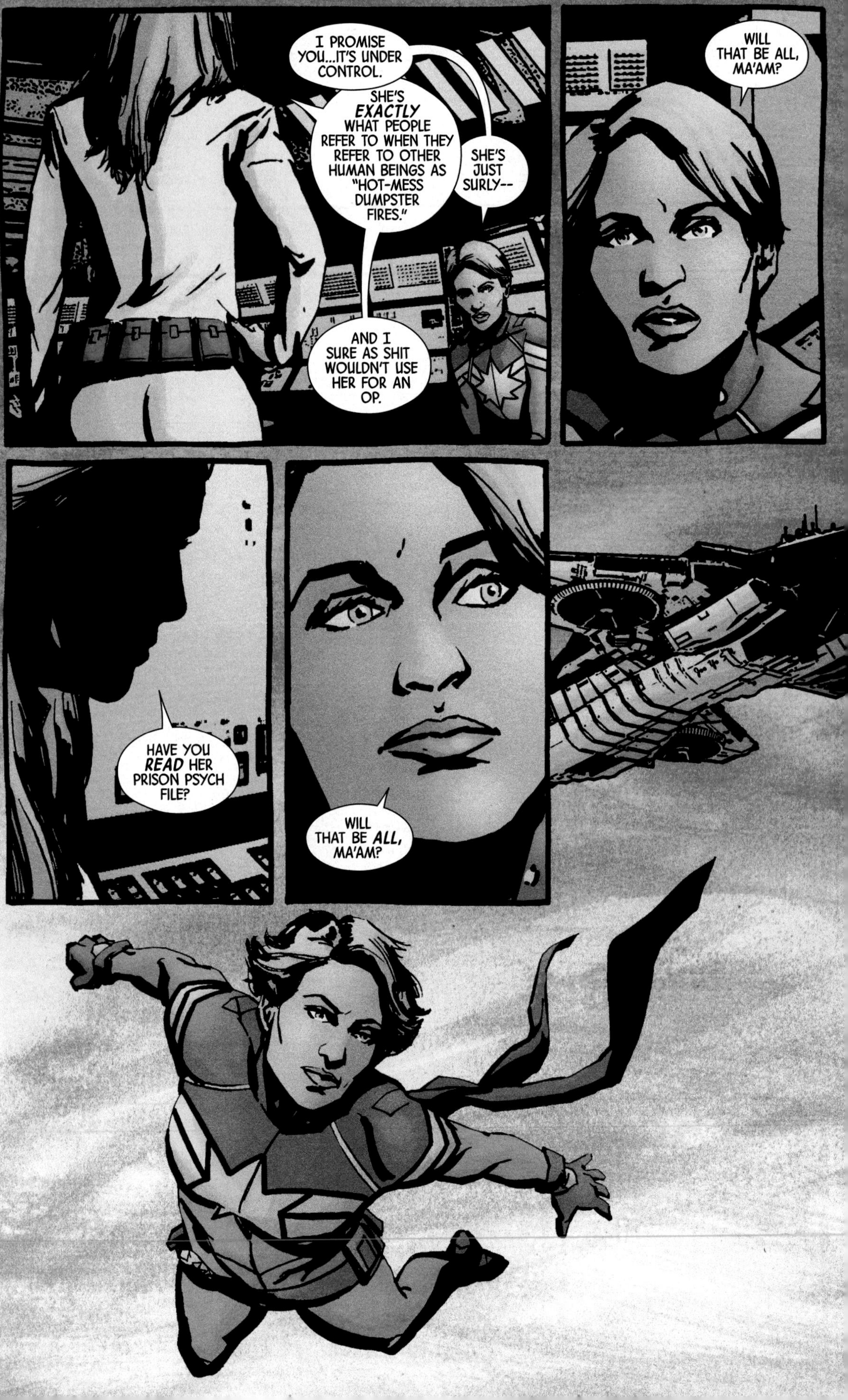
I PROMISE YOU...IT'S UNDER CONTROL.
SHE'S JUST SURLY--
SHE'S EXACTLY WHAT PEOPLE REFER TO WHEN THEY REFER TO OTHER HUMAN BEINGS AS "HOT-MESS DUMPSTER FIRES."
AND I SURE AS SHIT WOULDN'T USE HER FOR AN OP.
WILL THAT BE ALL, MA'AM?
HAVE YOU READ HER PRISON PSYCH FILE?
WILL THAT BE ALL, MA'AM?

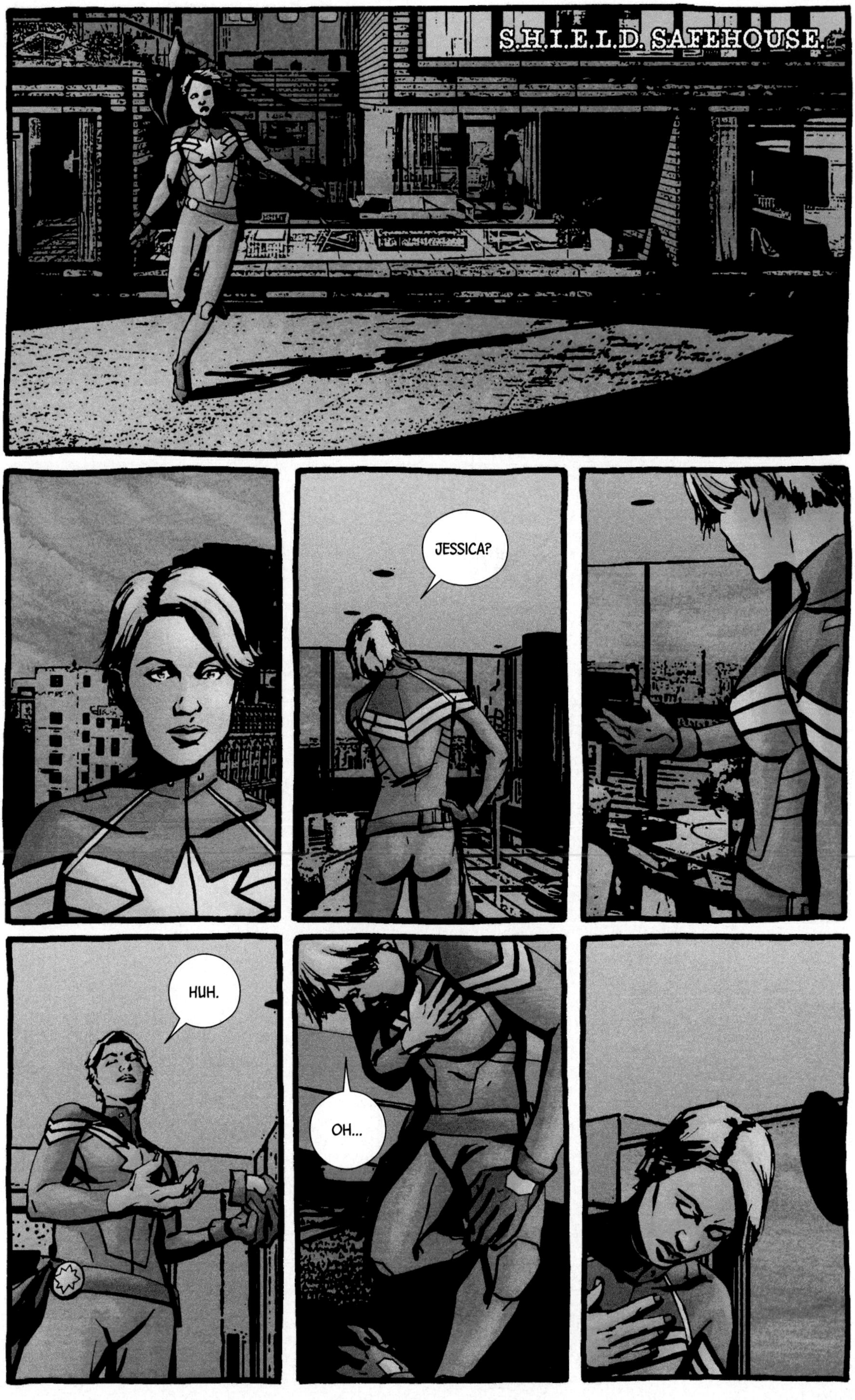
S.H.I.E.L.D. SAFEHOUSE.
JESSICA?
HUH.
OH...

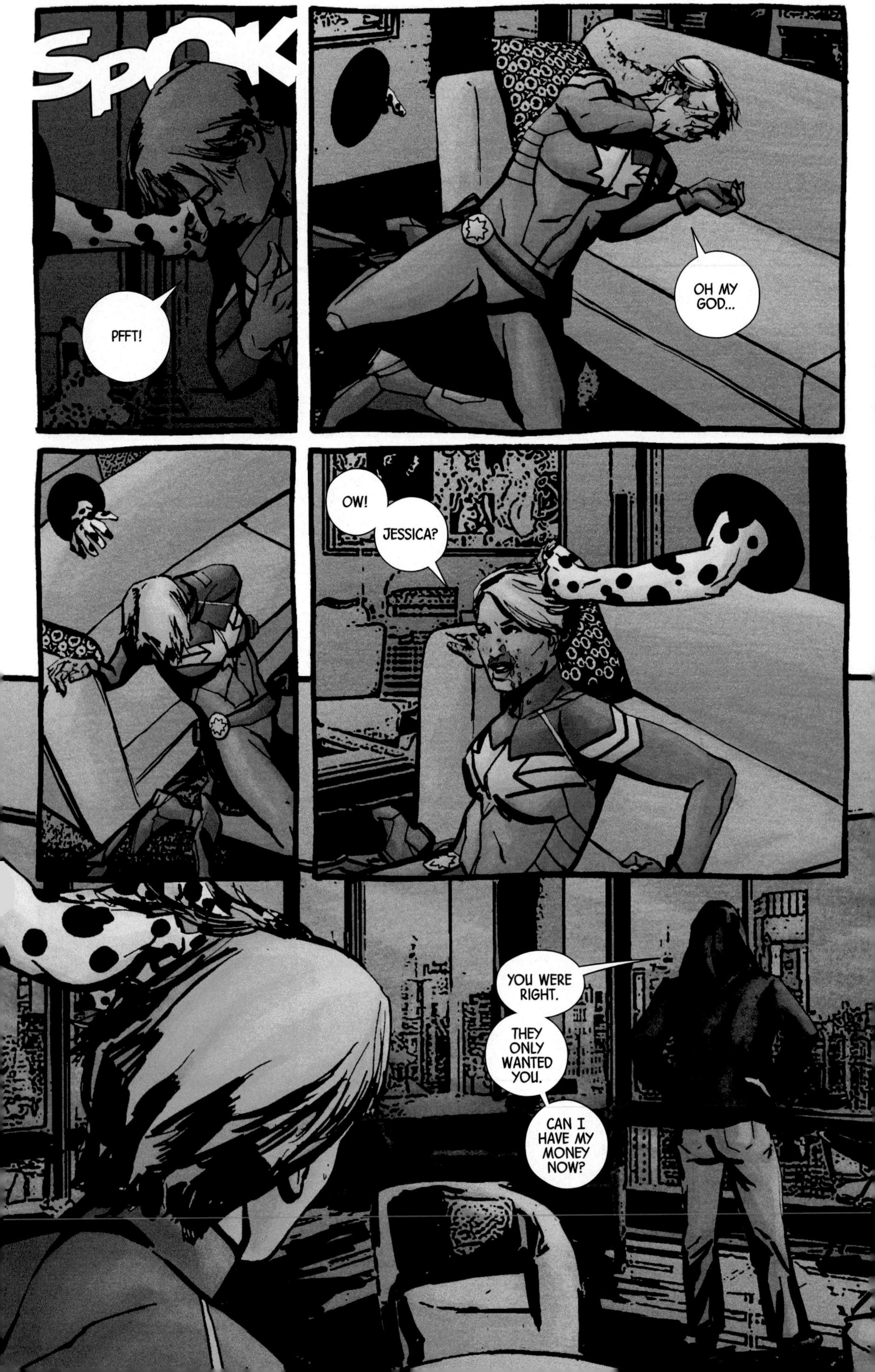
SPOK
PFFT!
OH MY GOD...
OW!
JESSICA?
YOU WERE RIGHT.
THEY ONLY WANTED YOU.
CAN I HAVE MY MONEY NOW?

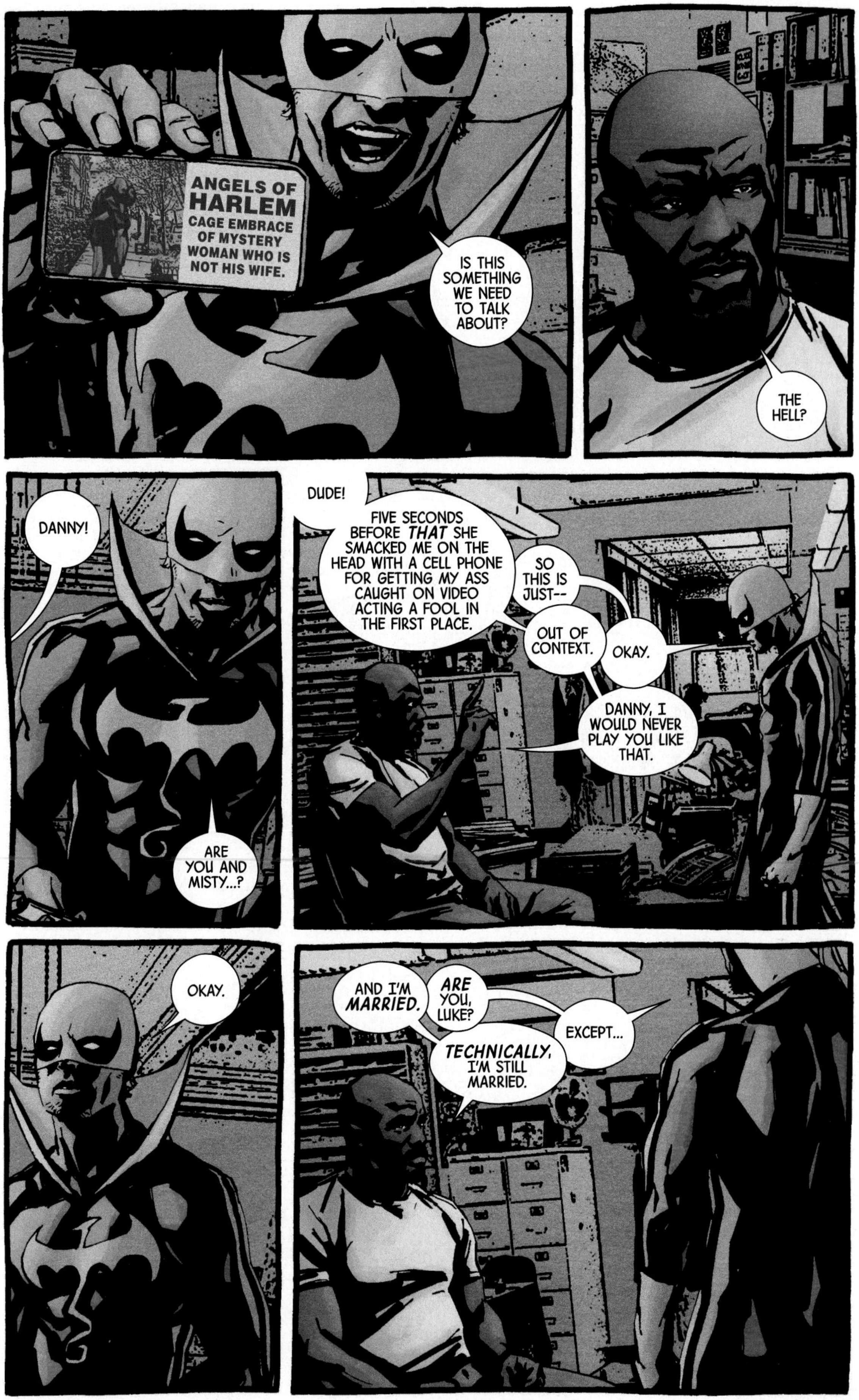
ANGELS OF HARLEM
CAGE EMBRACE OF MYSTERY WOMAN WHO IS NOT HIS WIFE.
IS THIS SOMETHING WE NEED TO TALK ABOUT?
THE HELL?
DANNY!
ARE YOU AND MISTY...?
DUDE!
FIVE SECONDS BEFORE THAT SHE SMACKED ME ON THE HEAD WITH A CELL PHONE FOR GETTING MY ASS CAUGHT ON VIDEO ACTING A FOOL IN THE FIRST PLACE.
SO THIS IS JUST--
OUT OF CONTEXT.
OKAY.
DANNY, I WOULD NEVER PLAY YOU LIKE THAT.
OKAY.
AND I'M MARRIED.
ARE YOU, LUKE?
EXCEPT...
TECHNICALLY, I'M STILL MARRIED.

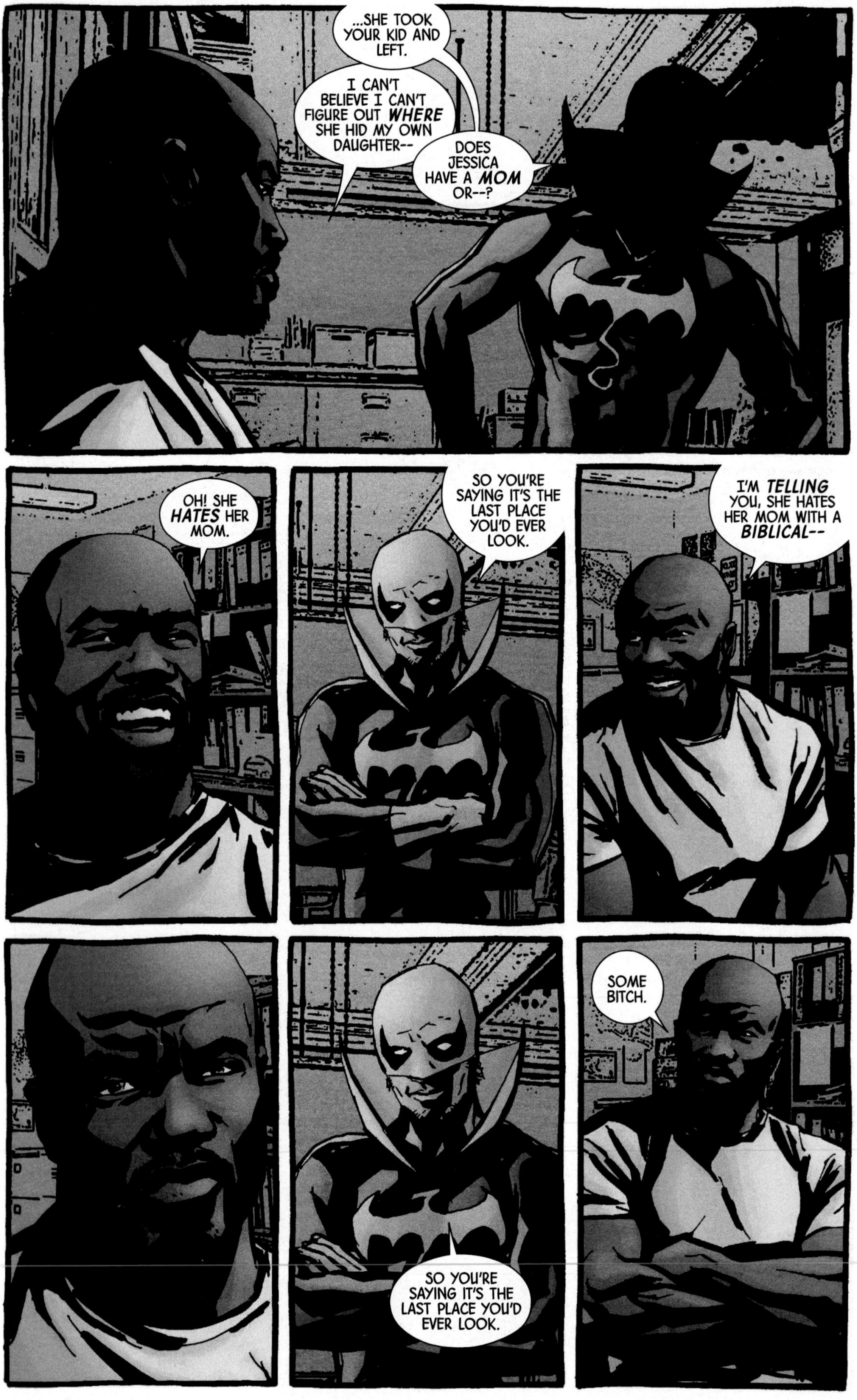
...SHE TOOK YOUR KID AND LEFT.
I CAN'T BELIEVE I CAN'T FIGURE OUT WHERE SHE HID MY OWN DAUGHTER--
DOES JESSICA HAVE A MOM OR--?
OH! SHE HATES HER MOM.
SO YOU'RE SAYING IT'S THE LAST PLACE YOU'D EVER LOOK.
I'M TELLING YOU, SHE HATES HER MOM WITH A BIBLICAL--
SO YOU'RE SAYING IT'S THE LAST PLACE YOU'D EVER LOOK.
SOME BITCH.

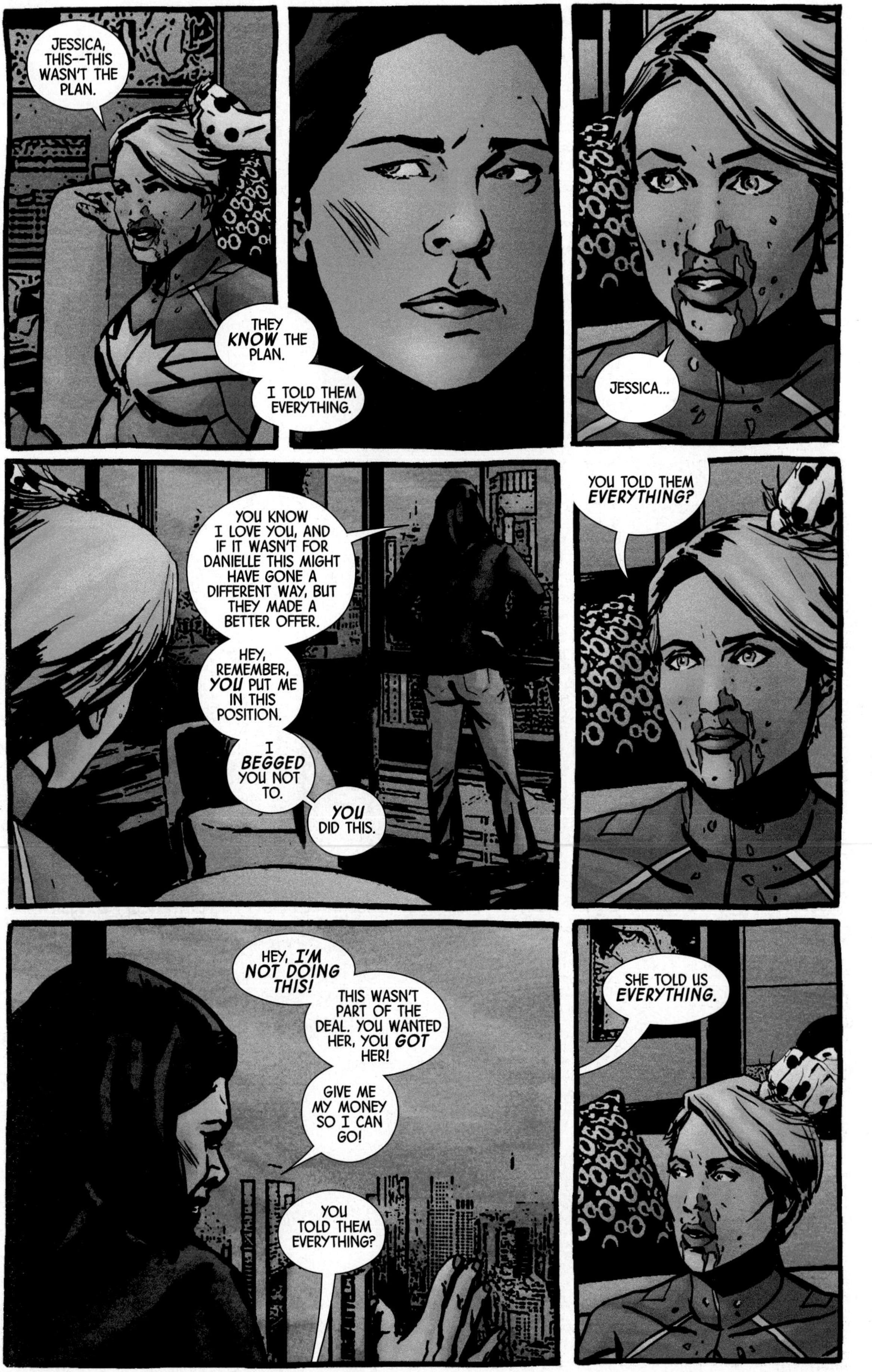
JESSICA, THIS--THIS WASN'T THE PLAN.
THEY *KNOW* THE PLAN.
I TOLD THEM EVERYTHING.
JESSICA...
YOU KNOW I LOVE YOU, AND IF IT WASN'T FOR DANIELLE THIS MIGHT HAVE GONE A DIFFERENT WAY, BUT THEY MADE A BETTER OFFER.
HEY, REMEMBER, *YOU* PUT ME IN THIS POSITION.
I *BEGGED* YOU NOT TO.
YOU DID THIS.
YOU TOLD THEM *EVERYTHING?*
HEY, *I'M NOT DOING THIS!*
THIS WASN'T PART OF THE DEAL. YOU WANTED HER, YOU *GOT* HER!
GIVE ME MY MONEY SO I CAN GO!
YOU TOLD THEM EVERYTHING?
SHE TOLD US *EVERYTHING.*

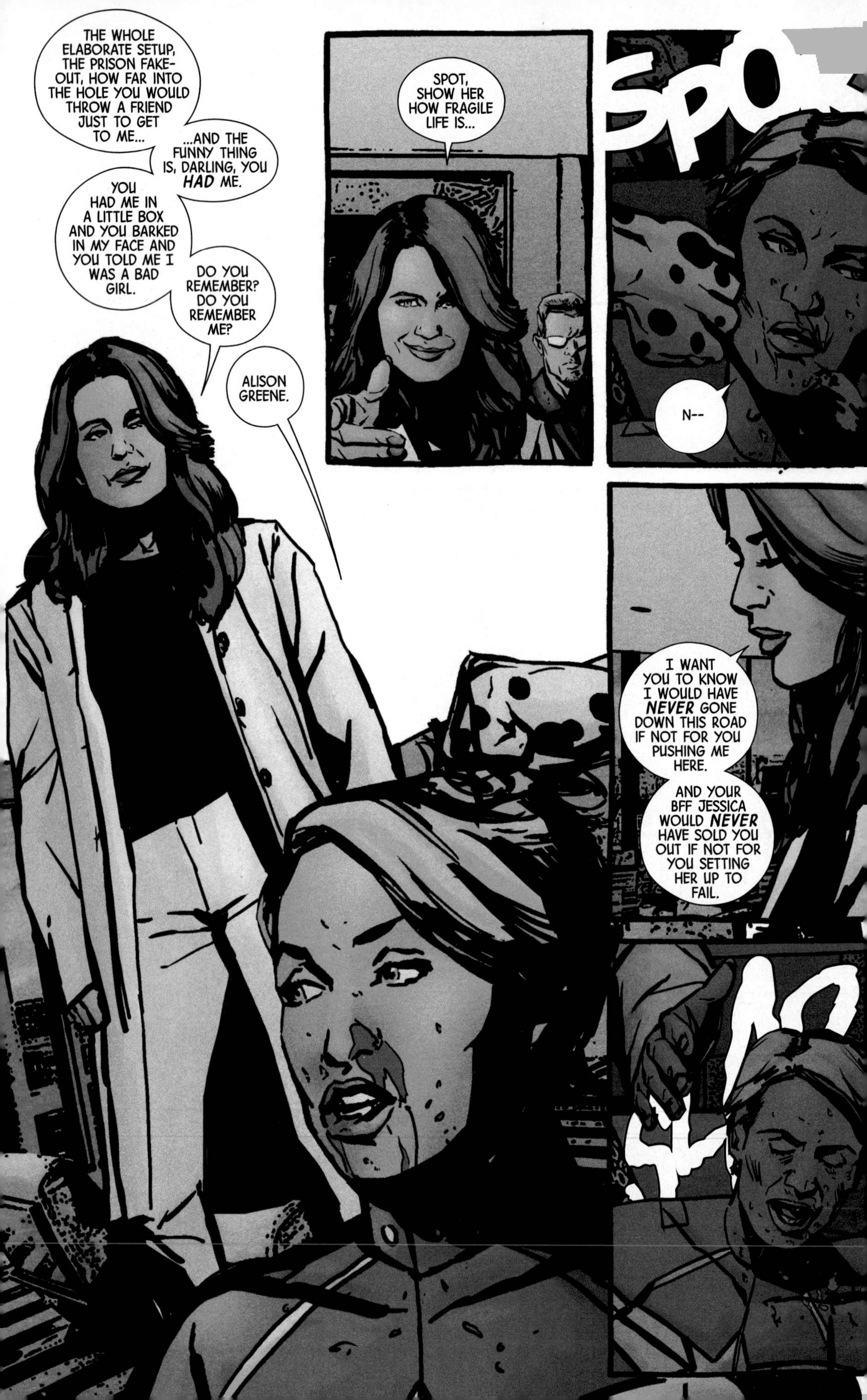
THE WHOLE ELABORATE SETUP, THE PRISON FAKE-OUT, HOW FAR INTO THE HOLE YOU WOULD THROW A FRIEND JUST TO GET TO ME...
...AND THE FUNNY THING IS, DARLING, YOU *HAD* ME.
YOU HAD ME IN A LITTLE BOX AND YOU BARKED IN MY FACE AND YOU TOLD ME I WAS A BAD GIRL.
DO YOU REMEMBER? DO YOU REMEMBER ME?
ALISON GREENE.
SPOT, SHOW HER HOW FRAGILE LIFE IS...
SPO
N--
I WANT YOU TO KNOW I WOULD HAVE *NEVER* GONE DOWN THIS ROAD IF NOT FOR YOU PUSHING ME HERE.
AND YOUR BFF JESSICA WOULD *NEVER* HAVE SOLD YOU OUT IF NOT FOR YOU SETTING HER UP TO FAIL.

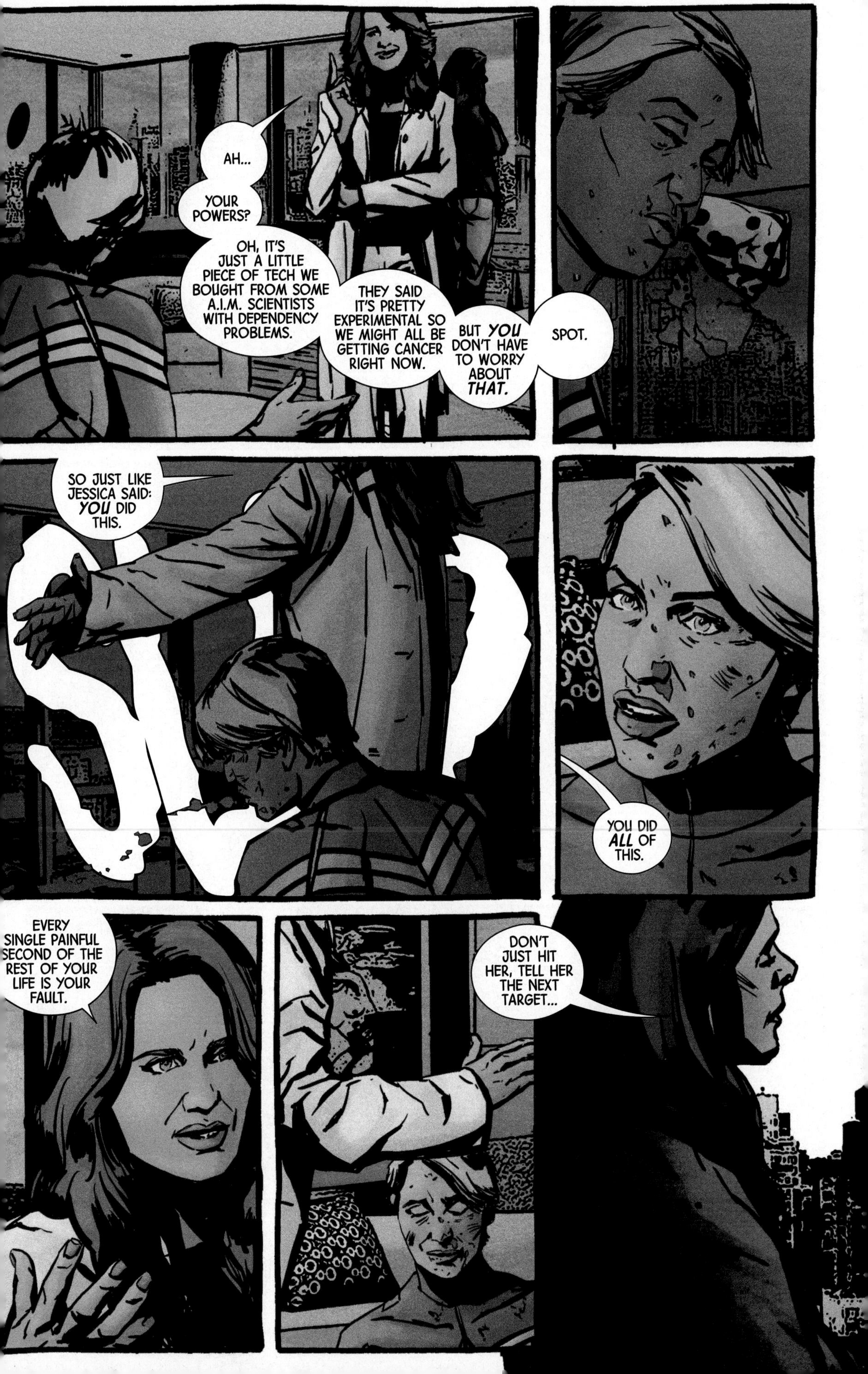
AH...
YOUR POWERS?
OH, IT'S JUST A LITTLE PIECE OF TECH WE BOUGHT FROM SOME A.I.M. SCIENTISTS WITH DEPENDENCY PROBLEMS.
THEY SAID IT'S PRETTY EXPERIMENTAL SO WE MIGHT ALL BE GETTING CANCER RIGHT NOW.
BUT YOU DON'T HAVE TO WORRY ABOUT THAT.
SPOT.
SO JUST LIKE JESSICA SAID: YOU DID THIS.
YOU DID ALL OF THIS.
EVERY SINGLE PAINFUL SECOND OF THE REST OF YOUR LIFE IS YOUR FAULT.
DON'T JUST HIT HER, TELL HER THE NEXT TARGET...

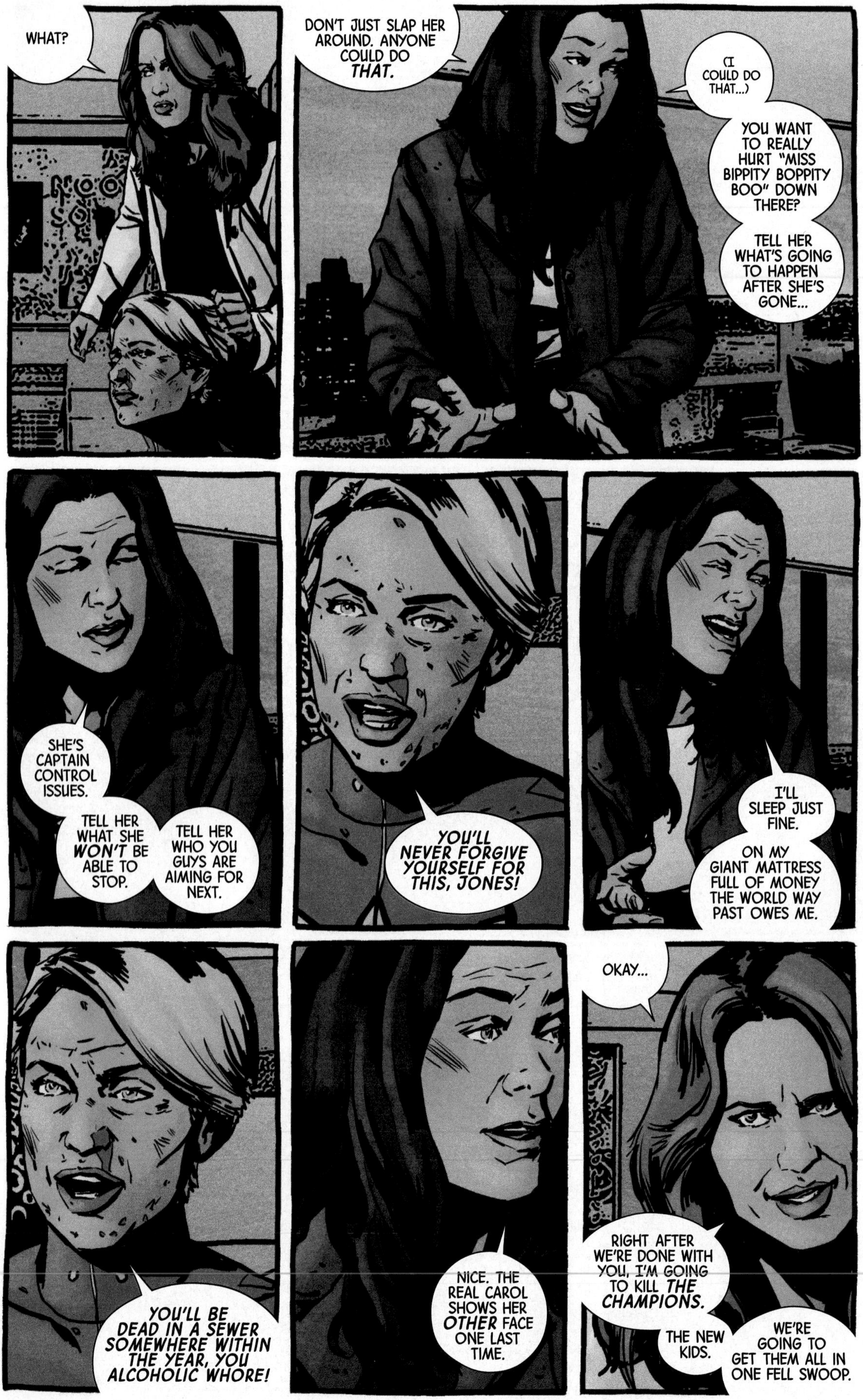
WHAT?
DON'T JUST SLAP HER AROUND. ANYONE COULD DO THAT.
(I COULD DO THAT...)
YOU WANT TO REALLY HURT "MISS BIPPITY BOPPITY BOO" DOWN THERE?
TELL HER WHAT'S GOING TO HAPPEN AFTER SHE'S GONE...
SHE'S CAPTAIN CONTROL ISSUES.
TELL HER WHAT SHE WON'T BE ABLE TO STOP.
TELL HER WHO YOU GUYS ARE AIMING FOR NEXT.
YOU'LL NEVER FORGIVE YOURSELF FOR THIS, JONES!
I'LL SLEEP JUST FINE.
ON MY GIANT MATTRESS FULL OF MONEY THE WORLD WAY PAST OWES ME.
YOU'LL BE DEAD IN A SEWER SOMEWHERE WITHIN THE YEAR, YOU ALCOHOLIC WHORE!
NICE. THE REAL CAROL SHOWS HER OTHER FACE ONE LAST TIME.
OKAY...
RIGHT AFTER WE'RE DONE WITH YOU, I'M GOING TO KILL THE CHAMPIONS.
THE NEW KIDS.
WE'RE GOING TO GET THEM ALL IN ONE FELL SWOOP.

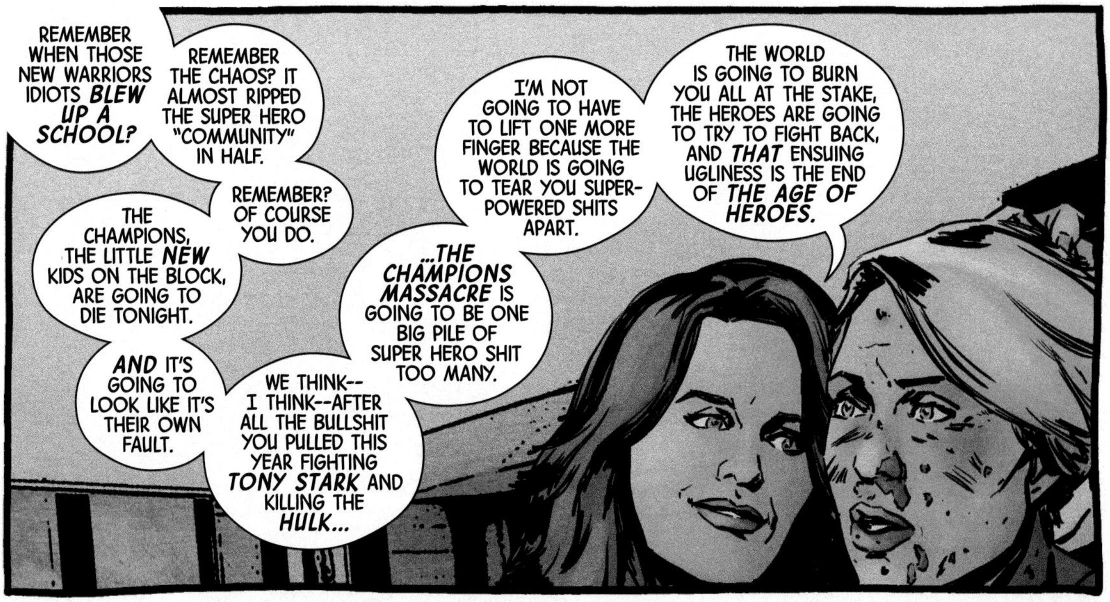
REMEMBER WHEN THOSE NEW WARRIORS IDIOTS BLEW UP A SCHOOL?
REMEMBER THE CHAOS? IT ALMOST RIPPED THE SUPER HERO "COMMUNITY" IN HALF.
REMEMBER? OF COURSE YOU DO.
THE CHAMPIONS, THE LITTLE NEW KIDS ON THE BLOCK, ARE GOING TO DIE TONIGHT.
AND IT'S GOING TO LOOK LIKE IT'S THEIR OWN FAULT.
WE THINK-- I THINK--AFTER ALL THE BULLSHIT YOU PULLED THIS YEAR FIGHTING TONY STARK AND KILLING THE HULK...
...THE CHAMPIONS MASSACRE IS GOING TO BE ONE BIG PILE OF SUPER HERO SHIT TOO MANY.
I'M NOT GOING TO HAVE TO LIFT ONE MORE FINGER BECAUSE THE WORLD IS GOING TO TEAR YOU SUPER-POWERED SHITS APART.
THE WORLD IS GOING TO BURN YOU ALL AT THE STAKE, THE HEROES ARE GOING TO TRY TO FIGHT BACK, AND THAT ENSUING UGLINESS IS THE END OF THE AGE OF HEROES.

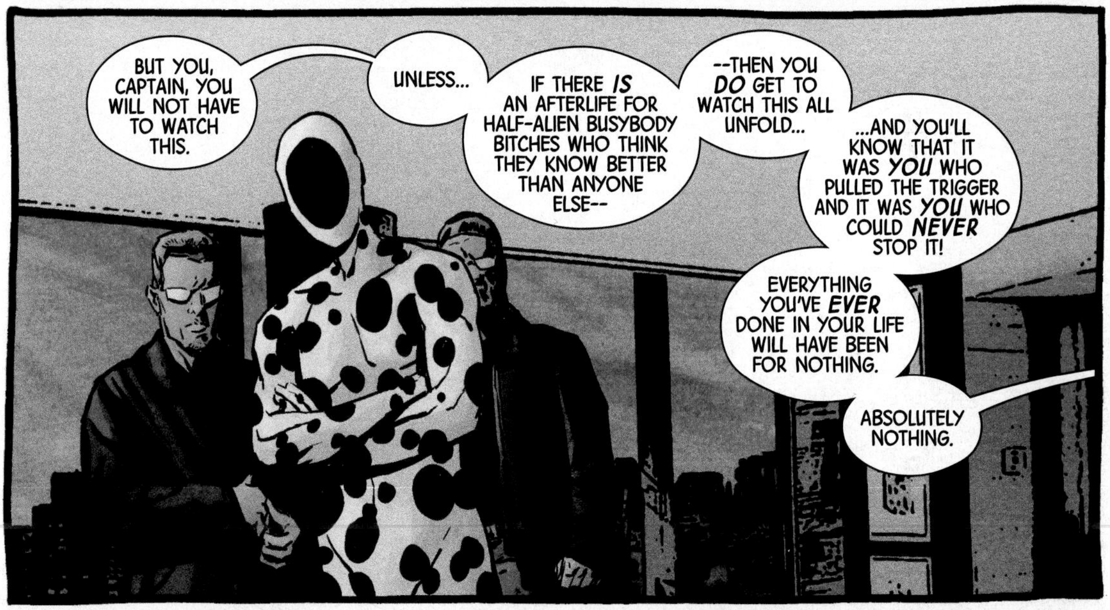
BUT YOU, CAPTAIN, YOU WILL NOT HAVE TO WATCH THIS.
UNLESS...
IF THERE IS AN AFTERLIFE FOR HALF-ALIEN BUSYBODY BITCHES WHO THINK THEY KNOW BETTER THAN ANYONE ELSE--
--THEN YOU DO GET TO WATCH THIS ALL UNFOLD...
...AND YOU'LL KNOW THAT IT WAS YOU WHO PULLED THE TRIGGER AND IT WAS YOU WHO COULD NEVER STOP IT!
EVERYTHING YOU'VE EVER DONE IN YOUR LIFE WILL HAVE BEEN FOR NOTHING.
ABSOLUTELY NOTHING.

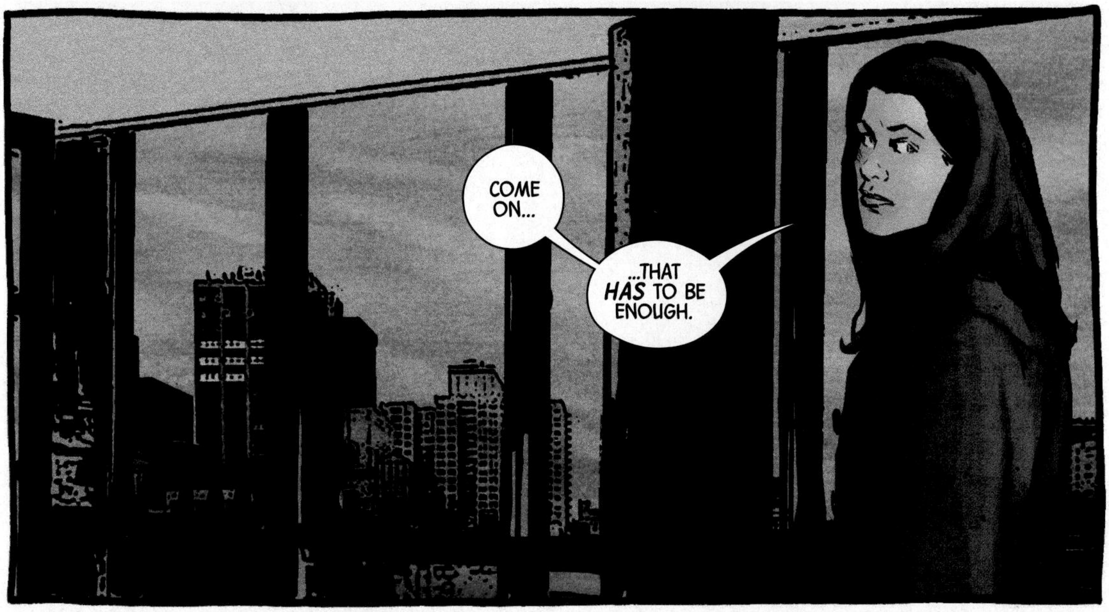
COME ON...
...THAT HAS TO BE ENOUGH.

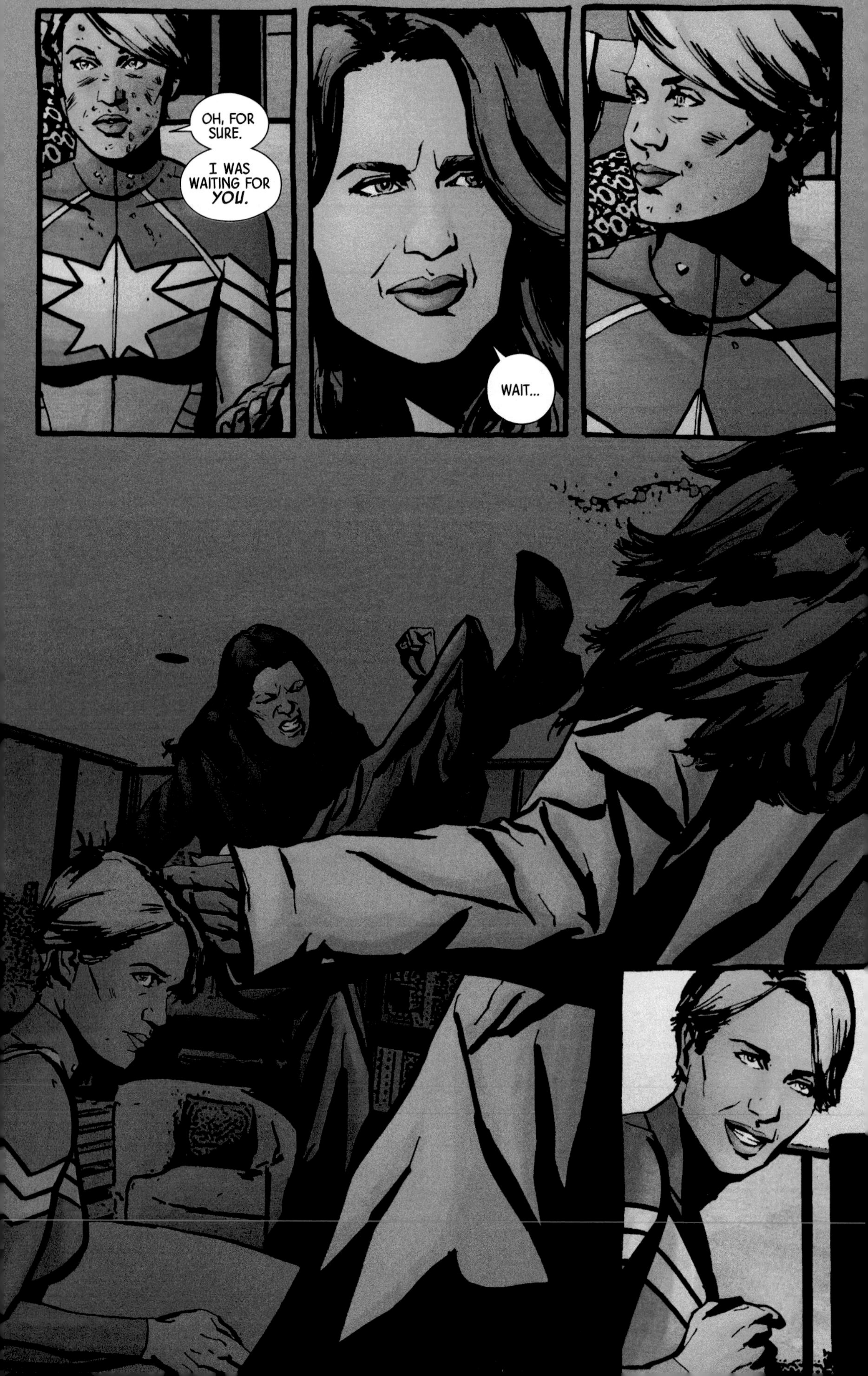
OH, FOR SURE.
I WAS WAITING FOR YOU.
WAIT...

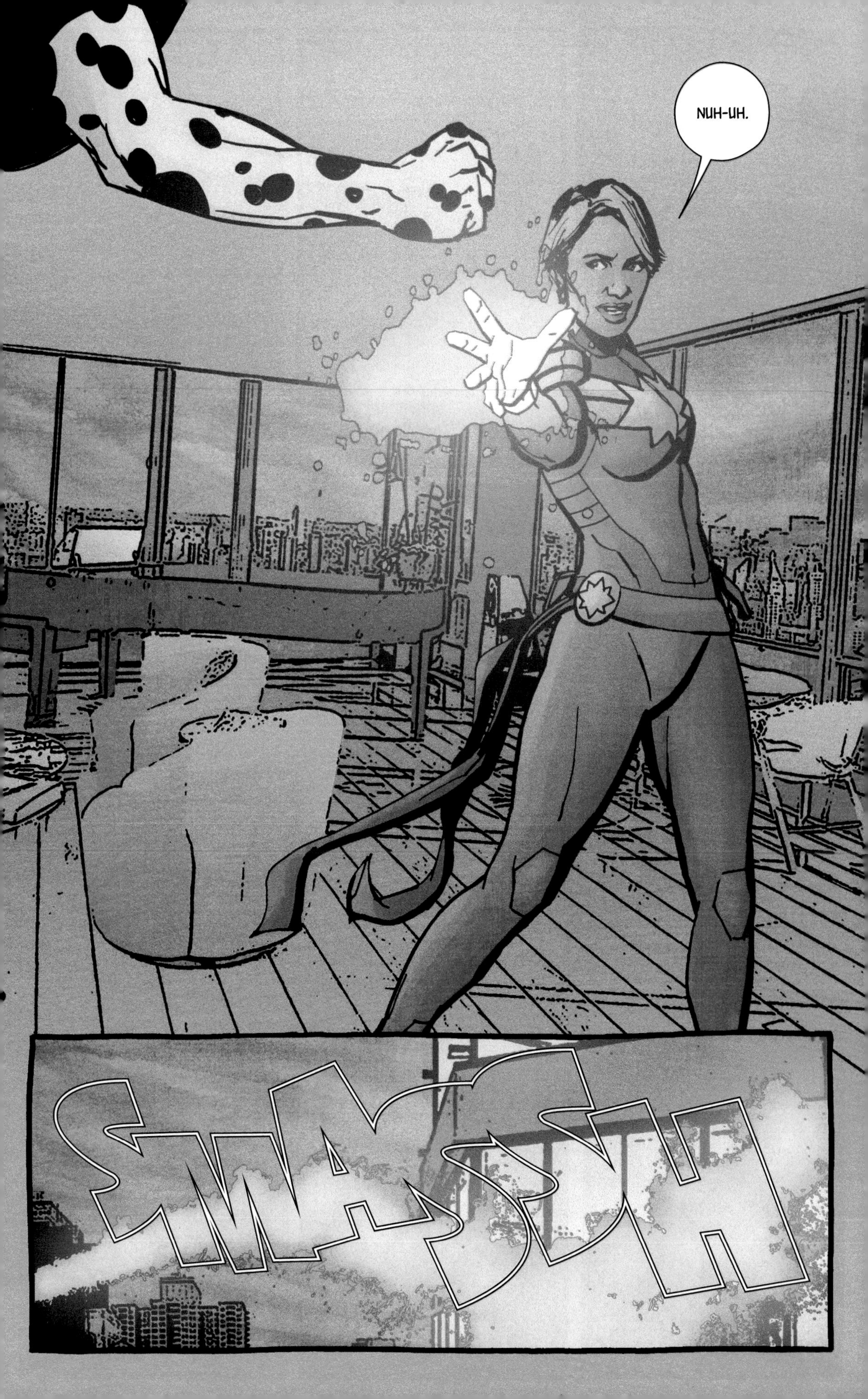
NUH-UH.
SWASH

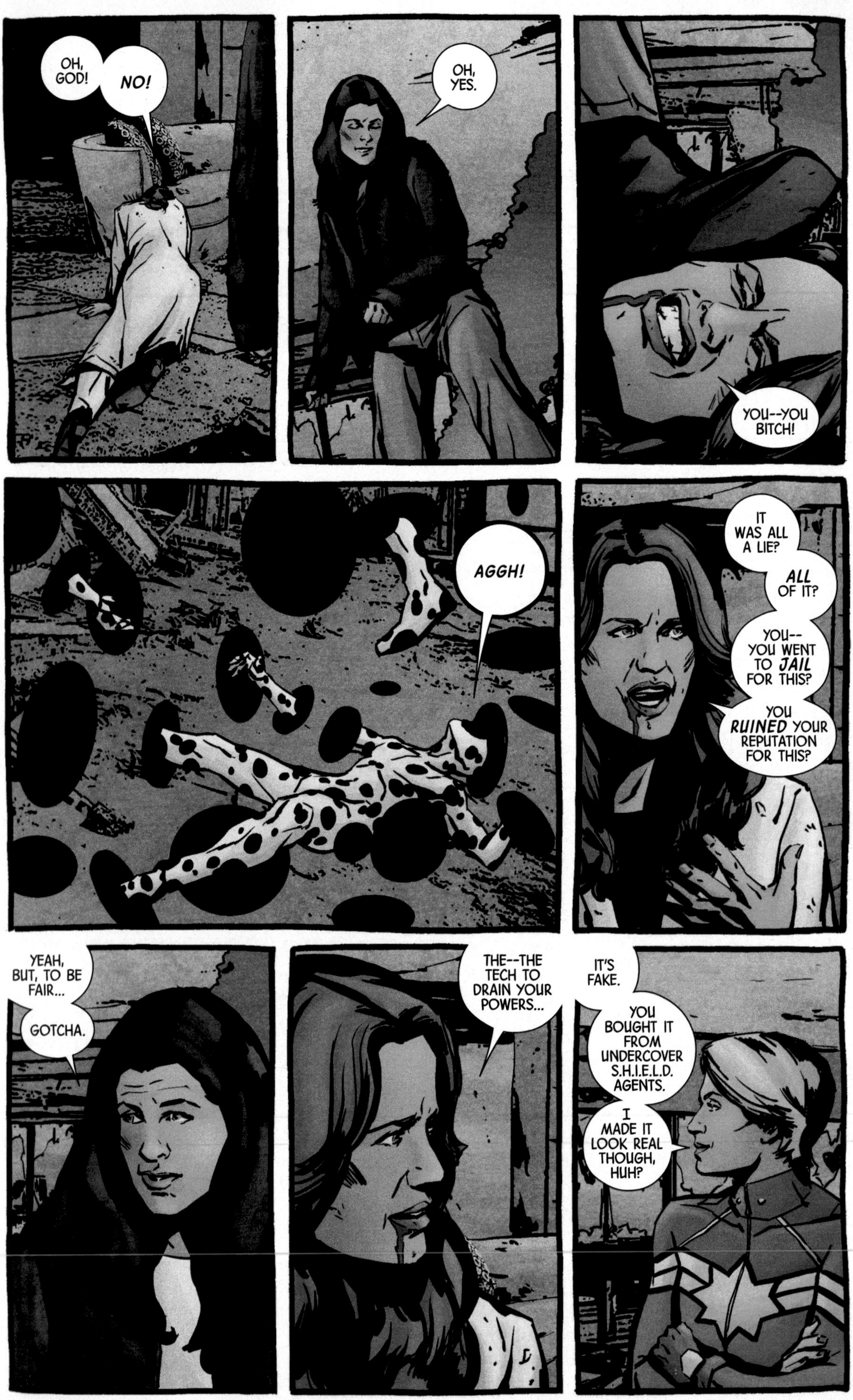
OH, GOD!
NO!
OH, YES.
YOU--YOU BITCH!
AGGH!
IT WAS ALL A LIE?
ALL OF IT?
YOU-- YOU WENT TO JAIL FOR THIS?
YOU RUINED YOUR REPUTATION FOR THIS?
YEAH, BUT, TO BE FAIR...
GOTCHA.
THE--THE TECH TO DRAIN YOUR POWERS...
IT'S FAKE.
YOU BOUGHT IT FROM UNDERCOVER S.H.I.E.L.D. AGENTS.
I MADE IT LOOK REAL THOUGH, HUH?

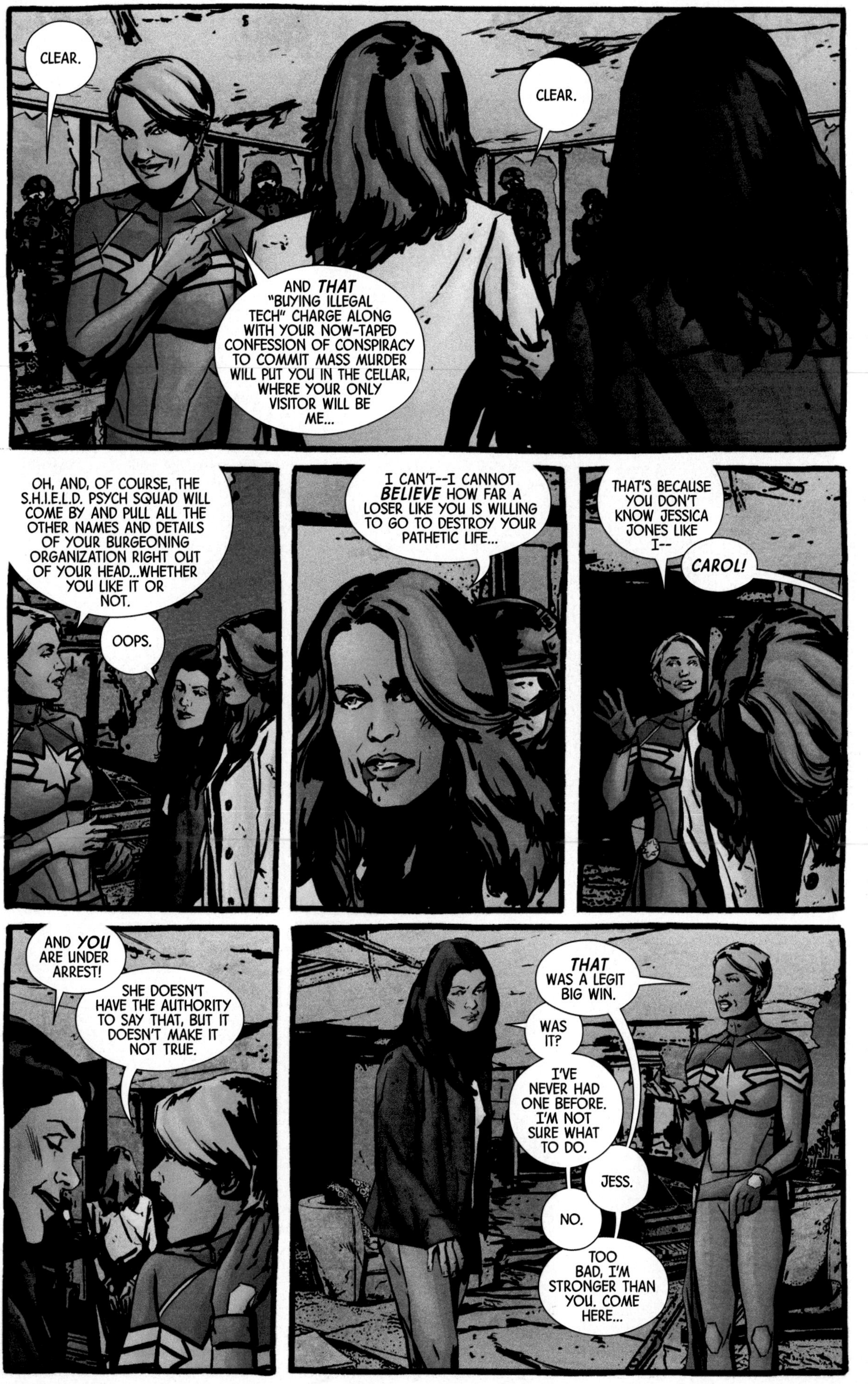
CLEAR.
CLEAR.
AND THAT "BUYING ILLEGAL TECH" CHARGE ALONG WITH YOUR NOW-TAPED CONFESSION OF CONSPIRACY TO COMMIT MASS MURDER WILL PUT YOU IN THE CELLAR, WHERE YOUR ONLY VISITOR WILL BE ME...
OH, AND, OF COURSE, THE S.H.I.E.L.D. PSYCH SQUAD WILL COME BY AND PULL ALL THE OTHER NAMES AND DETAILS OF YOUR BURGEONING ORGANIZATION RIGHT OUT OF YOUR HEAD...WHETHER YOU LIKE IT OR NOT.
OOPS.
I CAN'T--I CANNOT BELIEVE HOW FAR A LOSER LIKE YOU IS WILLING TO GO TO DESTROY YOUR PATHETIC LIFE...
THAT'S BECAUSE YOU DON'T KNOW JESSICA JONES LIKE I--
CAROL!
AND YOU ARE UNDER ARREST!
SHE DOESN'T HAVE THE AUTHORITY TO SAY THAT, BUT IT DOESN'T MAKE IT NOT TRUE.
THAT WAS A LEGIT BIG WIN.
WAS IT?
I'VE NEVER HAD ONE BEFORE. I'M NOT SURE WHAT TO DO.
JESS.
NO.
TOO BAD, I'M STRONGER THAN YOU. COME HERE...

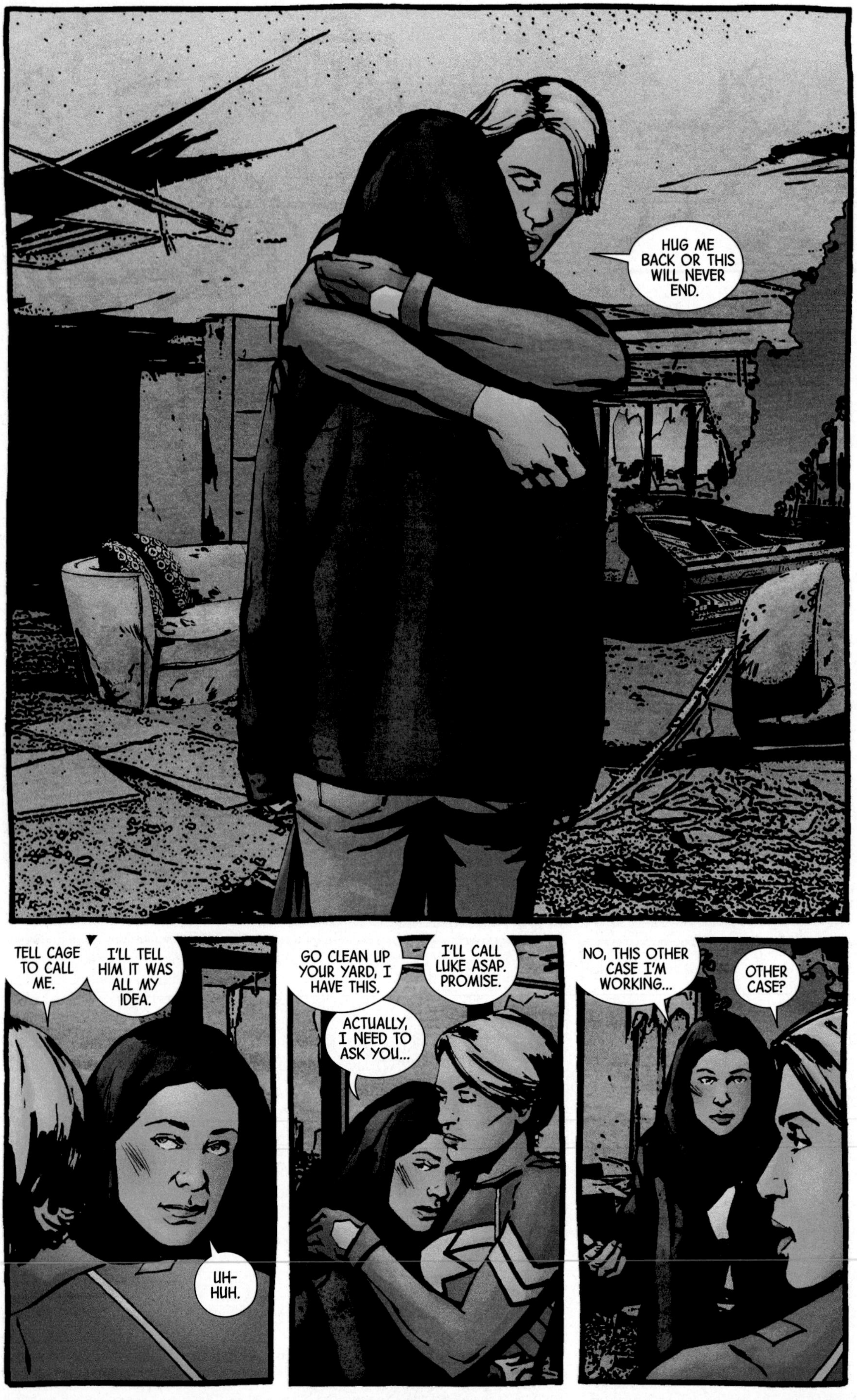
HUG ME BACK OR THIS WILL NEVER END.
TELL CAGE TO CALL ME.
I'LL TELL HIM IT WAS ALL MY IDEA.
UH-HUH.
GO CLEAN UP YOUR YARD, I HAVE THIS.
I'LL CALL LUKE ASAP. PROMISE.
ACTUALLY, I NEED TO ASK YOU...
NO, THIS OTHER CASE I'M WORKING...
OTHER CASE?

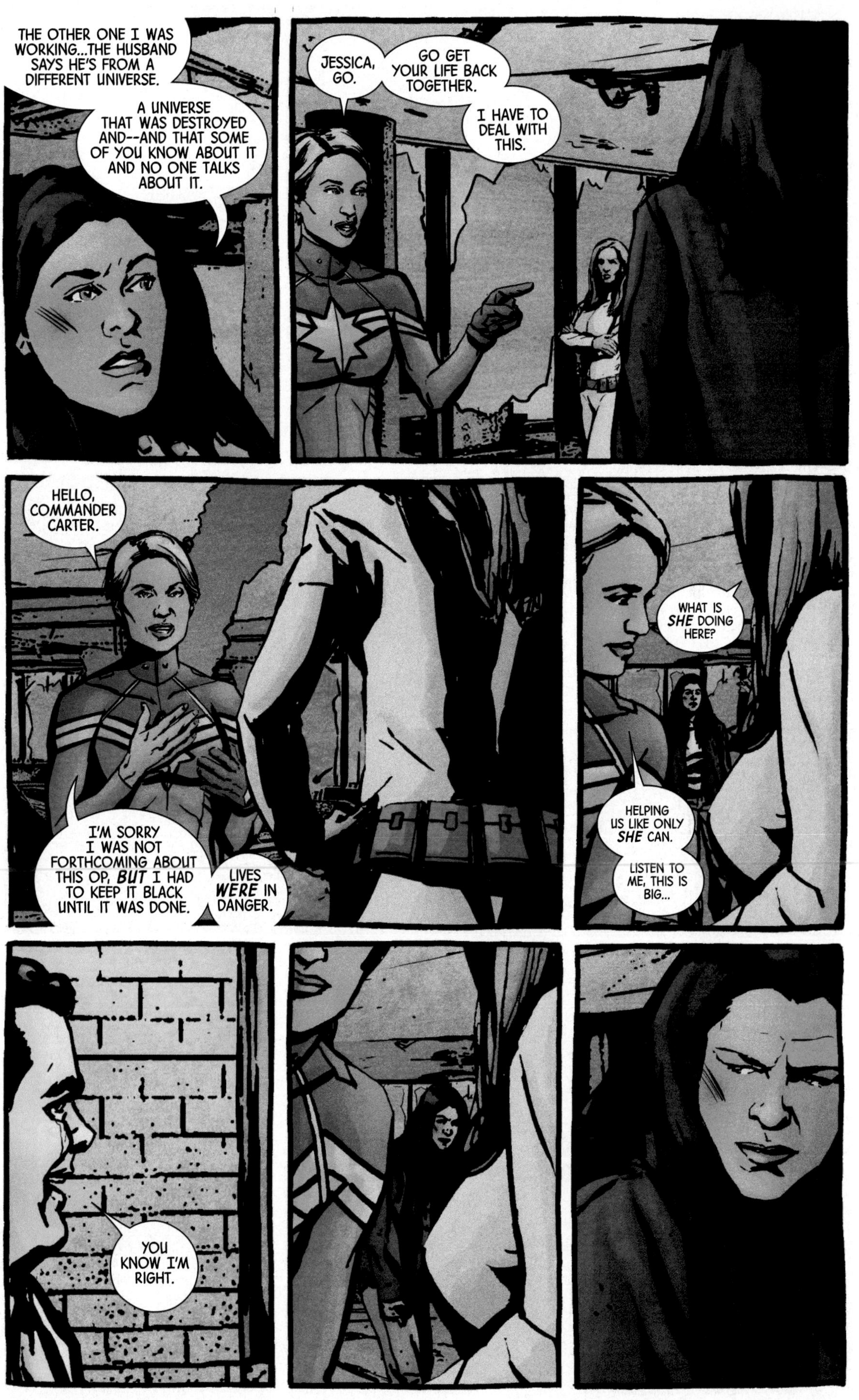
THE OTHER ONE I WAS WORKING...THE HUSBAND SAYS HE'S FROM A DIFFERENT UNIVERSE.
A UNIVERSE THAT WAS DESTROYED AND--AND THAT SOME OF YOU KNOW ABOUT IT AND NO ONE TALKS ABOUT IT.
JESSICA, GO.
GO GET YOUR LIFE BACK TOGETHER.
I HAVE TO DEAL WITH THIS.
HELLO, COMMANDER CARTER.
I'M SORRY I WAS NOT FORTHCOMING ABOUT THIS OP, BUT I HAD TO KEEP IT BLACK UNTIL IT WAS DONE.
LIVES WERE IN DANGER.
WHAT IS SHE DOING HERE?
HELPING US LIKE ONLY SHE CAN.
LISTEN TO ME, THIS IS BIG...
YOU KNOW I'M RIGHT.

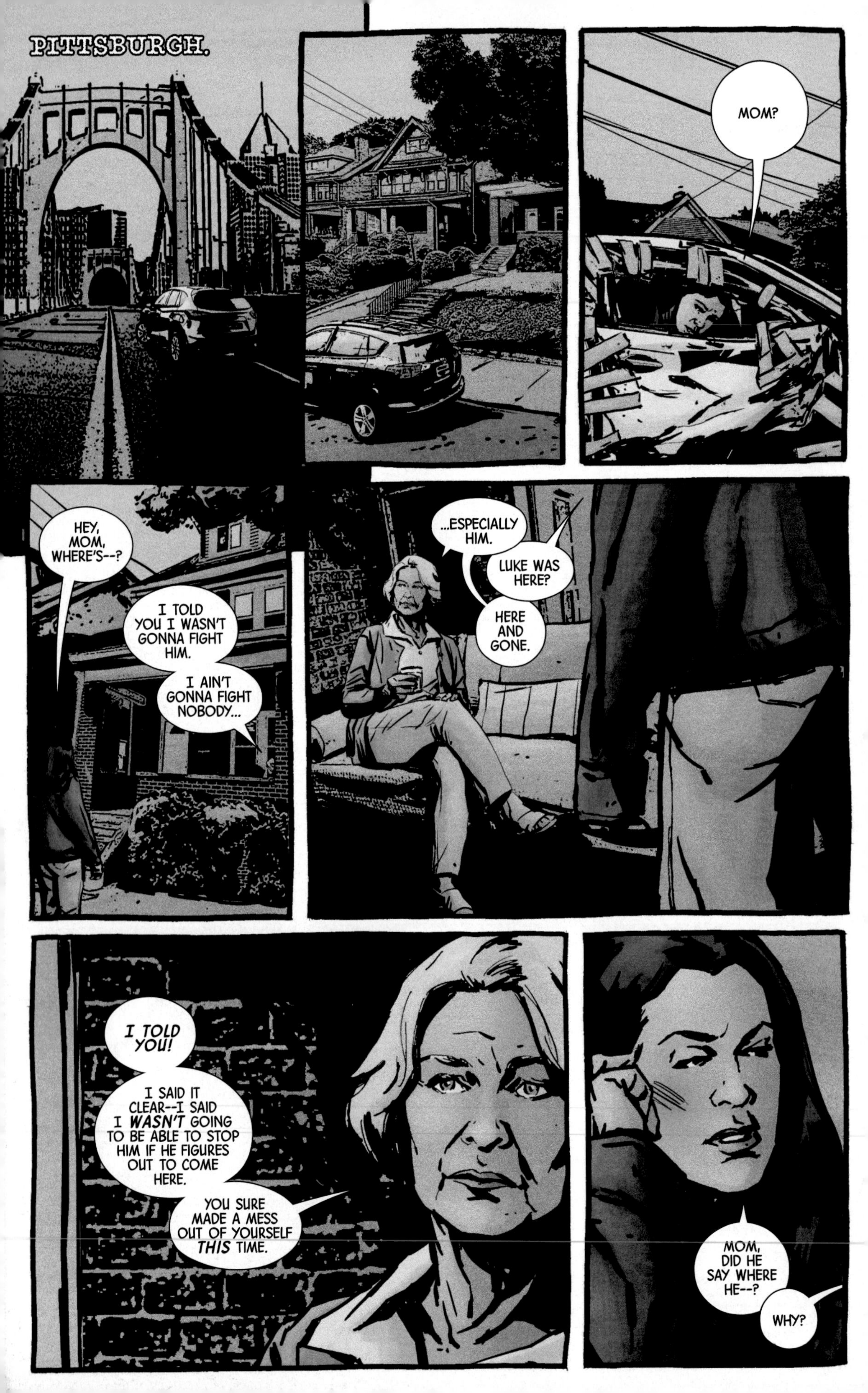
PITTSBURGH.
MOM?
HEY, MOM, WHERE'S--?
I TOLD YOU I WASN'T GONNA FIGHT HIM.
I AIN'T GONNA FIGHT NOBODY...
...ESPECIALLY HIM.
LUKE WAS HERE?
HERE AND GONE.
I TOLD YOU!
I SAID IT CLEAR--I SAID I WASN'T GOING TO BE ABLE TO STOP HIM IF HE FIGURES OUT TO COME HERE.
YOU SURE MADE A MESS OUT OF YOURSELF THIS TIME.
MOM, DID HE SAY WHERE HE--?
WHY?

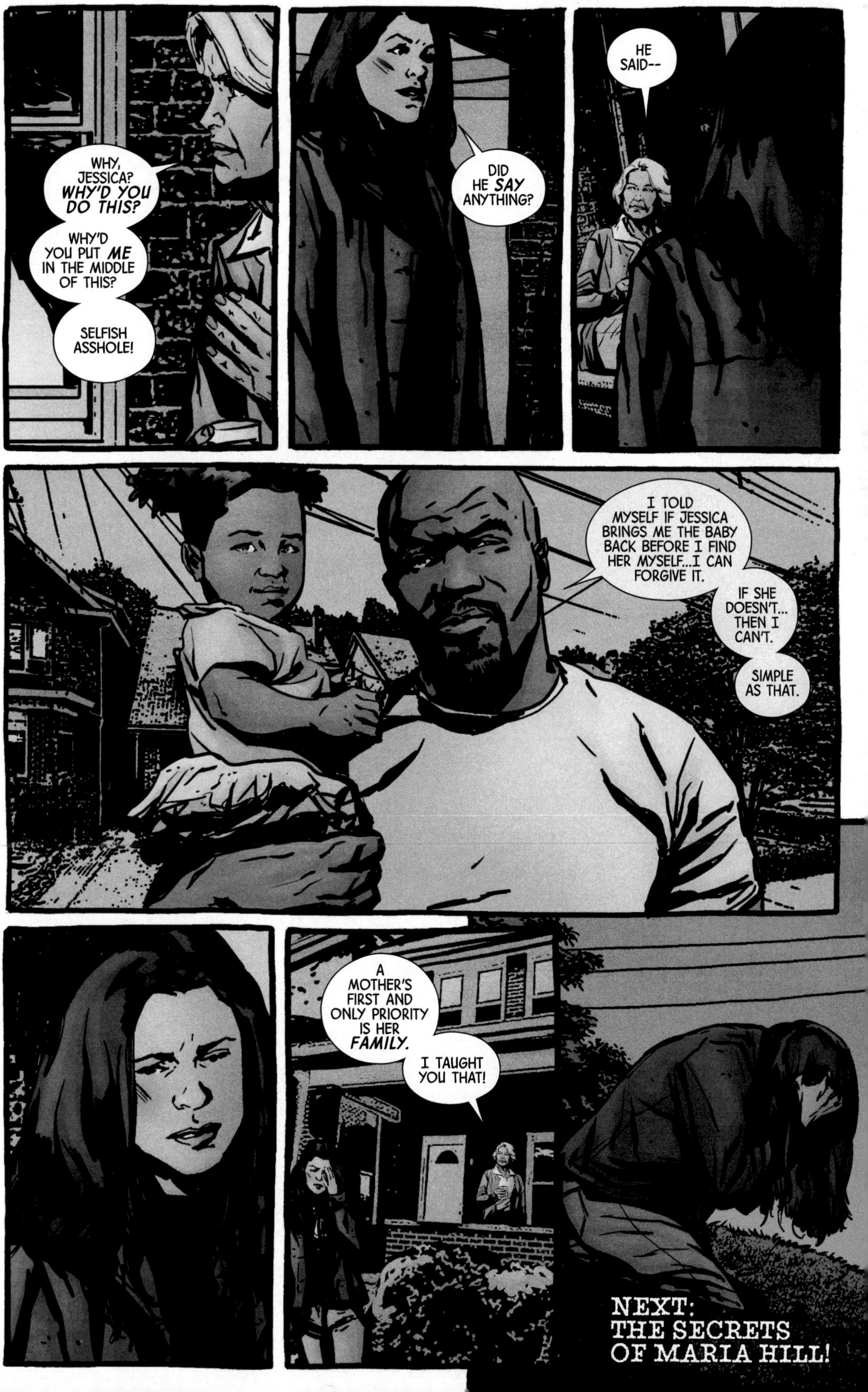
WHY, JESSICA? WHY'D YOU DO THIS?
WHY'D YOU PUT ME IN THE MIDDLE OF THIS?
SELFISH ASSHOLE!
DID HE SAY ANYTHING?
HE SAID--
I TOLD MYSELF IF JESSICA BRINGS ME THE BABY BACK BEFORE I FIND HER MYSELF...I CAN FORGIVE IT.
IF SHE DOESN'T... THEN I CAN'T.
SIMPLE AS THAT.
A MOTHER'S FIRST AND ONLY PRIORITY IS HER FAMILY.
I TAUGHT YOU THAT!
NEXT: THE SECRETS OF MARIA HILL!

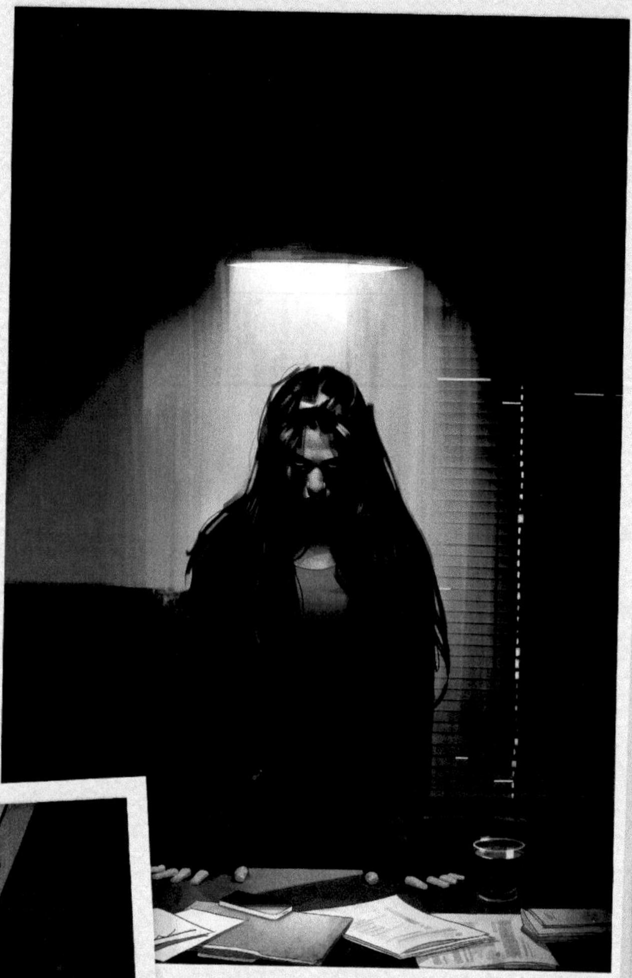

#4 variant by **Jeff Dekal**

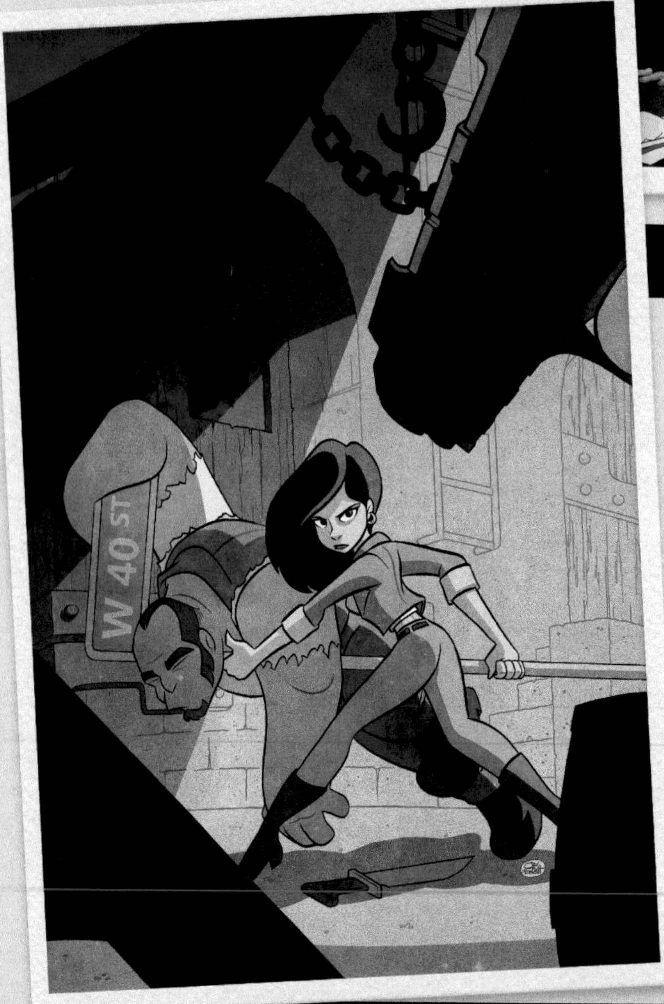
W 40 ST

#5 variant by **Jay Fosgitt**

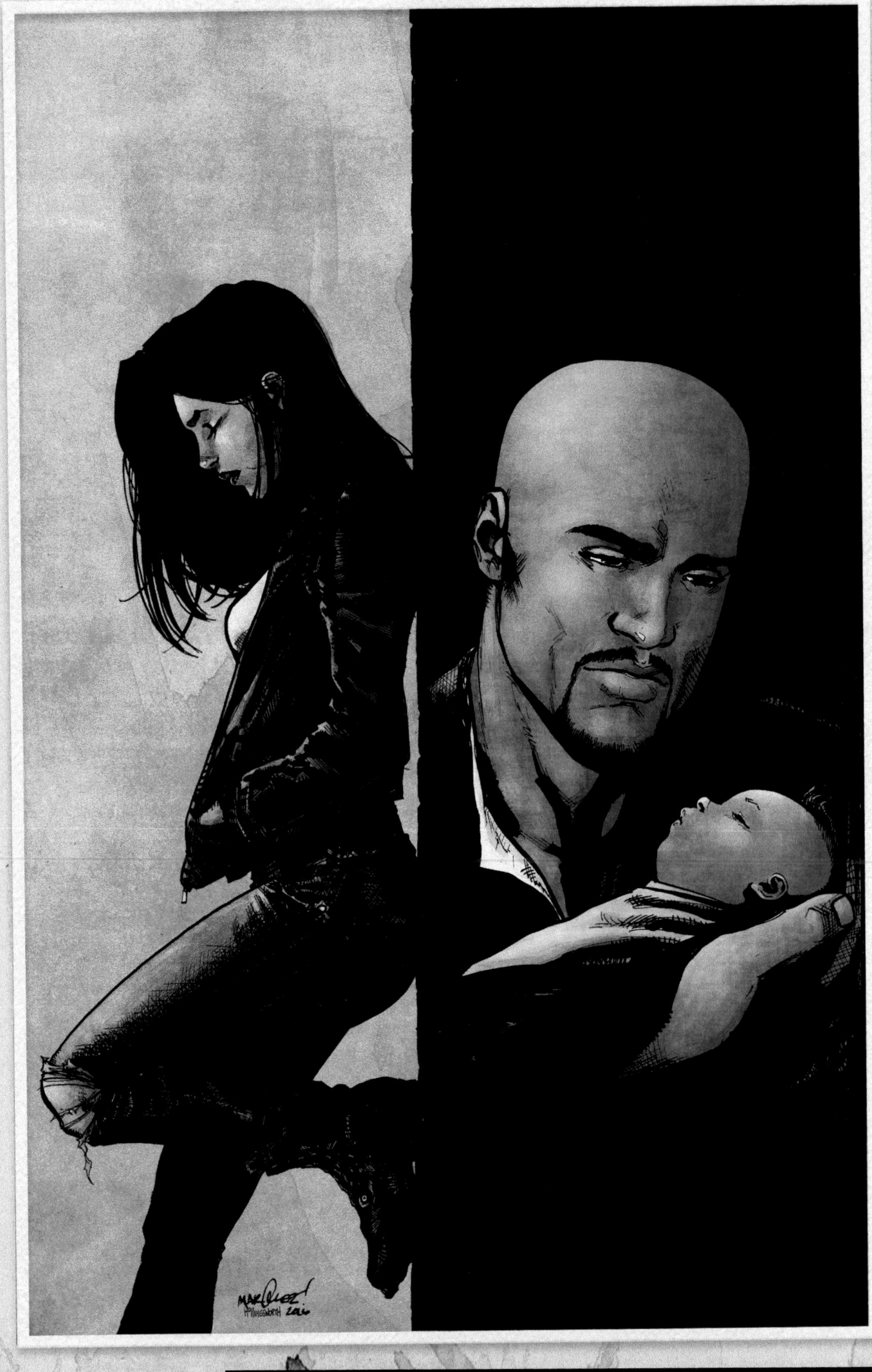
MARQUEZ!
HOLLINGSWORTH 2016

#6 variant by **David Marquez** & **Matt Hollingsworth**

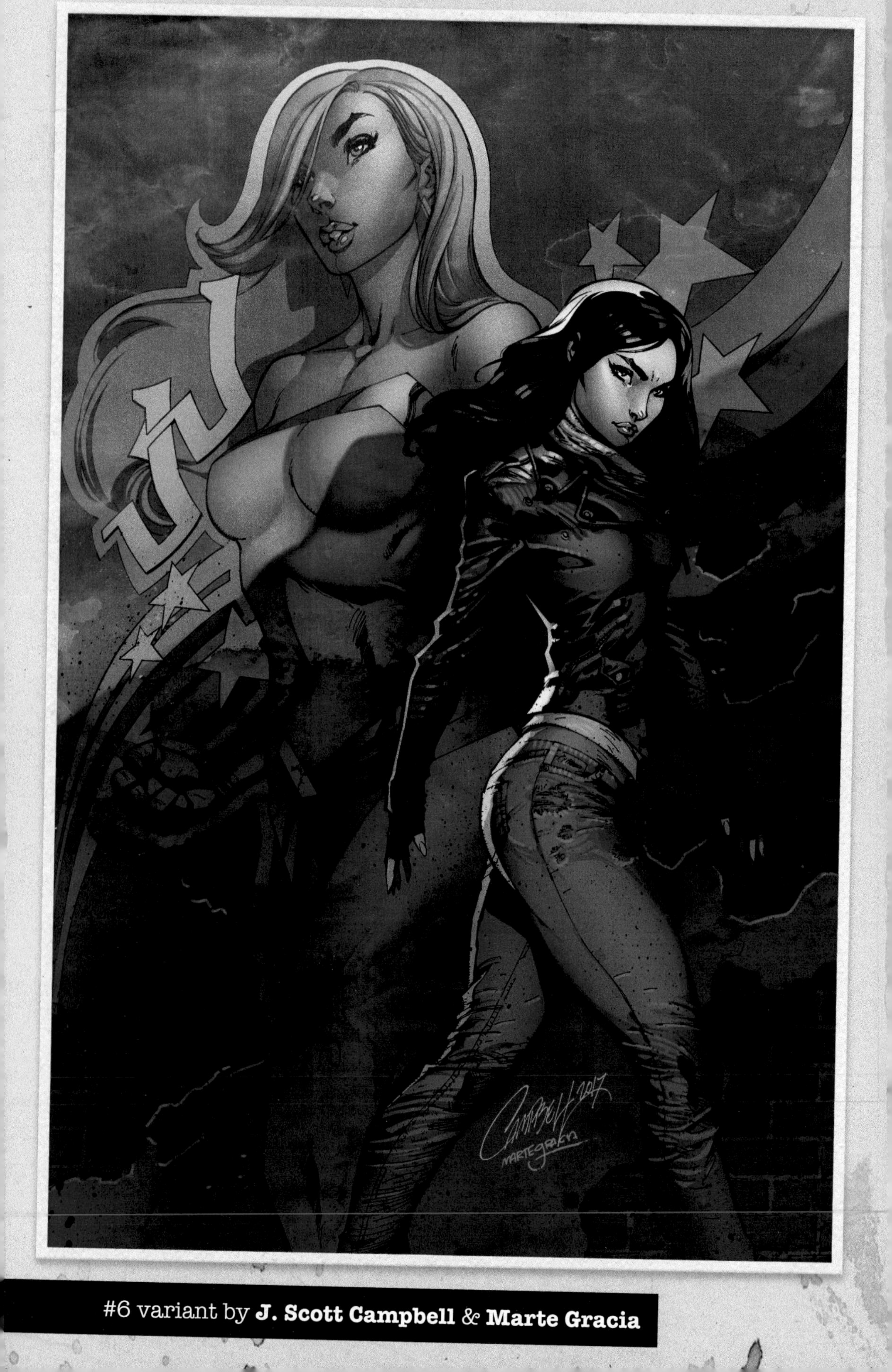

#6 variant by **J. Scott Campbell** & **Marte Gracia**